Clothing as Material Culture

Clothing as Material Culture

Edited by
Susanne Küchler and Daniel Miller

Oxford • New York

First published in 2005 by
Berg
Editorial offices:
1st Floor, Angel Court, 81 St Clements Street, Oxford OX4 1AW, UK
175 Fifth Avenue, New York, NY 10010, USA

© Susanne Küchler and Daniel Miller 2005

All rights reserved.
No part of this publication may be reproduced in any form
or by any means without the written permission of Berg.

Berg is the imprint of Oxford International Publishers Ltd.

Library of Congress Cataloging-in-Publication Data
Clothing as material culture / edited by Susanne Küchler and Daniel Miller.
      p. cm.
   Includes bibliographical references and index.
   ISBN 1-84520-067-5 (pbk.) -- ISBN 1-84520-066-7 (cloth)
   1. Clothing and dress. 2. Material culture. I. Küchler, Susanne.
II. Miller, Daniel, 1954-

GN418.C58 2005
391--dc22   2004030414

British Library Cataloguing-in-Publication Data
A catalogue record for this book is available from the British Library.

ISBN-13 978 184520 066 4 (Cloth)
ISBN-10 1 84520 066 7 (Cloth)

ISBN-13 978 184520 067 1 (Paper)
ISBN-10 1 84520 067 5 (Paper)

Typeset by JS Typesetting Ltd, Porthcawl, Mid Glamorgan
Printed in the United Kingdom by Biddles Ltd, King's Lynn

www.bergpublishers.com

Contents

List of Figures vii

Notes on Contributors ix

1 Introduction
   Daniel Miller 1

2 Looking Good: Feeling Right – Aesthetics of the Self
   Sophie Woodward 21

3 The Other Half: The Material Culture of New Fibres
   Kaori O'Connor 41

4 Aesthetics, Ethics and Politics of the Turkish Headscarf
   Özlem Sandıkcı and *Güliz Ger* 61

5 Cloth That Lies: The Secrets of Recycling in India
   Lucy Norris 83

6 From Thrift to Fashion: Materiality and Aesthetics in Dress Practices in Zambia
   Karen Tranberg Hansen 107

7 *Nga Aho Tipuna* (Ancestral Threads): Maori Cloaks from New Zealand
   Amiria Henare 121

8 Relative Imagery: Patterns of Response to the Revival of Archaic Chiefly Dress in Fiji
   Chloë Colchester 139

9 Pattern, Efficacy and Enterprise: On the Fabrication of Connections in Melanesia
   Graeme Were 159

Contents

10 Why are there Quilts in Polynesia?
Susanne Küchler — 175

Index — 193

List of Figures

4.1a	Rectangular foulard	68
4.1b	Rectangular foulard	68
4.2	Small square scarf	68
4.3	Traditional scarf	68
4.4a	Large scarf	69
4.4b	Large scarf	69
4.5a	Foulard with brooch	70
4.5b	Asymmetric style	70
4.5c	Asymmetric style	70
4.6	Inner bonnet	73
5.1	Waghri women spread their kitchen wares out on the ground to tempt passing women into bartering their old clothes in return	87
5.2	Recycling imported Western clothing in India	89
5.3	A bale of old clothes from the UK waits to be sorted at the factory in Panipat	95
5.4	Once the clothing has been sorted by colour, women cut it up into small squares	96
5.5	A baby's blanket woven from recycled thread and sold in Indian markets	98
7.1	Finely woven *aronui* or *kaitaka* cloak, made in the nineteenth century, possibly for a child. 625 × 1107mm	121
7.2	*Whatu* or Maori finger-weaving	127
8.1	'A Fijian Mountaineer', showing how *masi yarabalavu* was used by photographers to project an image of Fijian identity to the outside world	145
8.2	A posture adopted for stencilling in Natewa 1998	149
8.3	Preparing the clothing for a Natewan wedding	150
8.4	Two examples of the way that T-shirts are used to provide a commentary upon the contemporary manufacture of archaic barkcloth clothing in Fiji.	151
8.5	Making connections. The tui Vuna's House 1914	153
8.6	Using visual analogy subversively. A contemporary domestic display of archaic chiefly dress	155
9.1	'Church and people at Fagani, San Christobal'	163

List of Figures

9.2	'Malaitan native "a labour man" in Fiji'	168
9.3	Solomon Islands men wearing patterned cloth	169
9.4	'British New Guinea bride and bride groom'	170
10.1	Tivaivai *taorei* (patchwork), Cook Islands, ca. 1965	179
10.2	Detail of tivaivai *tataura,* cut out with rich embroidery, 2003	185
10.3	Tivaivai *manu,* 2003, Rarotonga, Cook Islands	187

The Contributors

Chloë Colchester was a research associate at University College London working for the ESRC funded Clothing the Pacific Project. She is now a freelance writer. Her research work involves using both Pacific and foreign clothing as a framework to assess the impact of Protestant missionary actitivity upon indigenous practice and belief. She recently edited *Clothing the Pacific* (Berg, 2003) and is currently preparing *Textiles for the Twenty-first Century* (Thames and Hudson) and an ethnographic monograph on the history of Fijian indigenous cloth for the University of Hawaii Press.

Güliz Ger is Professor of Marketing at the Faculty of Business Administration at Bilkent University, Ankara, Turkey. She has published on sociocultural dimensions of consumption, especially in transitional societies/groups, and the related issues of globalization, modernity and tradition. She is currently working on Islamic consumptionscapes, consumption among immigrants, production and consumption of cultural products, and historical analysis of consumer culture.

Karen Tranberg Hansen is Professor of Anthropology at Northwestern University. She has conducted most of her research in Zambia on different dimensions of urban life. She is the author of *Distant Companions: Servants and Employers in Zambia 1900–1985* (Cornell University Press, 1989), *Keeping House in Lusaka* (Columbia University Press, 1997), *Salaula: The World of Secondhand Clothing in Zambia* (University of Chicago Press, 2000) and editor of *African Encounters with Domesticity* (Rutgers University Press, 1992).

Amiria Henare is a curator at the University of Cambridge Museum of Archaeology and Anthropology. She has written on the history and contemporary importance of artefact-based research, and her research interests include visual and practice-based methodologies, indigenous anthropology and the dynamics of cultural change. Her book *Museum, Anthropology and Imperial Exchange* is about to be published by Cambridge University Press.

Susanne Küchler is Reader in Anthropology at University College London. She has published on art and memory in Melanesia and has been conducting research on quilting in eastern Polynesia over the last three years as part of an ESRC funded

Notes on Contributors

project entitled Clothing the Pacific. She is currently preparing a publication for Thames and Hudson on Pacific Pattern, as well as a manuscript on Cook Island quilting.

Daniel Miller is Professor of Material Culture at the Department of Anthropology, University College London. Recent books include *The Sari* written with Mukulika Banerjee (Berg, 2003), and he has edited *Materiality* (forthcoming, Duke University Press).

Lucy Norris is a postdoctoral fellow in the Department of Anthropology, University College London, where she was awarded her PhD. Her research investigates the life cycle of clothing in contemporary urban India, focusing on practices of disposal, recycling and the transformation of clothing into hybrid products in the global market. She is currently preparing a manuscript of her PhD thesis and devising a collaborative exhibition looking at related themes.

Kaori O'Connor studied anthropology at Reed College, Oxford University, and University College London, where she is a postdoctoral fellow. She has extensive experience of contemporary fibres and fashion, having worked on *Vogue* magazine and as a designer of handknits. She is the author of seven books on various aspects of fashion and design and is currently working on an intensive study of Lycra.

Özlem Sandikci is Assistant Professor of Marketing at the Faculty of Business Administration at Bilkent University, Ankara, Turkey. Her work addresses various social and cultural aspects of advertising and consumption. She is currently conducting research on Islamic consumptionscapes, production and consumption of rituals, and space-consumption relationship.

Graeme Were is an ESRC Postdoctoral Fellow in Anthropology at Goldsmiths College, University of London. His research interests are museum collections, ethnomathematics and material culture.

Sophie Woodward studied anthropology at Cambridge University and University College London, where she is now completing her PhD into women's wardrobes. She is also Research Associate at Nottingham Trent University, carrying out research into fashion as practice.

–1–

Introduction
Daniel Miller

Material Culture

The principle aim of this volume is to put an end to what now seems a rather unnecessary if ancient antagonism. Material culture studies (see Buchli 2002) has roots in two quite distinct trajectories. Many researchers have a background in specialist institutions such as textile conservation, design or museum collections. There they may have gained considerable expertise in the analysis of cloth and textiles. By contrast there are many students whose background lies more in cultural studies, sociology or social anthropology with training in semiotic and symbolic analysis and an interest in the 'social life' of clothing. Specialists in textiles may have very little respect for those disciplines they lump together as 'cultural studies'. They see this social analysis as merely mapping differences in clothing and fashion onto social categories such as class, ethnicity and gender. Such mapping removes any specificity to clothing studies since much the same mapping can be achieved with, for example, food or housing. In turn, social scientists may denigrate scholars of textile, pattern, form and technology as 'positivists' who study such things merely because they have collections. They see such attention to detail as emulating the assumptions of objectivity in the natural sciences and thus as a kind of 'right wing', failure properly to appreciate the politicized nature of all such research, which they have been trained to elicit from the material as what really 'matters'.

The aim of this book is to show how contemporary material culture studies transcends and refuses this simplistic dualism. In our book the dissection of clothing into pattern, fibre, fabric, form and production is not opposed to, but part of, its consideration as an aspect of human and cosmological engagement. The sensual and aesthetic – what cloth feels and looks like – is the source of its capacity to objectify myth, cosmology and also morality, power and values. We are concerned with what might have been termed the political, or the study of gender, but view these as diminished by being abstracted as separate academic 'debates'. Rather we see integrity in the complex interweaving of what can rarely be separated out into distinct material and social domains. The underlying claim is that such transcendence represents a certain maturity of perspective, one that recognizes the virtues of various disciplines and forms of expertise and seeks to bring these together within the larger project of academic understanding. It also represents a new confidence within material culture studies more generally, as more than a meeting point, rather an alloy from which can be forged a sharper instrument whose point can strike further towards these goals of understanding.

Underlying these possibilities has been a deeper transformation of material culture studies and general approaches to materiality within anthropology. In a recent volume, (Miller in press) I focus upon the meaning of materiality itself. Using this to complement the common critique of the concept of culture with a more specific critique of terms such as society, social relations and the subject. A series of case studies ranging from the study of religion to that of finance demonstrates what is gained by taking on board the intrinsic materiality of what are otherwise regarded as social relations. This is defended both on philosophical grounds and also pragmatically as often closer to the way peoples in many parts of the world understand themselves and struggle with the relationship between what they regard as the spiritual and material aspects of their lives.

Within that volume are two papers that are specifically concerned with the topic of clothing and textiles. Webb Keane (in press) argues against the idea that clothes are signs or representations of social relations. This has been the baleful legacy of many approaches labelled 'semiotic', although Keane argues that the work of Peirce was never limited in this way. The problem with such studies is precisely that clothing becomes reduced to its ability to signify something that seems more real – society or social relations – as though these things exist above or prior to their own materiality. In effect, Keane is saying, not just that the emperor had no clothes, but that the clothes should no longer have an emperor; that they are not merely the handmaidens to the study of society, or culture or identity. Rather we are prepared now to see clothes themselves as having agency, as part of what constitutes and forms lives, cosmologies, reasons, causes and effects.

Küchler's chapter (in press) takes this still further through a critique of our privileging of humanity as *homo sapiens*, those who are distinguished through their possession of intelligence. By focusing upon new forms of textile that include elements that can respond to and anticipate their environment, she shows how intelligence can also be considered an aspect of materiality, and that it is not just the social but also the intellectual characterization of humanity that needs to be reintroduced to its own materiality in order to transcend a false dualism that impedes rather than facilitates our understanding.

Behind the clash of prejudices found among students lies what is often already an assumption and thereby an assertion about what really 'matters'. In colloquial discussion of clothing, the principle problem has been precisely that the whole topic doesn't really matter. Since it is used as a covering or as a surface, clothing

Introduction

is easily characterized as intrinsically superficial. This may be connected to a wider critique of the concept of surfaces that can be related to architecture and other domains (e.g. Wigley 1995). We struggle with what might be called a depth ontology, a very specific Western idea of being, in which the real person, myself, is somehow deep inside me, while my surface is literally superficial, a slight, transient aspect that is shallow, more contrived, somehow less real and certainly less important. Politics as abstract and explicit debate is profound, while attention to forms such as clothing is trivial and self-indulgent. This denigration of surfaces has been part of the denigration of clothing and, by extension, of those said to be particularly interested in clothing, often seen as women, or blacks or any other group that thereby come to be regarded as more superficial and less deep. But I have argued (Miller 1994) that Trinidadians for example, see things very differently. What they regard as real, the real person, is considered to be on the surface. It is here that you can honestly appraise them, find out who or what they are. By contrast, that which is held deep inside them is seen as false, being hidden from public scrutiny. It is not the real self but the site of lies and deceptions. So for Trinidadians clothing is the very best route to finding out who a person really is, both for others viewing them and even for oneself, since it is through dressing that one confronts who one is, and reveals how certain self-representations and pretensions are really delusions (compare also Strathern 1979 for a similar critique based upon Melanesian evidence). This indicates that there is little point in suggesting it is right or wrong to talk in terms of the morality of surfaces. Rather we simply cannot assume that the way Western philosophy and conversation uses these concepts will necessarily apply to any other society. Indeed in a marvellous reconstruction of the history of France in terms of its attitudes to clothing, appearance and the site of reality, Richard Sennett (1976) showed how much these assumptions have changed over the last few centuries within the West itself.

Similarly we recognize that some of these distinctions pertain to a difference in the material being discussed. Writers such as Simmel (1977), or more recent commentators on fashion such as Davis (1994) or Entwistle (2000) may at times give less attention to the details of fabric when the primary interest is how quickly these change as part of a fashion system, where it is the temporality of knowledge that commands respect, not the form taken by fashion at any given moment. It is not surprising that in the early studies of folk costumes, which were one of the origin points of modern semiotics, or in anthropological decoding of colour and patterns of weaving, more attention is given to parameters of difference that are relatively stable (e.g. Weiner and Schneider 1989). On the other hand in creating modern material culture it is often those who work against this grain, such as an anthropologist who focuses upon the development of new fibres (Schneider 1994), that provide the best precedent for the current volume. It is those who may be

−3−

devoted to the study of class, but understand that appearance can be the substance and not just the mechanism of class, and those whose primary concern is lustre within a collection of fabric, but realize that lustre may have been understood as the idiom for sweat and thereby relations of labour, that paved the way for contemporary material culture approaches.

I have portrayed this clash and its resolution from the very specific perspective of material culture studies. It is not my intention to provide a general survey of disciplinary work on the topic of dress and cloth, but clearly there are many trajectories here and in each case there will be a different variant upon these tensions, so that although the contributions in this volume may not follow so clearly upon this trajectory I suspect it will also have a place in resolving tensions that exist elsewhere. With regard to the broader study of dress and cloth in anthropology, we are fortunate in that there has been a very survey of the literature by Hansen (2004), which complements works by Eicher both as collections (e.g. Eicher 1995) and as synthesis (e.g. Eicher 2000). Since as Eicher notes one of the main contributions of anthropology fostered by its concept of culture is to emphasize the social context of material, these studies are changing with the transformations of the societies anthropology works with. So there was a time when such studies would largely have focused upon rituals, ancestors and kinship, something evident in the final set of papers within this volume, but many of the recent studies summarized by Hansen, are acknowledgements on a regional basis of the increasing importance of fashion and mass consumption as reflected in the early section of this volume (e.g. Freeman 2000 for Barbados, Heath 1992 for Senegal, Kondo 1992 for Japan and Liechty 2003 for Nepal). Of course this is only a trend, one of the earliest influential anthropologists to work on clothing A.L. Kroeber (1919) actually studied contemporary fashion.

The amount of relevant work more generally coming out of dress and textile studies has grown hugely; in particular through the work of Berg, the publisher of this volume, both in its book series and through the journal *Fashion Theory*. As Attfield (2000) has shown there are many points of integration between such work and the kind of material culture studies discussed here. The historical study of dress and fashion has itself undergone radical changes that are reflected in this literature (e.g. Taylor 2002, 2004), which has also involved rethinking the relationship between form and context. Taylor (1998), in particular, has argued for a movement beyond the older form of object-based research, which parallels the case made here. One strong component of this is the emphasis upon materiality that comes from a focus upon clothing and the body, a topic which Entwistle (2000) discusses in general and which is treated in an exemplary manner by Summers' (2001) study of the Victorian corset. There has always been a clear interdisciplinary focus in these studies, which continues to be reflected in both the Berg catalogue which includes ethnographic work such as McVeigh (2001) on

Introduction

uniforms in Japan or Haynes (1998) on debutant balls in the USA, and in *Fashion Theory*. But this interdisciplinarity is equally true of the tradition of studies represented here and more generally in the *Journal of Material Culture*. Thus, in general terms the attempt by this volume to reach a new form of transcendence through an emphasis upon materiality that has little in common with the earlier fetishism of things in themselves should have resonance across a wide spectrum of current debates and studies.

In reference to this interdisciplinarity it is clearly one of the intentions of the present volume to ensure that, for its own part, the study of fibre such as 'wash and wear' fabrics and clothing such as a Maxmara skirt as used in New York or London can and should be subject to the same kind of understanding as barkcloth and Cook Island quilts. Here too issues of cosmology, morality, or the objectification of a generation may be better excavated through a sensitivity to the nuances of form and fibre. So the volume starts with the clothing of mass consumption. For this reason also it ends with a more concentrated regional case study that helps elaborate upon some of these ideas, through a series of papers concerned with the constitution of Pacific persons. Here the richness of anthropological approaches to regions such as Melanesia is brought to bear on the intricacies of cloth production, pattern and form.

The World beneath 'Haute Culture'

In contemporary material culture studies the challenge has been as much to reunite work on designer labels with work on traditional ikat, as it has been to reject the dualism of society and materiality. Our understanding of both barkcloth fibre and a Maxmara skirt is considerably enhanced by their juxtaposition and both have been denuded by the artificial separation that tends to correspond also to the division between anthropology and sociology. The way Woodward, with her anthropological training, understands this skirt is after all largely derived from her interpretation of writings by Strathern and Gell. Importantly, and unlike most writers on contemporary fashion, her focus is on people wearing these labels, not the producers and firms. She is not drawn upwards to the study of either haute couture or haute culture. Furthermore her examples are largely of social failure, of how these items betrayed and failed to accomplish their expected and intended effects.

In the two most extended studies within Woodward's paper we are introduced to individuals with strong desires as to who they want to be, and a clear sense of themselves. But in both cases the clothing is the superior agent, its very materiality thwarts them and prevents them from becoming those persons. Rosie has seven wardrobes, and is facing what is for her a key occasion. Yet such an expert strategist gets everything wrong. She fails to see how a retreat to clothes such as this Maxmara skirt, which have always worked in the past, is completely inappropriate for facing up to a context that is unprecedented and that really did demand something new. As a result the new Rosie that she looks forward to fails to come into existence. Vivienne is the inverse of Rosie, the person who will not buy clothes or dress up for an occasion. But as a result she also suffers from extraordinary constraints. At least Rosie got to the Ivy Restaurant, Vivienne cannot even go to the Sony award ceremony, since her clothing dictates again what she cannot be and by extension where she cannot go. There is no postmodern freedom here, rather highly constrained, highly anxious acts, which in stark contrast to the promise of the postmodern, are moments when you cannot escape responsibility to claims to authority, since these are foisted upon you by the judgements of others – exactly the point made earlier with regard to superficiality (Miller 1994, O'Hanlon 1989, Strathern 1979).

As Woodward notes this reveals another side to Gell's (1998) theories of the extended person. For Gell the emphasis upon this permeable relationship between the individual and their externality was the way in which their creative work could extend them outwards to influence others. But seen through Woodward's example this same theory reveals the extent to which the individual is thereby equally made vulnerable to the penetrating criticisms of others. So just as in the Pacific cases we see here the key attributes of cloth is its connectivity not its setting apart. Clothing is the carapace that often conducts and connects (Thrift in press) rather than separates our sense of what lies within and outside ourselves.

To position Woodward's chapter before O'Connor's accords well with O'Connor's own point – that the natural tendency to treat production as prior to consumption can often be misleading. Similarly in the final papers of this volume concerned with the Pacific there is no assumption of directionality. Pacific people may shred their fibres so that clothing can enact their understanding of relationships; technology is a creative and expressive medium and not just a means to a previously determined end. The final cloth may be there to justify the technology as well as the other way around. O'Connor starts from the observation that most contemporary clothing is the product of new artificial fibres, and the relationship between fibre and product is not given. It is not that one day Lycra is better suited to making girdles and the next day it is better suited to making leggings (see O'Connor 2003). There is no technological determinism here. The fibres do not determine whether they are used to hold a stomach in or assist in aerobic exercises. Rather for garments made of artificial fibres simply to exist in any real quantity, there had to develop an effective connection between the demand for particular kinds of clothing and the ability to make these. As in optical fibres this social economy can only work if people can see the light at both ends of the thread.

Introduction

To be entirely new is in a sense to be entirely old. Fibres at first could only be artificial silk because they had no resonance of their own. To come into being in their own right meant not just the study of the new propensity of fibre but just as much a study of the new propensity of women. They too were inventing themselves in many unprecedented ways, they too were discovering new ways in which they could gain stretch and flexibility – for example in the management of time – and needed new labels to designate and thus understand who they had become as a generation. Indeed what O'Connor shows is that it wasn't some new fashion or style that matched production to consumption, it was the emerging concern with 'convenience'. The new system of production that came not from manufacturing, but from the technologies of housewifery, became the critical selling point of these new materials. The production system of manufacture had to accord with the changing production system of women as consumers, So to understand innovation as much as to understand custom we need to see the resonances by which people develop themselves as material culture, and become the 'wash and wear' generation.

One of the primary difficulties in juxtaposing the study of the self-designated modern with more traditional anthropological work is the degree to which the fields we study become abstracted and designated as distinct. With much of the Pacific material we do not need anthropologists to insist upon a seamless connection between religion and clothing, because it is the designation of these as two separate categories that appears artificial. When fibres, fabrics and ways of wearing are the medium for one's relationships to other people and to the gods, we cannot have 'cloth' and 'religion' we can only have the materiality of cosmology.

In the self-designated modern societies, by contrast, the tendency is to see things and discuss them as separated out domains, so that being religious and being fashionable seem naturally opposed rather than naturally integral. It becomes increasingly clear that the process of categorization is itself deeply political, or more properly ideological, the attempt to gain hegemony for one or other view as to the 'natural'. The modern movement in Turkey, which took its political form through Atatürk, tried hard to designate religion and its unity with everyday life as antiquated and opposed to modernity. So as Sandikci and Ger demonstrate, the radicalism of their informants as contemporary urban women lies less in their explicit avowal of religion, and more in their espousal of religion as a legitimate and alternative form of modernity. Unlike the secular modernity that starts with the separation of these categories, such as politics and religion, we find cloth being used as an expression of interconnectivity. Once again we see an insistence upon a unifying cosmololgy, which takes a material and aesthetic form.

So for these women there is no contradiction between the espousal of fashion and having collections of scarves, used for veiling, to match the collections of clothing that Woodward studies in the UK. The rise of the mass market does not diminish, but rather makes possible, the fulfilment of religious ideals. In this case the problem for these women is how to conform to the commandment to be modest and avert the male predatory gaze, while simultaneously embodying the Islamic ideals of beauty and order, and thereby to express and embody Islam's aesthetic understandings. Consider, for example, the way calligraphy has traditionally also been used to resolve the problem of expressing the beauty of Islam without the profanation of representing the body (a dilemma fictionalized recently in Pamuk 2001). What industrial capitalism provides is a vast array of materials, shapes, colours and forms that can help women interpret these injunctions so as to resolve them. How to have colour without being gaudy, to have elegance of shape without sexualized allure, to have opacity and also lightness, comfort and also convenience. As Sandikci and Ger show, the work of 'interpretation' is simultaneously verbal and material. These women can explain what they are doing and how it relates to their struggle to understand and interpret Koranic commands, but the most eloquent testimony is in their practice, what is termed their 'beauty work'. The interpretation constructed from the richness of practice is often far more nuanced than anything that they can say about their relationship to religious text. Outsiders see a contradiction between the assumed materialism of mass consumption and religious spirituality, but insiders welcome the provision of new forms and materials as God's blessing that enables them to resolve contradiction and as a furtherance of cosmological imperatives. When we step back and consider the centrality of the headscarf to political struggles from Iran to France today, we can see that this appropriation by no means diminishes the political impact. On the contrary, it is the very essence of its politics. There is nothing superficial about headscarves.

Local Wearing, Global Tearing

This general refusal to 'see' the materiality of clothing as part of the politics of clothing but instead to assume that to be political is to suppress the material makes the end-point of Sandikci and Ger's chapter the starting point of the chapter by Hansen. Hansen begins by considering the way the phenomenon she has been studying tends to be represented in the media as the international clothing trade. The point she makes is that for the journalists such trade is simply abstracted as a 'symbol' for their stance on the state of the world, for example, exploitation. But as such, there is no specificity to their enquiry and thus no understanding of why clothing, why this clothing. What is ignored by such a glib reduction of this complex encounter is any realization of how clothing is constructed by the way it is combined and worn to create an effect. The materiality of cloth is manifest in the emphasis upon appearance. The very term *salaula* or sorting, makes reference

Introduction

to the active component of selection and recombination that makes such clothing in essence performative.

To illustrate this point Hansen looks at the development of what she calls 'clothing competence' in circumstances ranging from young men considering suits and jeans to older women's sensitivities to the various contexts for which they need specific clothing. From the point of view of these consumers, the important quality of *salaula* is not that they have been worn, but given the vast range of sources, it is that compared to high-street clothing in other countries this clothing has a much higher percentage chance of being unique within the universe of clothing worn in this region. The interactive nature of this aesthetic means that, in effect, the clothing becomes the summation of the reaction of others to one's attempt to carry it off, to appropriate it as one's new appearance in the world. To master this competence requires as much concern for the materiality of clothing, in this case of second-hand clothing, as it does in Woodward's analysis of clothing competences in first-hand clothing. Indeed Hansen, like Woodward is drawn to the instructive lessons to be learnt from clothes that fail when worn to a public occasion. But the irony in this case is that the specificity of clothing is heightened because second-hand clothes come to represent not lack of choice but greater choice than is available for first-hand clothes and thus a greater burden of expectations and responsibility upon those engaged in this work of reassembling clothes.

Several chapters in this volume echo with the sound of fibres being shredded. However, as made abundantly clear in the chapter by Norris, shredding is not just the apparent end of cloth, but often an unacknowledged beginning. That shredding old cloth creates the basis for new materials, but also releases their symbolic and social significance, so that fragility and reconstitution are made available again as warp and weft. An idea that is taken up again in Küchler and Henare's examination of the fibres of social connectivity. In the case of Norris, as also befits Indian social mores, whole castes are constituted by their precise place in this process of reconfiguring value; for example, the suspicion of that caste seen as responsible for removing old clothing as waste and replacing it with shiny new kitchen utensils. Particularly important is the way Norris uses her material to critique one more dualism that so far has been largely ignored, that between the study of social symbolism and political economy, since here it is the emphasis upon materiality itself that again serves to connect rather than separate off these two genres of academic study.

In comparing the reuse of old Indian clothing with, in parallel to Hansen, the reuse of imported Western clothes, Norris reveals the medium by which we can perhaps best understand materiality itself as an aspect of material culture. It is materiality as the form of value. While the term value sounds like the stripped-down substance from which economic, social and religious determinations of what matters to people can be built up, even at this most basic level, value is still material. It takes material form with inherent propensities, in which form it travels continents, becomes reconfigured, is reduced or substantially increased as value. Usually we think of abstraction as a loss of form, but in this book we can see that equally often it is materiality that constitutes rather than limits the very possibilities of value. For example, to pass through and accumulate value does cloth have to be first slashed and translated into the category of 'mutilated hosiery'? What regulations, national and multinational, attempt to control the relationship between these forms of materiality and their value potential? Who can see and identify themselves with opportunities to create value by entrepreneurial translations through selection, finding markets, relabelling or seeing the cachet in old labelling? Norris shows how these entrepreneurs have to become experts in translation. To secure value is to be able to sniff out the precise colour, texture or quality of the material and properly assess its potential in its next clothing life. Central to Norris's paper is its own revelatory quality. So much of what she describes was not only unknown to us, but is unknown to local buyers, and its value dependent upon not revealing certain aspects, such as its never having been washed, or the fact that it is not actually made from Indian materials. Shoddy comes over as a wonderfully ambiguous term in this account of clothing lies. It is these lies that permit the extraordinary cycle of cloth from the kinds of wardrobe studied by Woodword, to India and sometimes back again. During this journey key attributes such as labels may suddenly fade into insignificance, while other aspects of materiality rise up and make a claim to be the determinant quality of the material. In conclusion this chapter, as with all its predecessors, shows how much is gained by close attention to the fabric of identity.

The Constitution of Pacific Persons

The cumulative effect of the papers presented here is to overthrow conventional ideologies that have limited our perception of cloth. But we hope this is not some esoteric, theoretical gambit, resonant of academics trying to show how clever they are. On the contrary it most often arises as a tearing aside of what has prevented us coming closer to the way cloth and clothing is actually regarded by the people who produce and wear it. This is particularly evident in the series of papers that deal with cloth in the Pacific (see also Colchester 2003). In these papers the authors seek to convey the experiences of such peoples where cosmology, that is one's understanding of the nature of the universe and one's place within it, is often formulated through the making, wearing, displaying and destruction of fibres. The complexity of all manner of relationships is understood through the idiom of fibre and cloth, which is not therefore to be understood as representation or metaphor,

Introduction

but is that from which those understandings and expectations are woven. They tell you what an ancestor feels like, what it means to say a relationship is fragile. Such work has been considerably enhanced by Strathern's work in opening up our sense of the self as often only emergent through reflection upon appearance. Indeed it is worth remembering that many of Strathern's highly influential insights as to the partible and flexible nature of the self (1988) followed upon her earlier studies of self-decoration in Mount Hagen (Strathern 1979, also Strathern and Strathern 1971)

For Strathern this self emerges as a relational form that often knows what it is mainly through the impact of its own appearance. The materiality of presence, or personification, is what gives relationships their presence and their effects. But equally there have been important writings about materials and appearances, such as MacKenzie's (1991) book on netbags in New Guinea, or Gell (1993) on tattooing in the Pacific) or Thomas (1991) on exchange, that have given us a freedom in thinking about this same set of relationships from the perspective of the form and pattern that they take. These are in turn informed by a sense of relationships over time that make clothing and fibre something that embroiders the present, gives it shape and form onto fabric that is given by history and its embodiment in forms such as ancestors and custom.

A critical term in Strathern's work is personification, which responds to her focus upon the person as the form by which we come to see what constitutes relationships, but this is a more specific version of a more general term, that of objectification, which lies at the bedrock of material culture studies in its attempt to transcend subjects and objects and focus on this process of dialectical culture. But this word 'objectification' has also passed through quite different meanings. What does it mean, for example, to consider law as a form of objectification? When applied to law the word objectification is likely to connote its more 'Marxist' pejorative version of an object as a fixture from whose hard dry form the fluid humanity has been sucked out. We tend to think of law as static, as forcing people into a more object-like relationship to each other and to possessions. A kind of fall from the more dynamic, mutable relationships of customary understanding. But law and possession are all about relationships, and they are constantly transformed by a mixture of changing interpretation and changing moralities of fairness and appropriateness, saturated with moral, emotional and affective qualities. Consider the adjudication of possession in the case of an heirloom at the time of a divorce or inheritance. So law can equally well be associated with the more Hegelian sense of objectification, which sees objects and institutions as the sole means by which subjects create themselves, the very essence of creativity. The former narrow usage ignores the commonality of law and custom. In Australian Aboriginal society we see the well-defended rights of the painter as against the rights to oversee the painting and the rights to possession of the motifs being painted, all as integral aspects equally of Aboriginal kinship and Australian law (Myers in press).

For Henare this is why we must acknowledge that Maori cloth was treasured long before rights to cultural heritage were enshrined in state laws. Henare recognizes and partakes in the process of weaving as the means by which an object, the cloth or cloak, is brought into being. Genealogy, she argues, partakes in the same technical process. A raw material, the corporeal body, is subject to a whole series of rituals and additions that create its presence in a society as a living person or eventually as an ancestor. Indeed often the threads from which a body's persona is woven came through the positioning, wrapping, delineation of body and space with cloaks. The Maori language constantly recognizes the sameness of processes through which persons and cloth are produced. So cloth and persons are equally the products of objectification. As such they are not subservient to the processes within which they are employed. The perspective of objectification already presupposes the potential of objects in creating and reproducing relational subjects.

It should not be hard for anthropologists brought up on Mauss's (1966) interpretation of the Hau to concede Henare's further point here. The exchange of cloth is granted to be also an exchange of aspects of persons, since these same persons are partly constituted by their relationship created in that act of exchange. So also a cloth, or equally a technique of making cloth, that is held to come from an ancestor, is not just a representation or a memory, but an abiding presence of that ancestor. The very word ancestor speaks to a relationship joined to a descendent, a mutually constituting exchange, in this case, of temporalities. So in weaving a traditional pattern one's hands and their movements become the hands and movements of the ancestors who bequeathed the technique. A mistake is a ritual error, a failure to be that ancestor. This failure would be a breach of Maori law because it rends the cloth of the connectivity between present identity and the past, that which makes the fabric Maori. The claim to a right to inherit, that is to be Maori, is always a responsibility to an ancestral genealogy that wove one into being. To appropriately possess and employ the right cloak and to weave in the right way is to fulfil that responsibility to keep alive both ancestor and ancestry. So cultural heritage is an objectification, not because of the properties of Western law, but because it cannot ever have been anything else.

There are clear continuities between Henare's concerns and Colchester, since it is precisely the role of cloth in the objectification of power that lies at the heart of Colchester's paper, though here it is the ambiguities and competitive nature of that process of objectification that takes centre stage. Consistent with the previous chapter we see that to objectify is to constitute – that power exists in larger measure to the degree to which it can take a form – a form that reconfigures the authority of the past with that of the present. The situation Colchester describes is one of

Introduction

power inflation, in which power as a limited good was being reduced by virtue of the sheer number of attempts to express it in the form of projects such as church building for new denominations or cooperatives. This accounts for the paradox of *masi*, which was simultaneously a revival, to return as a new player in this game, but one which depended upon being deeply conservative, since only its apparently unmediated form bore witness to its capacity to bring back ancestral efficacy into the present. Its stability and continuity as customary legitimacy becomes still more important at a time when there is increasing uncertainty as to the normative form that should be taken by claims to power, a common fate for materials such as clothing under conditions of modernity (Clarke and Miller 2002).

Masi is effective also because it is substantive, it combines a kind of labour theory of value, where labour is itself both sign and substance of commitment, with a genealogical model of personhood, where objects act as rememberances. At a general level the chapter updates the anthropological discussion of the Pacific concept of mana as a local concept of objectification, that is the necessity of a material aspect to power. But Colchester shows that this implicates the specificity of the material itself. Here the stability of its pattern and form as materialization of the past takes on new aspects because of its juxtaposition with new materials such as photography. The change in context means *masi* could hardly be static for all its appeal to the past. This emerges in various creative, ambivalent and sometimes humorous and ironic effects. In turn this highlights one more synthesis, which is the necessity of such specific material forms as an essential component of general qualities such as power and spirituality. An ambivalence to materiality is itself central to Christian notions of spirituality (e.g. Engelke in press; Keane 1997). So understanding the precise materiality of *masi* become a means for understanding the nature of the emergent syncretism between Christian and pre-Christian forms of religiosity and power.

Central to Colchester's argument is the role of pattern, in particular the role of stability in relation to conditions of change. Pattern is even more evidently centre stage in the next chapter by Were. The gist of Were's arguments rests upon the ability of pattern to create connections rather than to be the bearer of differences and distinctions. Work on other media such as shells and ornaments, especially when considered in the light of recent theoretical work by Gell (1998), suggests the ways pattern might have been used in the Pacific to facilitate this work of connecting. But Were argues that with the European introduction of calico cloth in the region, pattern also becomes important for controlling the nature of the connection between the islanders and the newcomers.

There is a poignant contrast drawn here. On the one hand the impotence of islanders in the face of the violence exhibited, for example, in the practice of blackbirding, that is kidnapping men to work in plantations such as in Queensland. On the other hand the subtle means by which discriminating between different imported calicos and wearing these or reconfiguring these in accordance with prior custom allowed the islanders some degree of agency in determining the conditions of this colonial encounter. This follows the general argument of Thomas (1991) with regard to the two-way nature of selection and appropriation of material culture. As such the very goods that the islanders take from the Europeans become one of the means by which they seek to 'tame' the influence of missionaries and others and make this influence more appropriate to local sensibilities and customs.

These papers reach their conclusion in the essay by Küchler, which returns to our intitial and basic question of what we gain through a new openness to the materiality of relationships as constituted by fibre and cloth. What we do with materials such as fibre and cloth is often the means by which we come to 'see' the very nature of our relationships. This is a materiality that incorporates the process of production, shredding and recombining fibres that reflects the composition and decomposition of states of being, and is very different from our usual conceptualization of clothing in terms of surface and depth. Textile is not here an appearance. It is the form of an everyday experience. In this constancy of shredding, sewing and altering, appearance becomes also tactile and auditory: how we use our hands, what material feels like, the constant soundscape around the house. So recomposition is felt to be in the nature of relationships. Textile is a medium through which people think their anticipation of new and withdrawal from older connections. It is these threads of connection that perform the relative density of cultural substance.

Küchler shows how this applied equally to introduced sewn cloth as to traditional fibres such as barkcloth and mats, since the former were also reconstructed through tearing, sewing and quilting and thereby seen to express animacy. As such, clothing animated women's emotional and relational attachments to both the living and the dead. Intricacy in layering and pattern could 'stitch up' sensual and affective relationships between people and the materiality of houses, rituals and the general form taken by connectivity with gods, adopted children, ancestors and lovers.

Today Cook Islanders sew together quilts and quilts sew together Cook Islanders living in disparate lands. As such they use a new medium to replicate the same symmetry found in traditions where wrapping images of the gods had been the means by which people felt in turn wrapped up in the comfort accorded by being surrounded by spirits. Neither was simply a covering, they were forms of connection effected through the juxtaposition of layers and materials. Küchler illustrates the vision of material culture that this volume speaks to; fine attention to detail creates a phenomenological sense of how, for another society, being is experienced as a nexus of relationships in which the idea of living and the lightness of life is itself diffused. Dead people with a living presence, made cloth that is shredded and reconfigured, children that are removed from their past and

Introduction

reconfigured. A sewn cloth anticipates, acknowledges, constitutes, recalls and memorializes relationships; just as genealogy traces the threads of connection.

Conclusions

I want to conclude by making analogous points with reference to our recent study of the Sari (Banerjee and Miller 2003), a study that adds one further dimension to this reintegration of materiality with sociality. This is the dimension of wearing, which also can be seen to internalize aspects of the materiality of clothing, a point also made by Sandikci and Ger and also by Woodward. The chapters of this book set in the Pacific make clear that these material culture approaches are as much about returning to a sense of the materiality of the person as to the materiality of the cloth. This is not simply the materiality of the body. The material presence in question may equally well be an ancestor or an aspect of kinship. The point is that there is no simple boundary or distinction between persons and their environment.

This becomes very clear when we look at cloth that stands at the very place of this 'boundary'. In examining the South Asian sari, one is always drawn to what is called the *pallu* (Banerjee and Miller 2003: 29–41). This is the end of the cloth that normally has far more elaborate decoration than the rest and, in the commonest style of sari draping today, is also the part of the sari that appears to be 'semi-detached', draped over the shoulder as a loose item of cloth. It is the part of the sari that stands at this ambiguous boundary, simultaneously part and not part of the person. Investigated in its own right, the pallu is seen to be in constant use as a functional, sort of third hand, for wiping chairs, holding keys, protecting from the sun, or holding hot pans in the kitchen. It is equally in constant use as a means of shifting the appearance of the wearer in relation to those around her and thereby indicating both attitude and emotion. It can be tucked in to the waist to make one authoritative, held between the teeth to indicate modesty and veiling, it can be used to flirt or to demonstrate confidence as a 'power sari' in an office. Finally the pallu turns out to be 'instrumental' in examining the relationship between mothers and infants. It can be played with by a child, in a peek-a-boo game to create affection, it is what an infant may hold on to while sleeping with their mother or learning to walk. Like the famous 'transitional object' of psychoanalysis (Winnicott 1971, best known as Linus's blanket in the cartoon *Peanuts*), it becomes that aspect of the mother that appears semi-detachable and thus semi-appropriated by the child.

In all three cases we see the sari not simply as the cover of the individual but as the mediation between the individual and that which lies outside them, their child, their kitchen, their office workers. This semi-detached nature means that a pallu may extend the individual, but can also betray them, for example, by catching fire or being caught in a car door or stepped on by a malicious male. So it is not simply an extension of will. What this implies is not just a difference in clothing, but a significant difference in what it means to be a woman. To have clothing that has this dynamic built into it, so that one can radically change one's appearance several times in a hour, if need be, has no equivalent in the relatively fixed, tailored clothing that dominates the West, which also has none of the ambiguity central to the sari. As argued in *The Sari* this has an impact on how individuals relate to themselves, to others, and to wider issues such as the nature of rationality or modernity.

But none of this is an intrinsic feature of draped clothing. Another draped cloth in another place or time may exhibit none of this dynamism. So the materiality can be considered a propensity but not simply a cause. And this has been true of every chapter in this book. As O'Connor showed, artificial fibres too have propensity as materials, but this does not determine what they have become over the decades. Biological anthropology tells us every year more about how people have propensities, given their genetics and the course of human evolution, but no amount of biological anthropology will ever account for the diversity and the extraordinary possibilities of culture that are detailed in this book. Propensity does matter, and it is the way in which matter becomes integral to cultural processes. It would be a shallow analysis that failed to understand how and why the pallu, or rayon, or barkcloth or cotton lend themselves to what they have become, or in some cases how a usage has had to overcome the intractability of material. Indeed many of these chapters are about tearing, shredding, reconfiguring and transforming the potential of fibre and textile as it moves from one context to another, often hiding and denying its own story. We need to respect biological anthropology but always with a clear understanding of its limitations. In the same way to refocus upon materiality is in no sense a return to determinism.

This then is the current state of material culture studies as they pertain to textile and clothing. They lead to a new respect for the scholarship involved in the precise analysis of the propensities of fibre, shape, texture and pattern. They lead to a new scholarship that considers draping, feel, comfort and assemblage. The technologies of wearing and of genealogy are reintroduced to those of weaving. The result is immeasurably richer, because we can now understand genealogy as technology, weaving as a form by which patterns of value are created not just patterns of style, Assemblage emerges not just as craft but also as a thwarted or failed expression of will in the face of stronger forces, whether that of elite society or of colonial authority. But to produce this richness of texture demands our acknowledgement of one more technology. We have also reintegrated the technology that we term scholarship, found in anthropology and other social sciences that investigate the nuances of kinship, cosmology, death and commensality. We are forcing

Introduction

the scholarship that pertains to analysing kinship and social distinctions, and that which pertains to understanding fibres and style and that which pertains to exchange and international trade, not just to respect each other but to be interwoven into a thereby much stronger material culture. None of these technologies can be appraised over any other. All become requisite. We do not reduce to a simple category of cloth for the same reason we do not reduce to a simple category of gender, class or ethnicity.

When we go out into the world we want, even as academics, to look good, and looking good and stylish depends upon our ability to wear new garments; a material culture that no longer unravels into the warp of materiality and the weft of society, but is there to accentuate and express every subtle contour of that body of understanding we bring out into the public gaze.

References

Attfield, J. 2000 *Wild Things*. Oxford: Berg.
Banerjee, M and Miller, D. 2003 *The Sari*. Oxford: Berg
Buchli, V. (ed.) 2002 *The Material Culture Reader*. Oxford: Berg
Clarke, A and Miller, D. 2002 'Fashion and Anxiety'. *Fashion Theory*, 6: 191–213.
Colchester, C. (ed.) 2003, *Clothing the Pacific*. Oxford: Berg.
Davis, F. 1994 *Fashion Culture and Identity*. Chicago: University of Chicago Press.
Eicher, J. (ed.) 1995 *Dress and Ethnicity: Change Across Space and Time*. Oxford: Berg.
—— 2000 'The Anthropology of Dress'. *Dress*, 27: 59–70.
Engelke, M. (In press) 'Sticky Subjects and Sticky Objects'. In D. Miller (ed.) *Materiality* Durham, NC: Duke University Press.
Entwistle, J. 2000 *The Fashioned Body*. Polity Press, Cambridge.
Freeman, C. 2000 *High Tech and High feels in the Global Economy: women, work and pink-collar identities in the Caribbean*. Durham, NC: Duke University Press.
Gell, A. 1993 *Wrapping in Images: Tattooing in Polynesia*. Oxford: Clarendon Press.
—— 1998 *Art and Agency: An anthropological theory*. Oxford: Oxford University Press.
Hansen, K.T. 2004 'The World in Dress: Anthropological perspectives on clothing fashion and culture'. *Annual Review of Anthropology*, 33: 369–92.
Haynes, M. 1998 *Dressing up Debutants*. Oxford: Berg.
Heath, D. 1992 'Fashion, anti-fashion, and heteroglossia in urban Senegal'. *American Ethnologist*, 19(1):19–33.

Keane, W. (1997) *Signs of Recognition: Hazards and Risks of Representation in an Indonesian Society*. Berkeley: University of California Press.

—— (in press) 'Signs are Not the Garb of Meaning: On the Social Analysis of Material Things'. In D. Miller (ed.) *Materiality* Durham, NC: Duke University Press.

Kondo, D. 1992 'The aesthetics and politics of Japanese identity in the fashion industry'. In J. Tobin (ed.) *Re-Made in Japan: Everyday Life and Consumer Taste in a Changing Society*. New Haven: Yale University Press, pp. 176–203.

Kroeber, A.L. 1919 'On the principle of order in civilization as exemplified by changes in fashion'. *American Anthropologist*, 21(2): 235–63.

Küchler, S. (in press) 'Materiality and Cognition: The Changing Face of Things'. In D. Miller Ed. *Materiality*, Durham, NC: Duke University Press.

Liechty, M. 2003 *Suitably Modern: Making Middle-Class Culture in a New Consumer Society*. Princeton, NJ: Princeton University Press.

MacKenzie, M. 1991 *Androgynous Objects*. Chur: Harwood Academic Press.

McVeigh, B. 2001 *Wearing Ideology*. Oxford: Berg.

Mauss, M. 1966 *The Gift*. London: Cohen and West.

Miller, D. 1994 'Style and Ontology'. In J. Friedman (ed.) *Consumption and Identity*. Chur: Harwood, pp. 71–96.

—— (in press) 'Materiality'. In D. Miller (ed.) *Materiality*. Durham, NC: Duke University Press.

Myers, F. (in press) 'Some Properties of Art and Culture: Ontologies of the image and economies of exchange', In D. Miller (ed.) *Materiality*. Durham, NC: Duke University Press.

O'Connor, K. (2003) 'Production, Consumption and Technology Innovation: The Material Culture of the Midlife'. PhD thesis, University of London.

O'Hanlon, M. 1989 *Reading the Skin: Adornment, Display and Society among the Wahgi*. London: British Museum Publications.

Pamuk, O. 2001 *My Name is Red*. London: Faber and Faber.

Schneider, J. 1994 'In and Out of Polyester: Desire, Disdain and Global Fibre Competitions'. *Anthropology Today*, 10(4): 2–10.

Sennett, R. 1976 *The Fall of Public Man*. Cambridge: Cambridge University Press.

Simmel, G. 1957 'Fashion'. *American Journal of Sociology*, 62: 541-58.

Strathern, A. and Strathern, M. 1971 *Self Decoration In Mount Hagen*. London: Duckworth.

Strathern, M. 1979 'The self in self-decoration'. *Oceania* 44: 241–57.

—— 1988 *The Gender of the Gift*. Berkeley: University of California Press.

Summers, L. 2001 *Bound to Please: a history of the Victorian corset*. Oxford: Berg.

Taylor, L. 1998 'Doing the laundry: A reassessment of object-based dress history'. *Fashion Theory*, 2(4) 337–58.

—— 2002 *The Study of Dress History*. Manchester: Manchester University Press.

—— 2004 *Establishing Dress History*. Manchester. Manchester University Press.

Thomas, N. 1991 *Entangled Objects*. Cambridge, MA: Harvard University Press.

Thrift, N. (in press) 'Beyond Mediation: Three New Material Registers and their Consequences'. In D. Miller (ed.) *Materiality*, Durham, NC: Duke University Press.

Weiner, A. and Schneider, J. (eds) 1989 *Cloth and Human Experience*. Washington: Smithsonian Institution Press.

Wigley, M. 1995 *White Walls, Designer Dresses: the fashioning of modern architecture*. Cambridge, MA: MIT Press.

Winnicott, D. 1971 *Playing and Reality*. London: Tavistock.

–2–

Looking Good: Feeling Right – Aesthetics of the Self
Sophie Woodward

The post-Barthesian emphasis on semiotic decoding has dominated accounts of Western fashion and clothing, seen in the prevalence of magazine analyses (Buckley and Gundle 2000) and the abundance of treatises on subcultural style (Cole 2000) – wherein understandings of clothing centre upon fashion's communicative capacities. However, often the clothing – ostensibly the subject matter of such accounts – remains a ghostly presence, coming to appear immaterial by the very lack of engagement with the physicality of clothing. Structuralist approaches are clearly problematic, in positioning clothing as a text with arbitrary signifiers (Barthes 1985). However, given that clothing is based upon assemblage, this focus upon relations between items remains particularly pertinent. The principle aim of this paper is to reconcile the structuralist emphasis upon the totality of clothing as a relational structure of meaning, with an exploration of the particular materialities of clothing. This is accomplished through investigating how clothes from women's wardrobes in London are put together as outfits that come to constitute a personal aesthetic. This aesthetic emerges as perceptions of what 'goes together', based upon colour, texture, style, cut, pattern. Rather than merely explaining the details of such an aesthetic, in the manner of costume history, what 'goes together' is taken in terms of what 'feels right'. As material culture, clothing is not seen as simply reflecting given aspects of the self but, through its particular material propensities, is co-constitutive of facets such as identity, sexuality and social role. Thus, instead of assuming a predetermined self, the question here becomes that of determining what anthropological conceptualization of the self would arise when viewed through the practice constituted by clothing.

The ways in which clothing is comprehended are fundamentally linked in to wider understandings of the relationship between the surface and personhood. The Western ontology divides the inner intangible 'self' located deep within, from the frivolity and inconsequentiality of the surface (Napier 1985, Wigley 1995, Miller 1994). Within popular and academic discourses, clothing and fashion are therein seen to be superficial and unimportant, as material objects situated at the periphery of the body. However, accounts that point to the problematics of interpreting appearances – where the self is potentially located yet simultaneously recognized as constructed (Sennett 1971, Peiss 1996) – suggest that a deeper understanding of surface and appearance is necessary. Through an understanding of the intricate processes of layering items of clothing, and the combinations of colours and textures that are made (Young 2001), the complex construction of the surface becomes apparent. Here I am investigating such processes of assembling clothing as part of the multifaceted surface, being the site where the self is constituted through both its internal and external relationships.

Gell's notion of a distributed personhood (1998: 21), wherein selfhood is externalized and distributed in space through different material objects, is useful here. As a collection of items of clothing, the wardrobe can be seen as such an externalization of selfhood. Gell (1998) refers to individual style (as opposed to generic artistic styles) as 'personhood in aesthetic form' (1998: 157). In this instance, the personal aesthetic I will be interrogating is the palette from which women paint themselves daily. In dressing, the daily creation of such 'art works' becomes a medium through which their intentions are externalized into a form by which they can impact upon the will of others. Following Gell, the items of clothing are not viewed as passive objects utilized by autonomous individuals, but rather are fundamental to the mediation and externalization of agency. However, the emphasis that would follow a reading of Gell, would be on clothing as a medium through which women can successfully impact upon others. The ethnographic material to be presented here shows this is far too straightforward and unidirectional. Putting on clothing is a form by which one exposes one's 'self' to the outside world. The clothing becomes a conduit that allows other peoples intentions to penetrate deeply into the intentions of the wearer. This often actually prevents the wearer of clothing from becoming the kind of self they would otherwise have wished to construct, let alone influence anyone else. As will be demonstrated, the result is very different from our usual assumption, as championed by postmodern accounts, that this would become simply a study of the self expressing itself freely through clothing.

Combinations of the Self

Through considering the material microscopics of particular women's personal aesthetic, the focus is upon how clothing mediates this relationship between the individual woman and the outside world. The assemblage of outfits involves negotiating whether an outfit is 'really me' and equally the expectations of the occasion of wearing, and the gaze of those present. The process of combining items to be worn involves the process of constructing the individual in the eyes of others. In tracing a 'personal' aesthetic, this does not entail a move from 'the

Aesthetics of the Self

social' to 'the individual', or a disciplinary shift from anthropology to psychology or psychoanalysis. Rather the daily dilemma of assembling clothing involves the mediation of factors such as social normativity and expectations, as dressing involves not only individual preferences but fundamental cultural competences (Entwistle 2001, Craik 1993, Goffman 1971, Mauss 1973). As clothing is worn next to the body, such 'external' factors cannot remain abstract but are necessarily brought within the realm of the intimate, experienced as an internal dilemma and ambivalence (Wilson 1985). My fieldwork made apparent that the moment of assemblage and dressing that takes place in front of the wardrobe or mirror occurs mostly alone, as a woman considers her clothed reflection, anticipating the imagined sartorial judgements of others.

One woman I worked with, Rosie, a married management consultant in her early thirties, was recently invited for the first time to dinner at The Ivy Restaurant (a renowned haunt in London of the fashionable and famous), with four of her female friends. Greatly excited by the prospect of attending such an exclusive location, the issue of what to wear was one of grave consideration. In selecting her outfit she wanted to look as if she belonged at such a venue, as adequate for the occasion in the context of such stylish people. Throughout her life Rosie has participated in a series of clearly defined subcultures: Goth, hippy, 'student', camp club culture, 'single girl on the pull', persistently dressing to fit in with various established groups. Such a desire to conform to the place and people that constitute The Ivy, can be seen to form part of Rosie's sartorial trajectory of adhering to categories of clothing. On this occasion her anxiety to fit in is exacerbated by the novelty of the occasion. As a highly paid professional with no financial dependants, a house in Hampstead, her concern does not centre on her financial position. She certainly possesses an abundance of designer clothes that would appear to befit the occasion.

However she remains unsure of what to wear and spends the next few hours futilely trying on various items from her seven wardrobes. In order for the unprecedented occasion of going to The Ivy to live up to its anticipated expectations, Rosie feels she needs to wear something new and dynamic. Overwhelmed by the mass of clothing, in a myriad of colours, patterns and styles, she is unable to differentiate between them and her usual capacity for aesthetic combination is lost. In this moment of panic she falls back on her favourite black leather knee-length Maxmara skirt as a lifeline of security in the ever-expanding vortex of clothing that engulfs her room, piling up on the bed and floor. The fit of the skirt is perfect, clinging to the hips, gradually triangulating out, ceasing just below the knees. Despite being leather, the refined shape and style and its blackness give it an understated effect when worn with her usual black cotton cap-sleeved top. Viewing her wardrobe through the lens of the unprecedented invitation, the vitality of her favourite outfit is drained. The sombre blackness fails to give voice to the ambiguous facets of her personality needed for the occasion: trendy, youthful, stylish, yet also successful. Resolving still to wear the skirt, the search begins for a suitably 'funky' yet fashionable top, as the increasing mounds of failed tops obscure her bedcovers.

The sheer mass of clothing leads her to panic, as she doubts whether a suitable top will ever be located. Finally, she resorts to another tried and trusted item, and opts to wear the skirt with her favourite one-shoulder khaki-look fitted top, which is dusted with silver glitter. The combination of khaki and glitter is unexpected: a casual combat look coexisting with the feminine and sexy. Khaki is ordinarily used by the army to stop the individual being noticed, whereas here the glitter, which catches the light as the contours of her body move in the light, enables the eye to be drawn ambiguously to her. In her panic Rosie end up resorting to two items that she knows how to wear and knows are 'her' – fitting her usual aesthetic: one from the 'funky' order of clothing thus enabling her exuberance, the other personifying chic stylishness – the skirt being made of luxuriant leather bought from an expensive boutique. To complete the outfit, she wears her knee-high leather boots and a three-quarter-length leather coat. Seeing as both are the same fabric and colour as the skirt, the combination seems like a safe one as the shiny blackness should all blend and merge into one, leaving the top to stand out.

However, the outfit was a failure. The leather skirt, jacket and boots, which Rosie thought would 'go', instead of placing prominence on the funky top, served to dominate the outfit, undermining the ordinary subtle sexiness of the skirt. She said she felt like a member of Liberty X (a 'raunchy' popular music band renowned for a self-conscious creation of an overtly sexualized style through the wearing of all-over leather). Rosie felt aware of her age in the outfit – being in her early thirties and having now adapted her ordinary aesthetic to her mature, more settled position in life, it was 'a bit glitzy and a bit too much like a young, clubbing girl for me'. The outfit harks back to her days as a younger woman 'on the pull', inappropriate to The Ivy where there is a sense of having 'arrived'. The crucial element in Rosie's discomfort here lies not in the items themselves, but in the way in which the items were combined. She failed to anticipate the dominance of the shiny heavy blackness, which swamped the outfit eliminating all pretence at subtlety, and extricating different facets of her personality. Instead of looking chic, stylish and sophisticated, she felt overdressed and uncomfortable; the smooth structured contours of her skirt, concretized into a perpetual physical awareness of the heaviness of the leather oppressing her. As part of her 'distributed personhood' (Gell 1998), the outfit should have externalized her intentionality in order to impact upon those present so that they saw her as a chic, fashionable individual. However here the agency of the clothing becomes apparent; Rosie failed to anticipate that the leather in the boots, the skirt and the boots would articulate together in such a way as to impede her own intentions and create unwanted effects.

Aesthetics of the Self

The failure of the outfit also relates to the particularities of place. By opting for those garments that had become most unequivocally expressions of herself, ironically Rosie ended up neither looking nor feeling like herself, because, by definition, a safe self could not create what needed to be an unprecedented self, where 'fit' had to include place as well as person. An aspect of the self here is therein anticipatory – seeing herself as who she could be at The Ivy: fashionable, chic, successful – refracted back onto her wardrobe. Rosie instead looks backwards to previous successful events; here the self is temporally not merely the succession and culmination of past events as is often assumed. Rather, through clothing, the self may be forward looking: an imagined potential self as seen through the eyes of others, projected backwards onto the clothing in the wardrobe.

Rosie's example is one of aesthetic disjuncture; however equally common among my informants were joyous moments when an outfit 'is me', when the combinations made constitute an aesthetic fit with the wearer. Mumtaz is a married mother of two in her mid-forties; she has lived extensively in Paris, Kenya, Uganda and India for the majority of her life. Her husband was made partner in a prestigious law firm in London four years ago, which was the impetus for their move from Paris to London, where they now live with Mumtaz's parents and their own two children. Last year she was invited back to the wedding of one of her husband's former colleagues in France. The decision over what to wear incorporates the normative expectations of what is acceptable wear to a wedding. In addition she will be re-encountering friends after an absence of several years. Mumtaz confides that when living in Paris the significant investment women made in their appearance led to her own constant rigorous maintenance programme. Even a trip to pick up her children from school turned into an event wherein clothing had to be closely considered. Having been out of this cycle for a significant period, Mumtaz feels the imagined expectations of the others particularly keenly.

As someone who loves clothing and fashion, Mumtaz relishes the opportunity to create an outfit afresh. Rather than purchasing anything new, she searches through her many wardrobes: three of which contain 'Western clothing' the other one containing 'Indian clothing'. The final outfit she decides upon consists of a white linen short summer dress, with thin spaghetti straps, worn over her 'ethnic' trousers – fitted black cotton trousers with colourful embroidery encircling her ankles (the trousers are in fact from *New Look*, a standard UK chain with no particular Asian connection). To finish the outfit off, she drapes one of her *chunis* (the scarf part of one of her many *shalwar kamiz*) round her shoulders. The particular *chuni* is jade green with round embroidered sections that shimmer in the light (her 'spotty scarf'). The monochrome effect of the dress and trousers is invigorated by the playful shimmering of the *chuni* and the embroidery that surrounds and defines her ankles. Mumtaz has drawn on her pre-existing wardrobe yet has made a unique combination: wearing a dress over trousers, mixing her Indian and her Western clothing.

On this occasion the outfit was a considerable success, she spent the afternoon basking in the admiring glances and comments of her friends. Not only did she manage to conform to the social mores, yet she also managed to look chic, stylish and most importantly individual; she looked and felt 'like herself'. What Mumtaz is combining here is not just colours and fabrics; she is also combining in aspects of her self: former parts of her biography – her life in India, her global existence – bringing together the diverse items within one outfit. The 'surface' of her body here is the site for the construction and presentation of her self, constituted biographically and relationally. Strathern (1979), writing on self-decoration in Mount Hagen in Melanesia, demonstrates that for the people of that region appearance is regarded as anything but superficial. Focusing explicitly upon body decorations employed by men on formal ritual occasions, Strathern points out that such elaborate make-up is not a form of disguise, but rather this is seen to be where the self is displayed, 'bringing things outside' (Strathern 1979: 249). Although the context considered in my ethnography is vastly different, an analogous process can be seen to be happening. The different facets of Mumtaz's self – her past, her ethnicity, her global travels – are objectified in the clothing hanging in her wardrobe. In the act of dressing, she hangs her self around her body, bringing attributes of her personality and aspects of her self into the surface of her outfit. Others will regard her work of selection as an expression of her intent, which thereby makes visible to them things which on other occasions may remain private and concealed.

In this moment of selection Mumtaz is able to draw together disparate threads from her four separate wardrobes. Rather than expressing recidivist tendencies like Rosie, going for items that are 'safe', Mumtaz makes a novel, bold combination. Such eclectic assemblage is something Mumtaz does frequently, befitting the multiple facets of her self. Furthermore eclecticism is a defining feature of fashion, the fortuitous consequence of her diverse combinations lead to her outfits appearing fashionable and original. The self is here backwards looking – through considerations of her previous experiences of dressing in France, and through her past sartorial biography. Yet simultaneously Mumtaz's imaginary projection of herself in the eyes of others at the wedding, successfully refracts back on her wardrobe to lead to the unprecedented assemblage. Like Rosie on the actual occasion of wearing the clothes – in this case the wedding – wearing her self round her body, she is exposed to the judgements of others; the adulation she receives reinforces her sartorial confidence, vindicating her decision.

Vivienne's Wardrobe

Rosie and Mumtaz reveal instances of aesthetic disjuncture and aesthetic 'fit' respectively; the moment of assemblage incorporates the particular anxieties

Aesthetics of the Self

and concerns engendered by significant social occasions. However, the example to be considered next centres on a delineation of an entire personal aesthetic, from which emerges specific moments of actualization. While for both Rosie and Mumtaz, their clothing is fundamental to their self-conception, Vivienne, a retired political researcher in her fifties, appears to be the opposite. Politically aware and motivated, she insists that her appearance – clothing and otherwise – is not fundamental to her beliefs or values. The real important self is 'inner', intangible and invisible. She professes to have no interest in fashion, despises shopping, and states she just 'throws on whatever' every day from her one and only wardrobe. She relates with relish instances wherein her work colleagues roll their eyes in despair at the sight of her in ripped jeans and fraying old sweaters. It has become so important to demonstrate that clothing does not matter to her, she now actively cultivates the unkempt look of the 'unlooked'. Vivienne's paradox is that so fixed is her idea of wanting not to be judged by appearance, in fact she has consciously to cultivate such a 'natural' unthought look. Vivienne wears such clothing with the intention of convincing others that she does not care about her appearance – the outcome being that she in fact cares a great deal what others think of her appearance.

Her sole wardrobe contains her skirts, shirts and dresses. Piled at the top are various jumpers and fleeces, with many of her pairs of shoes rammed at the bottom. Her only other receptacle for clothing being her chest of drawers, containing her underwear, Yoga clothing, winter jumpers and T-shirt tops. Now retired, she partakes only in the odd freelance political research project. Even during her full-time working days, as there was no dress code, Vivienne did not have separate work/casual clothing. The clothing she wears is continuous across the different domains of her life: whether she is going in to work, having dinner with a friend, seeing one of her daughters or spending time at home. The styles, fabrics and colours tend to cohere around particular configurations, defined by her own aesthetic. The main points of disjuncture from this are clothing worn to weddings or when travelling – where the external influences of social, cultural and religious expectations come into play. However, even in these cases, in order for her to feel 'comfortable', Vivienne's dominant aesthetic widens to incorporate such events. The notion of 'comfort' incorporates a physical sensation of comfort; but also in a more nuanced sense, comfort involves the notion of aesthetic fit: the wearing of clothes which are 'you'.

Vivienne articulates comfort as linked to practicality and eschews any notion that she has a defined aesthetic where 'how I look' links in to 'how I feel'. Claiming she makes no effort with what she wears, what emerges from an analysis of her wardrobe is that in fact the 'natural', thrown together look involves a great deal of cultural work and cultivation. Ordinarily Vivienne wears her Rohan trousers and perhaps a sweater in the day in the winter time; she asserts that the trousers are 'comfortable and practical', being loose, navy blue, cotton trousers. Large combat-style pockets protrude on either side of the hips; such bulky evident pockets, allied with the multiple toggles and zips that cover the trousers, create an aesthetic of functionality. Not only are the trousers practical – being of a hardy fabric, loose with large pockets – they are also designed to look functional. Vivienne was given them by her niece who used them during her gap year. Although initially she only wore them in the garden, she now wears them all the time, much to the dismay of her daughters, and niece who complains, 'they don't do anything for you!' Vivienne evidently revels in this response to her clothing, as she actively creates an image of herself as being purely practical, with no interest in the combinations of her clothing. However, central to the creation of this image is the appearance of the trousers to others; the anticipated effect of the trousers is to make others think she has made no effort; the incredulity of her niece makes apparent the efficacy of the trousers as an objectification of this intention.

Vivienne's clothing falls primarily into three colour domains: dulled down colours (black, navy and grey), 'earthy' colours (stone, olive green, browns) and 'warm' colours (red, burgundy, yellows). Although such colour palettes do not solely correspond to certain events or domains, Vivienne does express a tendency to favour the brighter, lighter colours in the summer months. Rather than being an isolated preference, the dominance of darker, duller clothing throughout Britain in the winter months is overwhelming. In tandem with the practicalities pertaining to the weather (darker colours absorbing heat and therefore being inappropriate to the summer; lighter colours becoming ruined in rain and bad weather) is an overwhelming sense of social appropriateness. Such a normative expectation is manifest in the colours available in retail outlets; almost without exception every woman I interviewed divided her wardrobe primarily into winter and summer clothing – many having a biannual switch of wardrobes in around May and September. In effect Vivienne is part of a broader trend wherein the clothing practices and shifts in colours, fabrics, wearing of open-toed shoes in effect creates the seasons (given that the division between summer and winter is characterized more by unpredictability than by binary weather polarities). Here there is a semiotic 'fit' to the outer environment; just like in Rosie's case, where clothing is selected to be appropriate to the occasion and the people she will be meeting, here the 'sunny clothes' are worn to greet the anticipated sun. Comfort here involves the fit to external factors rather than internal.

The ways in which Vivienne wears colours are quite particular: in strong contrasting blocks. Such contrasts are made either through combination, or are often co-present within one item of clothing. She possesses a long flowing cotton Afghan dress – the predominant colour of the top half is burgundy with defined green, burgundy and blue rectangles printed on. The bottom half is backed by a striking arterial red colour, and terminates at the ankles with strong bands of

Aesthetics of the Self

burgundy and navy. Rather than being colours that merge into each other, the harsh blocks of colour stand in stark juxtaposition, challenging the viewer. Although she no longer wears this dress (given the political connotations of wearing a dress that is evidently Afghan) she loves the colours, patterns and style of it. Seemingly in contrast to the uncompromising boldness of the colours, the fabric itself is soft, worn cotton, falling in loose flowing waves around the body. This stylistic paradox is central to Vivienne's aesthetic, as will become apparent.

Another facet of this aesthetic paradox is that while the colours exist in strong blocks, Vivienne's penchant for habitually wearing the same items of clothing for periods often in excess of twenty years leads to a softening of the material, and fading of the colours. When she was sixteen her then actor boyfriend gave her a long-sleeved loose cotton tunic, purchased in Nigeria. The predominant colour is bright orange, with large yellow circles printed across the top. During summer, when the weather turns slightly cooler she always wears this top because 'it is the colour of sunshine. It cheers me up so much to wear it'. On wearing the jumper her mood is lifted by the brighter colours, and the coolness of the weather is balanced out by the sunshine of her top. Having worn the top frequently in the summer for the last thirty-five years, the fabric has softened to the touch, and the colours faded through exposure to light, and persistent washing. The orange colour has become diluted. Vivienne has had similar sartorial preferences all her life, a practice that is confirmed by the presence of numerous tops she has had for over thirty years. The seeming contradiction of the harsh blocks of bold colours, on the soft, faded worn fabric is symptomatic of her wardrobe. Furthermore such continuity of styles is evidenced in the sartorial coherence of her wardrobe.

Assembling Aesthetics

As Rosie's example makes apparent, the ways in which combinations are made are crucial in realizing a particular aesthetic. Despite Vivienne claiming she will 'throw on whatever', and that she has no concern with what colours go together, there are certain combinations that are always made. She possesses three red shirts in total, and each one is only ever worn with black trousers or a skirt. All of Vivienne's skirts are floor length, with a slit running right up the back of the skirt, ceasing half way up the thigh. When she walks the trailing leg is almost entirely exposed. This facilitates ease of movement, yet simultaneously Vivienne confesses she likes exhibiting her legs. Her daughters Sandra and Tamsin regularly buy her skirts with a slit, insisting this is her best bodily feature. While being appropriate for a woman of her years and status, the outfit is practical in not impeding her bodily movements, yet at the same time is sexualized. As regards the colours, not only is the contrasting effect of red and black quite striking but the combinational potential of the shirts is severely limited. Although the red shirt and black skirt were not bought as an outfit, they only find communion with each other. Vivienne feels that neither item 'goes' with anything else. McCracken (1988) points to the need to understand the complementarity of goods; Vivienne's sense of 'what goes' is based upon her particular sense of order. The internal categorization of the wardrobe along such lines is common to all wardrobes investigated in my fieldwork. Vivienne's example here shows that this sense of 'what goes' can be extremely constraining. The colours (black and red), and the styles (a loose shirt and a skirt) articulate with each other in such a way that she feels she cannot intervene. What she feels to be the logic of the clothing means that she will only combine these items together.

In this instance it is both the colours and the styles of the items that are restrictive; more generally throughout Vivienne's wardrobe the stylistic combination of a loose, relatively unstructured shirt with a long skirt is a common one. She has an array of silk shirts: one purple one, which hangs alone on a hanger, and a collection of four, all hung together, in the following colours: camel, olive green, pale brown and a darker brown. They were acquired explicitly for travelling, in keeping with local cultural and religious sensibilities, predominantly within the Middle East, where she recently carried out political research on Islam. In Iran, given the extreme heat, she wore flimsy cotton summer dresses beneath the obligatory long coat that concealed the body. However, in Pakistan and Egypt, she borrowed a couple of pairs of raw silk trousers off a friend, which she wore with her silk shirts: clothing that was comfortable, yet would not draw attention to her. Here the 'fit' is functional, as part of her job the clothing has to coincide with Muslim sensibilities.

These shirts are also now her standard wear for when she is compelled to dress more formally. Although Vivienne's clothes are relatively continuous across domains, slight moderations are made for formal wear. A particular combination she favours is her long grey skirt, with one of her greenish shirts and her fitted grey woollen waistcoat, from Monsoon. The thickness of the waistcoat's material, and rigid seaming, serves to structure and formalize the waistcoat – designating its appropriateness for smarter occasions. Yet, it is covered with delicate embroidery, consisting of small red flowers with yellow centres and green ivy growing up the front. Vivienne admits that she loves to wear a green shirt with this waistcoat in part due the coordination between the green embroidery and the selected shirt. This outfit recapitulates the ambiguity at the heart of Vivienne's aesthetic hinted at earlier: the fluidity of the draping shirt and skirt coupled with the rigidified structure of the waistcoat, which is further softened by intricate floral embroidery.

This outfit is appropriate to formal occasions, yet simultaneously is one in which Vivienne feels comfortable; the 'comfort' is enabled by the ease of movement, and by being a particular look which Vivienne habitually wears. This issue of comfort is crucial to understanding Vivienne's wardrobe. She is in possession

Aesthetics of the Self

of a range of poncho-style tops, all purchased about fifteen years ago from a South American shop in Camden Town (North London). The authenticity of the items, being made in South America, from llama wool, is important to Vivienne in her self-conceptualization as a global, politically astute person. Only one of them is an actual poncho (wherein the head goes though a neck slit at the top, and the material falls like a cape over the shoulders, leaving the arms free). Two of the others follow the principle of a pashmina (a large strip of material which is flung around the shoulders like a shawl). However, the commonality lies in the fabric and patterning, and similarly in the effect and function of wearing them. She tends to wear all of them in autumn and winter time; made from llama wool they are rough to the touch, and are worn over her usual clothes for an extra layer of warmth. Being impractical in the rain (merely getting sodden and waterlogged) she favours them on dry winter days, and often doubles them up as rugs in the park.

The material of the poncho consists of wide vertical stripes in a dark brown, camel and stone colour. The stripes run down vertically from the neck, yet as the material slopes over the shoulders, so too do the stripes, resulting in them curving with the arms, as they become diagonal and gradually horizontal as they reach her lower arms. As the neck is a wide V-neck, in conjunction with the softening of the shoulders through gently curving stripes, the effect is to make the neck area expansive, and the overall look is unstructured. The shape of the body is softened, rounding off the shoulders, physically engendering a sense of casualness. When worn, particularly on winter evenings in at home when there's a chill in the air, the masses of woollen fabric enswathe and enclose her body – still allowing the free movement of her arms. The cosiness of the poncho is further facilitated as she is able to hug her own body with her liberated arms, while still being subsumed by a layer of fabric. Similarly the other poncho-style tops permit such a sense of comfort and of being surrounded in cosy warm layers of fabric. The pashmina-style items are thrown around the shoulders, thus enveloping the body when worn. This sense of the voluminousness of fabric and looseness is prevalent in a great deal of Vivienne's clothing. As already mentioned, the silk shirts she wears are wide and baggy, as are the other shirts she wears informally. Her primary concern is to remain unfettered and unrestrained by the clothing she wears; the clothing she selects enables movement, allowing this feeling of comfort, as the clothing embraces her clothed body.

The ponchos materially enable comfort and cosiness, in particular in the home (where Vivienne often wears them). The 'comfort' engendered is not merely an obvious physical sense (in particular given that the material is harsh), but rather as something with coincides with her ordinary aesthetic. The ponchos are wrapped round the body; as 'ethnic' clothing, authentically obtained, in the autumnal colours she favours – the ponchos therein 'fit' her self-conceptualization. Weaved within the ponchos is her sense of the global, her political awareness.

The looseness of the fabric is crucial; even in her more formalized items, already discussed, rigidified structured shapes are not those Vivienne favours. The relationship between structured formality, as required by an evening/smart event, and soft fluidity is encapsulated in her skirt, silk shirt and waistcoat combination already discussed. Here, through appropriate combination, Vivienne is able to feel appropriately smart, and aware of the formality of the occasion through the rigidity of the waistcoat. Yet she is simultaneously allowed her usual 'comfort' through the flowing shirt in her usual blocks of colour. The fact that it is silk, a sensation apparent as it sensuously caresses the skin, makes it again defined as a smart or special occasion. Sexuality is heightened through the slit in the skirt, her legs are suggestively revealed only when she walks. The physical style of the skirt, with its slit, allows it to be practical but at the same time, by taking a healthy stride, a glimpse of the leg is revealed and the skirt is elevated beyond the level of mere function. Both factors are equally important to Vivienne. Within this look it is not merely that each individual item allows distinct facets, rather it is within the surface of individual items (the shape of the waistcoat yet covered with delicate ornament) that this happens. Comfort involves a combination not only of particular colours and fabrics, but also a complex interplay within the surface of each item: the complexities of the items ambiguously contradict and enhance each other. Part of what is being combined are aspects of her self and biography, cultivated through this aesthetic. Such an outfit shows the complexities of the surface through clothing – not only are different items layered upon each other to differential effect, but within each item the nuances and subtle antagonisms – of function and sexuality – interact and interchange with each other within the feature of a single item of clothing. Also players in this interchange are aspects of her biography, of her personality. As in Strathern's (1979) discussion where attributes of the person are brought to the surface, here with the movement of Vivienne's leg to a different angle, such attributes may be activated, then temporarily submerged, only to resurface again.

One of the most striking factors about Vivienne's clothing is the means through which she acquired it. The vast majority has been passed up to her by her two daughters – items they no longer wear or want, yet which are not yet completely threadbare, often things which are already second-hand. Many of her items are faded through perennial washing and wearing. Like the orange top discussed earlier, along with many items procured from charity shops, the biography of many items in her wardrobe is already extended over a long period of time, testing the durability of fabrics to their limit. Until clothing has physically disintegrated, Vivienne perseveres in wearing it. In wearing her clothing, Vivienne is bringing her familial relationships, her political orientations, her ecological moralities all within the act of dressing. Combinations of clothing involve a moment of totalization: of incorporating the diverse threads of her life within her clothing.

Aesthetics of the Self

Given that Vivienne's aesthetic is relatively coherent and continuous, the aesthetic totality that constitutes her wardrobe is able to bring together multiple facets of her self – as constituted biographically, relationally, politically and ethically. Like Mumtaz, what she is combining is not just colours, and fabrics, but fragments of her self.

Such an aesthetic totality only crystallizes over time, as the clothing softens through wearing, so too the clothing becomes integral to being a part of her. In wearing the same clothes over a period of time, the fabric starts to relax. The persistent washing and wearing of a sweater starts to drain the colour, softening both the appearance and the texture. Through perpetually wearing the same items of clothing it is as if they age with the wearer, becoming like a second skin. On wearing them there is no awareness of constraint, or a seam that rubs or chafes; rather the items soften in the places where the body is most harsh on the clothing: the elbows of a jumper, or the knees on trousers. The relationship between the clothing and person becomes symbiotic, the hardness of the body being softened by the fabric. Having occupied such a relationship to clothing all her life, Vivienne loves not to have to feel conscious in the clothing she is wearing. When the clothing is already worn and aged, the boundary that separates the clothing and the person starts to disintegrate, and the clothing is able to 'become' the wearer. Bayly (1989) has pointed to the links between biography and clothing, wherein the porosity of cloth, and as something worn by individuals next to the body, enables a fusion between person and clothing. Through clothing's capacity to age, yet being similarly durable this symbiotic relationship between person and clothing is created, where the wearer feels comfortable in her clothing. What Vivienne makes apparent is that she is equally able to do this when someone else has worn the clothing in for her. Although her favourite item is still a fleece she bought in Camden market twenty years ago, and is now so ripped and torn, it cannot be worn, but hangs – not quite dead – on the back of her door.

Isolated Nodules of Clothing

Given that she no longer works full time, Vivienne is able to wear such clothing all the time; however as has already been suggested when discussing her more formal wear, she widens her ordinary aesthetic to accommodate such necessities. Within her wardrobe Vivienne does possess certain isolated 'outfits', compelled by particular social occasions. Despite despising wearing rigidified formal clothing, on the occasion of her brother's wedding, her anticipated potential discomfort is subsumed to familial relationships. The purchased outfit consists of a cream top and burnt umber coloured skirt, both made of cotton which shimmers slightly in the light. The top is short sleeved and hangs loosely, yet at the bottom where it is at its fullest the top is layered with asymmetrical jaggered fabrics. The natural undulations of a loose top are enhanced by the extra layer of material present at the bottom. The skirt is in exactly the same style, and falls to near the floor. When wearing such an item, the body of the wearer recedes in prominence and instead the overlapping waves of fabric dominate and become the focus of attention. Moreover the body is still able to move freely underneath, albeit with the material swishing and catching against the legs with every step. Vivienne has worn this outfit to two weddings and would probably wear it to another, as she felt sufficiently comfortable in it, although professes she would not wear it to any other occasion as she would feel too 'self-conscious' in it, 'over the top'. Although such a domain forms a distinct nodule of her wardrobe, it is apparent that it still corresponds to her particular personal aesthetic: the colours and the style. While she ordinarily favours clothing that is like a second skin, here the 'fit' to the external event, and the expectations of those attending, means she is able to feel comfortable wearing it.

Such relatively formalized wear is able to be incorporated within Vivienne's overall personal aesthetic; while only wearable for particular occasions, she still feels comfortable in them. Vivienne's wardrobe constitutes an aesthetic totality in the convergence not only on particular colour combinations, but in her incorporating her family and her global political orientations into her clothing. So tyrannical is this aesthetic totality that more often than not Vivienne turns down invitations to formal events if she is not able to wear her everyday clothes. She turned down an invitation to a very prestigious media awards ceremony last year, solely on the basis that she did not want to get dressed up. She hated the thought that she would be forced to walk in a 'mincing way', wearing shoes she would be unable to take a full stride in, 'I just wouldn't be able to be!' On this occasion Vivienne vividly imagines the discomfort she would feel at the event, and is able to opt not to attend. The way in which she moves and stands is fundamental to her 'being', and is enabled and facilitated by the clothing she wears. Despite professing to throw 'whatever' clothing on, here an entire decision to not attend an important event is based upon clothing, and the 'discomfort' the wearing of formalized clothing would entail for her.

Conclusion

The very fact that Vivienne turns down prestigious invitations based upon her refusal to wear certain clothes makes it clear that clothing is just as significant for her as it is for the explicitly clothes conscious Rosie or Mumtaz. For all three women their wardrobes have been analysed as forms of extended personhood – wherein clothing becomes a means through which disparate facets of their

Aesthetics of the Self

selfhood are objectified (Gell 1998). Gell's theory points to the ways in which a person's intentionality may be distributed through objects, thus highlighting the immense potential to influence the minds of others through a particular medium. Such actualized potential is seen in Vivienne's cultivated image of lack of cultivation, resulting in the despondent groans of her daughters. However what becomes apparent through closer analysis of all three cases is that 'how I look or feel' turns out to be anything but merely a personal and free expression of the self. One of the supposed characteristics of postmodernity is that 'everyone can be anybody' (cited in Featherstone 1991), which translates sartorially into the wealth of often contradictory styles and identities to experiment with. What the examples here make clear is that there are numerous constraints that prevent this free exertion of agency through clothing.

The first constraint comes at the moment of assemblage: the individual has to commit to a particular outfit, combinations which in turn are unequivocally associated with that person. On any particular occasion one cannot be all the possibilities or looks that are present in the wardrobe. Although a degree of ambiguity can be incorporated within one outfit, the multiple identities offered by fragmented and ephemeral fashions cannot all be co-present within the one assemblage. Rosie's many wardrobes are overburdened with postmodern possibilities – offers of identities or selves Rosie may try on. Though for others who are aware of her affluence in clothing this makes her selection that much more specific, they know how easily she could have chosen something else. In the case presented in this paper, rather than this abundance of choice leading to greater freedom, it is this very profusion of clothing that leads to her inability to choose and indeed in the end making what seemed like a 'safe' choice, but was in fact unsuited to the occasion. What is constraining here for Rosie is the fact that in the moment of dressing she has to perform an act of aesthetic totalization to create her self. In Vivienne's case the opposite appears to be going on – her entire wardrobe constitutes a totalized aesthetic, rather than this merely being required at the moment of dressing. Such a totality incorporates not only particular colour domains and softening, flowing fabrics, but incorporates all aspects of her existence – an aesthetic 'comfort' materially cultivated through a lifetime of wearing. However, what becomes apparent is that such a complete aesthetic coherence can be just as constraining as Rosie's multiple possibilities. So enclosed are her aesthetic parameters that she is unable to attend events where she cannot wear these clothes.

Vivienne's personal aesthetic is extremely restricted in terms of what colours and fabrics she will wear, this leads on to the second major area of constraint, which is the constraints of the clothing itself – in terms of both its material propensities and also its own internal logic of combinations. In positing the agentic capacities of objects, Gell (1998) critiques the assumption that autonomous human agents have intentions, which are imposed upon passive objects. Instead agency emerges in the context of a web of objects and people – and that 'agents thus "are" and do not merely "use" artefacts' (1998: 21). Through this he refers to objects as secondary agents; they are not therefore seen to have independent intentions of their own but rather are the material embodiment of this intentionality – part of the matrix of its generation and actualization. Implicit within this argument – that objects are part of the externalized mind which may impact upon the mind of others – is the potential for failure. As the objects carry people's intentionality – yet in Gell's own argument are not passive – then through their very materiality objects may thwart our intentions. This is clearly apparent in Rosie's case. She intended to look chic and sophisticated; while each individual item in itself had worked before, she failed to anticipate that through combination an entirely unwanted effect would be produced. The particular fabric from which the skirt was made – leather – sits heavily upon her. Throughout the whole night she cannot ignore its presence; the combination of three items that are all black and all leather leads to an unexpected consequence. In communion with each other, they come to dominate Rosie herself, and the subtlety of her top. Thus not only does the clothing not act as a medium for her own intentions, it produces quite the opposite effect, through its own logic – the blackness and the fabrics connect with each other. The black leather in combination through the items comes to have its own efficacy and takes over the outfit, submerging Rosie's own intentions.

Rosie's example shows both the constraints of the material propensities of clothing, and the internal combinational logic of clothing. All the women I have worked with have a clear sense of what can and cannot be combined together – in terms of colours, styles or fabrics. Vivienne has an evident tendency towards wearing silk shirts and loose cotton skirts. Stylistically the looseness of the shirt and skirt correspond to create an overall feeling of fluidity; the skirt is in a 'safe' colour (blue or black), which has a high combinational potential. Again it is the shirt that is of the different fabric – the outfit is both smart and 'special' – through the shirt, yet the skirt grounds this in a comfortable everyday aesthetic. The style, colour, fabric all articulate together to create a particular effect. More often than not however this sense of what 'goes' is extremely constraining. What women experience as an aesthetic logic inherent in the style of the clothes itself can considerably impede their sense that they are free to choose.

As already noted, Vivienne's clothing constitutes an aesthetic totality which in itself prevents her from attending an event as her clothing delimits her. Cultivated throughout her lifetime, the dominance within her clothing of items that are soft and worn is overwhelming. As she has worn the clothing over such a long period of time, she becomes inextricably interwoven with the item itself. She cannot have this relationship to newly purchased clothing, which impacts upon her purchasing patterns – if clothing is not handed up to her she often buys it from second-hand

Aesthetics of the Self

shops – so it is already worn. This in itself creates its own logic of narrowing, in that she rarely buys new clothing. Furthermore, if her old worn clothing 'is' her, the differential relationship she would occupy to a new item means that one of her pre-existing soft worn items could not coexist in one outfit with a new item. When new items are purchased they form distinct nodules within the wardrobe (and are usually 'smart' items). Only once items are worn are they able to be combined again with older items. What is apparent here, then, is that the aesthetic logic is not that the logic of the clothing is constraining Vivienne, but that she herself is part of this logic. It is the interactive process of Vivienne wearing the clothing that creates this aesthetic incompatibility between the new and old clothing.

The third aspect of constraint comes from the way the clothing interiorizes the anticipated judgements of others. Discussed earlier was the possibility that clothing may be a means by which women are able to externalize their intentions in order to impact the will of others. In terms of Gell's (1998: 96–153) theory, clothing opens up the person to wider layers of externalized, potentially distributed, mind. But this opening up has made them vulnerable to penetration by the anticipated gaze of others. In the moment of selecting an outfit, Rosie imagines this gaze so vividly that it rapidly turns into such immense anxiety not only is she not able to find an outfit, she ends up falling back on an assortment of 'safe' items. In imagining how she may impact upon those at the Ivy, she lets the anticipated judgments of others in. Here the clothing may be regarded as a conduit – which in opening up the potential impact upon the minds of others, also allows the fierce judgements of others to strike deep within. In order to select the outfit that will make Rosie feel fashionable and chic, she has to envision the clientele that attend, how she might appear to them. The result is that Rosie's usual capacity for combination and selection of outfits is lost. Despite having seven wardrobes, Rosie's selection not only failed to express her, but from her perspective quite betrayed her, turning her into what she imagined others saw as aspects of herself she would never have wanted revealed at that time. In understanding such moments of anxiety, we need to examine how clothing as a medium that relates surface to depth is as much the fibres that conduct the judgements of others to the inside, as the intentions of the self to the outside.

In Rosie's case this moment wherein the judgements of others penetrate within leaves her vulnerable. However such a moment can also be one of success. As Mumtaz makes apparent, on an equally important occasion, she is able to exert her own agency on her clothing. Rather than allowing the imagined opinions of others to impede her decisions, she is enabled to make a novel combination. Many of the constraints discussed earlier arise out of the material propensities of items of clothing, the perceived internal ordering of the wardrobe and the totalization necessary in the act of selecting an outfit. However, despite Mumtaz's wardrobe having clearly defined orders – such as an 'Indian' wardrobe separate from her 'Western' clothes – she is not confined by this aesthetic logic. She has the confidence to exert her own agency on the pre-existing ordering of her wardrobe, in order to make radical new juxtapositions. The logics of clothing do not dominate her choices. There are many instances therefore of success – of the clothing distributing the wearers mind to others – as well as of failure. When Rosie wore the leather items together, through combination they came to dominate and ultimately quash her externalized intentionality. However in Vivienne's case often the opposite is the case. Wearing the worn, softened clothing, which is losing its colour, or the Rohan trousers with the aesthetic of functionality, she is able to feel like her 'self', yet simultaneously influence others into thinking she does not care about clothing.

Through these three contrasting examples we can see the agency of the wearer – in selecting an outfit, and as objectified through the items of clothing to impact upon others – yet also the ways in which the materiality of the clothing brings about unwanted and unexpected effects. However, there is not a defined opposition between the agency of the wearer and that of the clothing; nor in each instance of dressing does the order of things comes to dominate the order of people or vice versa. Rather there is an intricate interaction between the two. In the earlier discussion of Vivienne, it becomes apparent that even what appears to be the structural logic of her wardrobe – the new clothing being incompatible with old favourites – is in fact more complex. As the clothing becomes worn through its relationship to her and her body, she cannot wear new clothing with this, because it is incompatible with the self that the worn clothing embodies. Therefore her self is part of, and in part created by, this aesthetic logic. This is extremely different from the situation with regard to either Rosie or Mumtaz, both of whom are deliberately attempting to create an outfit that will impact upon the will of others. However, for Vivienne the aesthetic logic has not only become sedimented over time. As the clothes become more worn the effect is twofold: the clothing externalizes her intentionality more efficaciously (as the unkempt look is enhanced), and her personal aesthetic becomes even more narrowed, delimiting further what cannot be combined. As items worn habitually over extended periods of time, she lacks the extreme self-consciousness that Mumtaz and Rosie express on instances of dressing; instead now Vivienne's clothing draws out facets of her self and biography through its own logics independent of the wearer. The slit in the long skirt allows the 'surfacing' of Vivienne's sexuality yet also of her practicality and desire for mobility. The fluctuating processes of surfacing and resurfacing of facets of the self are actualized within complex aesthetic dialogues that interweave the agency of the wearer and the logics that arise from the materiality of the clothing.

References

Barthes, R. 1985 *The Fashion System*. London: Cape.
Bayly, C. 1989 'The Origins of Swadeshi: Cloth and Indian Society, 1700–1930'. In A. Appadurai (ed.) *The Social Life of Things*. Cambridge: Cambridge University Press.
Buckley, R. and Gundle, S. 2000 *Fashion and Glamour*. In N. White and I. Griffiths (eds) *The Fashion Business: Theory, Practice, Image*. Oxford: Berg.
Cole, S. 2000 *'Don we now our Gay Apparel': Gay Men's Dress in the Twentieth Century*. Oxford: Berg.
Craik, J. 1993 *The Face of Fashion: Cultural Studies in Fashion*. London: Routledge.
Entwistle, J. 2001 'The Dressed Body'. In J. Entwistle and E. Wilson (eds) *Body Dressing*. Oxford: Berg.
Featherstone, M. 1991 *Consumer Culture and Post-Modernism*. London: Sage.
Gell, A. 1998 *Art and Agency: Towards an Anthropological Theory*. Oxford: Clarendon Press.
Goffman, E. 1971 *The Presentation of Self in Everyday Life*. London: Penguin.
Mauss, M. 1973 'Techniques of the Body'. *Economy and Society*, 2(1): 70–89.
McCracken G. 1988 *Culture and Consumption: New Approaches to the Symbolic Character of Consumer Goods and Activities*. Bloomington: Indiana University Press.
Miller, D. 1994 'Style and Ontology'. In J. Friedman (ed.) *Consumption and Identity*. Chur: Harwood Academic.
Napier, D. 1985 *Masks, Transformation, and Paradox*. Berkeley: University of California Press.
Peiss, K. 1996 'Making up, Making over: Cosmetics, Consumer Culture and Women's identity'. In V. De Grazia and E. Furlough (eds) *The Sex of Things: Gender and Consumption in Historical Perspective*. London: University of California Press.
Sennett, R. 1971 *The Fall of Public Man*. Cambridge: Cambridge University Press.
Strathern, M 1979. 'The self in self-decoration'. *Oceania*, 49(4): 240–56.
Wigley, M. 1995 *White Walls, Designer Dresses: the Fashioning of Modern Architecture*. Cambridge, MA: MIT Press.
Wilson, E. 1985 *Adorned in Dreams: Fashion and Modernity*. London: Virago.
Young, D. 2001 'The Colours of Things, Memory, Mentality & an Anthropology of the Senses in North West South Australia'. Unpublished PhD thesis, University College London.

–3–

The Other Half: The Material Culture of New Fibres
Kaori O'Connor

Clothing, as Dalby (2001) says of the Japanese kimono, is one of the richest aspects of material culture available to the anthropologist. Once viewed simply as mere artefacts, it is now recognized that cloth and clothing are culturally constructed commodities with complex symbolic properties, transmitting purity and pollution, linking past and present, transforming through belief, carrying fundamental values. Spanning worlds and time, a substantial anthropological record speaks eloquently of the ways in which cloth and clothing materialize social and political statuses, convey and consolidate identity, mediate social relations and not only reflect social change but also create it, acting as Schneider (1994) shows as an agent of history by giving cultural form to innovative dynamic moments. The very ubiquity, intimacy and materiality of cloth and clothing mean that by studying them we can obtain nuanced insights into the dynamics of society on many levels not easily arrived by other means, if at all. Yet although we know that cloth and clothing work like this in the culture areas anthropologists have traditionally studied, and excellent anthropological work of this kind continues (notably Hendrickson (ed.) 1996, Renne 1995; and see Hansen 2004 for a full review) there is as yet no established 'material culture of cloth and clothing' at home that looks in this specifically anthropological way at the things we wear and don't wear and their relation to the things we do and don't do.

This lack is all the more striking since it was an anthropologist, Kroeber (1919, also Richardson and Kroeber 1940), who was the first to study Western clothes in a detailed and systematic manner, noting the correspondence between social and political shifts and changes in fashion. However, since the 1970s, competing disciplines – notably cultural studies and sociology (see Wilson 1985, Entwistle 2000a for typical examples) – have sought to exclude anthropologists from the study of fashion at home through the use of a simplistic modernity paradigm that goes as follows. Western fashion changes and is modern. Non-Western clothing is fixed, traditional and does not change. Therefore, it is asserted, anthropologists can have nothing to say about modern, Western fashion. Even in its own terms, this argument cannot be sustained, as Bannerjee and Miller's (2003) recent benchmark study of the changing contemporary sari amply demonstrates. More importantly, the passage of time has revealed the limitations of these competing approaches which arise specifically from their historical development, and which I deal with here necessarily briefly (a detailed account is in preparation, O'Connor 2004a, see also 2004b), in fulfilment of the need, highlighted by Marcus (1998, 1999), for anthropologists working at home to acknowledge and critique competing representations in order to situate their own work.

The disciplines that have come to dominate the study of clothing in our society emerged during the theoretical debates of the 1970s and 1980s. Heavily influenced by academic Marxism and feminism, the field rapidly became historicized, politicized, gendered and theorized. Schooled in literary analysis, unaccustomed to ethnography and preoccupied with text, the nascent disciplines focused on images, privileging semiotics (Barthes 1985 being the seminal work in this field) and visual culture over material culture. In time, distinct approaches to clothing developed – fashion theory and the feminist perspective (Hollander 1978 and Wilson 1985 being influential works respectively); the masculinist orientation (Breward 1995, 1999, Nixon 1996); cultural and media studies (McRobbie 1991, 1994, 1998, Craik 1994, Hebdige 1978, 1988, Braham 1997, Warwick and Cavallero 1998, Bruzzi and Gibson 2000, Benstock and Ferriss 1994); design history and the new art history (Steele 1998, Breward 1998, Palmer 1997) and what can be called the new cultural sociology (Entwistle 2000a, 2000b, Entwistle and Wilson 1998, Campbell 1995, 1996, Rubinstein 1995). Despite differences that are outside the scope of this work, studies of this kind were generally productive of what Leitch (1996) has identified as the postmodern perspective on fashion, visually oriented and primarily concerned with the disaggregation and heteroglossia of dress codes and styles. Couched in the language of domination, hegemony, resistance, accommodation and negotiation, the corpus of work produced under this aegis tended to demonize capitalism (closely identified with the patriarchal), and to ignore the realities of life in our mass market, commodified culture. Thus, culture and commerce were kept entirely separate, with the latter virtually invisible (see McRobbie 1998 for a paradigm example). Producers were cast as manipulative profiteerers, and the origins of goods were left largely unexamined except for studies of labour exploitation. Consumption was valorized, with the wearing of clothes elevated to the status of performance art and the expression of personal politics. Cloth, deemed to be visually unexciting on its own, was sidelined in favour of clothes and, increasingly, *images* of clothes as epitomized by fashion photography. Clothing itself was split into two categories. The first, 'fashion' – a term that embraced both elite couture and reactionary streetwear and little in between – was never well-defined, but was nonetheless considered to 'matter more' than the second category, 'clothes', the everyday wear of ordinary people, which was largely overlooked. In addition to resisting hegemonic norms and breaking convention, these studies aimed to give voice to diversity and the marginal. There were many investigations of subcultures such as Punks and Goths (see Hodkinson 2002), but few of the mainstream culture to which they are sub-. There is a disproportionate number of studies of alternative areas of provisioning, such as charity shops, and of elite practices, such as what passes for *haute couture* today, but relatively few of mainstream, mass market arenas and activities, or of the middle class, which, contested though that term may be, still comprises the largest self-declared social grouping. In the literature, dress practices are presented as the cultural construction of embodied identity but this identity is highly restricted. For example, there is a plethora of studies of youth culture, but little on the sartorial culture of other age groups, begging the question of what happens to youths, their clothes and their bodies when they get older, a significant question in our society where there are more people over the age of forty than under it. And then there is the ever-increasing number of studies preoccupied with eroticism (see especially Summers 2001, Steele 1996, 2001, Kunzle 1982), sexual practice and fetish fashion – but is sex all there is to fashion?

Ironically, these studies, which aimed to widen the field, have effectively narrowed it. Undeniably, they introduced a dynamism missing from old-style costume histories, but by separating commerce from culture and practice from theory, by ignoring the mainstream, and by celebrating fragmentation and diversity while at the same time privileging some groups and subjects over others, they have created an analytic black hole. Theirs is a world of fashion as fuzzy logic, an insubstantial universe spinning on an axis of what Ortner (1999: 58) has described as vertiginous Baudrillardian process, driven by signifiers with no referents and images that never stabilize. There are fashions in the study of fashion, as with everything else. Still influenced by early postmodernism, these competing approaches have not developed to meet new concerns. Although we may now know more about individual practice, and the uses of clothing in identity formation, we know almost nothing about the mainstream processes by which cloth and clothing, however they are used, come into being in our society. It is now clear that the mapping of difference and elucidation of the personal produced by competing disciplines do not illuminate the nuanced workings of society as a whole as anthropologists are accustomed to seeing them, nor do they address the questions that cloth and clothes pose through their very specificity.

Appositely, it is just at this point in the social sciences generally that the inability of rationalist neoclassical economics as well as cultural studies and the other new disciplines to explain why we buy and don't buy – and why we produce and don't produce – is becoming apparent. This is where material culture comes to the fore, its very materiality countering the over-theorizing that has prevailed for so long, allowing us to look at our clothing in new ways, in order to ask the kinds of questions that anthropologists abroad have long been asking about cloth, clothing and society in other cultures. We are revisiting what Sahlins (1974) called 'an economics properly anthropological', which cannot be comprehended in its material terms apart from its social terms. In concentrating on the ways in which people realize themselves through consuming goods, it has been all too easy to forget, as Sahlins showed for the American clothing system, that capitalist production too is a cultural process in which mass-produced goods constitute a virtual map of the cultural universe. There is now a rapidly growing interdisciplinary interest in the relationship between culture and commerce, marked by calls for more ethnographies of practice in commodified worlds, specifically ethnographies that link production and consumption (see du Gay and Pryke 2002, Jackson, Lowe, Miller and Mort 2000). This is a perfect opening for studies of clothing at home that treat capitalism as a cultural system in which both production and consumption are part of the same process, allowing the analysis to focus on the dialectics between the two, a distinctively anthropological approach. And it is a perfect opportunity too for developing new material culture approaches to the understanding of the dynamics of contemporary society through the study of cloth and clothing. This contextualizes the section that follows, and the future development of the anthropology of cloth and clothing at home generally.

The Material Culture of New Fibres

In applying a material culture approach (see Buchli 2002), we are returning to the roots of anthropological practice, but in a new way. The new material culture is not concerned primarily with the mechanics of technology or the aesthetics of style, but with production in a larger, cultural sense, in which production is seen as a cultural process and mass-produced goods constitute social values in material form. Significantly, this universe is not limited by *literal* materiality. How and why are some things made and others not, why are some things successful and others not, who wears what and why, who does *not* wear what and why, and what do things or their lack say about people and society? The counterfactual is central here, for by looking at failures as well as successes, *the immaterial as well as the material,* we can appreciate the complexities that distinguish anthropology from cultural studies and sociology (see O'Connor 2004a).

Conventionally, material culture studies begin at the beginning. For clothing, that starting point is cloth, either woven or 'made', as with felt or *tapa*. In the case of anthropology at home, focusing on fabric is a useful way of avoiding the confusion induced by concentrating on constantly changing fashion styles. Fabrics have long been seen as artefacts, transformed as Ingold (2001) puts it, out of brute matter, in this case out of 'natural' fibres such as cotton, wool and silk, which are literally beaten into submission to culture. This is the nature-into-culture model, in which the physical and social processes of transformation are the objects of interest, not the materiality of fibres, which remains unexamined, and in which surfaces are deemed to be significant, not what lies beneath or within them. This model may work well enough in pre-industrial, artisanal and small-scale contexts, but is woefully inadequate for the society in which we live, where mass production is the rule and 'meaning' does not spring from long established tradition, or through the physical processes of making by hand, as for example with hand-weaving or quilting.

The challenge this poses to established approaches to cloth is seen in the fact that in the seminal anthropological work on the subject, Weiner and Schneider's (1989) *Cloth and Human Experience,* the examples of capitalist societies dealt with were either pre-industrial or involved handwork, as with hand embroidery done for tourists. Tellingly, all of the societies studied employed cloth made of natural fibres. At home today, the picture is very different. Regardless of consciously expressed preferences for natural fibres and fabrics, more than half of the fibres we wear today are man-made. Globally, 40 per cent of the world fibre production is cotton, 2.5 per cent is wool and 0.2 per cent is silk.[1] Apart from statistically insignificant fibres such as ramie and jute, the rest is comprised of man-made fibres in two main groups – synthetics (such as polyester) and cellulosics (such as viscose rayon) – along with speciality fibres such as spandex, the best-known brand of which is Lycra. And yet, to date, there has been only one anthropological investigation of the social and cultural aspects of synthetic fibres in our society, Schneider's (1994) pioneering study of polyester. Like Mintz, whose 1986 work on sugar she cites, Schneider goes beyond social and technological history to throw light upon the workings of capitalism as a cultural system, demonstrating how changes in the production and consumption of synthetic fibres in America – peaking in 1969, then declining steadily through the 1970s and 1980s – were coincidental with broader cultural movements and the formation of new social groups in which the category 'natural' took on highly charged symbolic meaning, and in which synthetic cloth and clothes came to carry negative moral values. Here, the very specificity and materiality of polyester – its feel; its mode of production, which raised environmental issues; its association in the public mind with science and modernity; the kinds of clothes for which it was used – illuminate wider issues and processes. In itself, this represents a substantial advance on understanding what cloth and clothing can tell us about our society as a whole, but it is possible to go further – to an even more basic form of materiality – the *fibre* of which cloth and clothes are made.

Man-made fibres fundamentally alter our understanding of the relationship between persons and things, because the difference between man-made and natural fibres is one of kind rather than of degree. While natural fibres such as silk are basically 'as found'[2] the unique feature of man-made fibres is that they can be created 'to order'. Instead of processing a natural fibre in hopes that it will fit requirements, requirements can be established in advance, and the fibre created specifically to fulfil them. Thus a fibre can be created to respond to changes in heat or light, to carry electronic information, to resist moisture or retain it, to destroy odour-causing bacteria or exude a perfumed aroma, to change surface colour and pattern under different conditions, and to stretch or contract. Easily characterized as 'active' in contrast to 'inert' natural fibres, these new techno-textiles have been described as 'smart', 'intelligent' and 'sapient' (e.g. Küchler 2003). Because the fibres have been created from scratch, the distinction between inner and outer, surface and interior, becomes less relevant. It is no longer a clear case of 'culture' being laid on the surface of 'nature' and indeed synthetic fibres blur the boundaries between them. This effectively moves the goalposts of material culture to a more fundamental level. Schneider's study began with finished cloth, and focused on the competition between producers of synthetic and of natural fibre fabrics. By beginning even earlier, with the very invention of a fibre, one can trace the interplay of culture and commerce entailed in the creation of new forms of materiality, and better understand the various factors that account for a fibre's success or failure in a wider social context. With man-made fibres, it is even more the case that, as Pastoreau (2001: xiv) said of clothes, 'there is nothing anecdotal or romantic, not to mention aesthetic, about clothing; it is a veritable social system'.

Usefully for analysis generally, the specificities of man-made fibres introduce or tie together a number of factors, contexts and agendas that an evolving critical anthropology at home is now having to address. For example, the economics of new fibres, which carry extremely high development costs, are such that for a fibre to be successful it must go into mass production. This situates studies in a broad and inclusive sector of society, the mass market, in a trajectory that begins with invention and finishes not with purchase, but with end use. By following a fibre through its many forms and stages – not all of which are successful – we gain insight into how a complex mass market works, and the ways in which producers and consumers are interdependent. Man-made fibres take a long time to bring to market and, usually, a long time to establish. This introduces time and process to the analysis, allowing us to see the ethnographic present as just one episodic moment in a larger stream (Moore 1994). Indeed, the sheer scale of the fibre industry makes it virtually impossible to understand what is going on in the ethnographic present without reference to the archival past. Studies of man-made fibres also oblige us to engage with the paradigmatic form of capitalism, big business. Despite the romantic image of the lone inventor, epitomized today by the iconic garage in Palo Alto where the first home computer was devised by the founders of Hewlett Packard, in the world of chemical fibres it has always been the case that only big business has the resources to develop and commercialize entirely new products. In the past, this process has been seen by the social sciences in one of three ways. Histories of innovation tend to portray technological development as part of an inexorable and untroubled scientific progress in which human agents appear to play no part (see Noble 1977 for a critical account; and Handley 1999 for an example relating specifically to fibres). In cultural studies, as we have seen, it is individuals and images that are privileged and the material world largely ignored, although at the same time capitalist production is decried as manipulation by big business of the consumer. Third, social histories engage the larger context and longer view with varying degrees of success (see Strasser 2000 for an exemplary example), but like technological histories they tend to deal only with successes not failures, and as such present only a partial view. A further attraction of man-made fibres is that they allow us to move beyond these limitations by introducing a form of archival resource little used by anthropologists to date – commercial archives.

Once considered almost archaic, archives, as Showalter (2001) notes, have become highly fashionable. Wardrobes are spoken of as personal archives, and fashion designers giving collections of their past works to museums speak of them as 'material archives'. This renewed interest in records and material objects can be seen, I argue, as a reaction to the excesses of postmodernism. Businesses in our society, particularly family businesses and those with strong corporate identities, have often created and maintained commercial company archives. What begins as a record of daily work becomes a memorial over time, and it is the latter quality that has often accounted for their preservation. The documents kept in these collections are frequently diverse, and can consist of personal and business correspondence, production records, salesmen's receipts, laboratory records, internal memoranda, market research reports, press releases, transcripts of meetings, promotional materials, sales aids and retail ephemera, company magazines and newsletters, advertisements, newspaper cuttings, radio and television transcripts, examples of products and even expense receipts. That advertisements are but one element among many in these collections is significant. Miller (1997) has argued that the importance of advertisements is overstated in studies arising in competing disciplines, which, using textual analysis as a primary tool, foreground the advertisement and its deconstruction, while ignoring the advertiser's intentions and other forms of commercial activity that present themselves to ethnographic and archival view. In these studies the producer-consumer relationship has been largely seen in terms of hierarchy, dominance and submission, framed by the discourses of capitalism (Miller 1997: 153), and also of gender, in which the producer is cast as wholly dominant and exploitative of consumers. O'Barr (1994) has noted that there is very little in the advertising-centred literature about the producer's intentions that is more than assumption or speculation and he has criticized historians and analysts of advertising such as Marchand (1985, 1998) for failing to consider the objectives and motives of producers from the perspective of the producers' own experience. Easily accessible in the public domain, and even more easily taken out of context, advertisements (or, more accurately, interpretations of advertisements) provide a partial perspective at best. It is only with the greater array of sources contained in a full commercial archive – combined with ethnographic observation and information from other sources – that a more detailed and nuanced picture begins to emerge about how material things come into being in our society, and what happens to them, their producers and their consumers over time. Commercial archives relating specifically to man-made fibres are a particularly important resource for understanding this process because of the specific properties of fibres alluded to above. Because fibres can be created to order, knowledge of consumer preferences and desires regarding both cloth and clothing, and an awareness of social change and values, become highly important to fibre producers. Technological expertise alone is not enough. As commercial archives show, producers have to engage successfully with culture in order to attain commercial success, and in the case of fibres this engagement is a highly complex process. A knowledge of how this process has worked in the past is essential to understanding what is happening in the present, where the dynamics of culture and commerce, production and consumption, are central to our constantly expanding material world, and where new fibres shape the way we live, and are shaped by us in return. In addition, because they deal with the mass market, reading a producer's archive is a useful corrective for those accustomed to the micro-perspectives of diversity. To date, academics have shown some reluctance to examine commercial archives on the grounds they are 'biased', but there can be no justification for ignoring the authoritative sources on production simply because they have been generated by the producer.

Man-made Fibres: The Early Years at Dupont and the Case of Wash and Wear

Many of the man-made fibres in our wardrobes have been produced by a single firm, E.I. du Pont de Nemours and Company, commonly known as Dupont. This transnational American corporation, the oldest industrial company on the Fortune 500 list, was until recently,[3] through its textile division, the world's largest integrated fibre business, operating in 50 countries and with an approximate annual revenue from fibres of $6.5 billion (US). As Charles O. Holliday Jr, the CEO of Dupont put it in 2002, 'We're not just the leader in this industry. We, more than anybody, created this industry'.[4] 'Not just producers of man-made fibres, Dupont were also inventors, with an unrivalled programme of applied and fundamental research. It was in Dupont's laboratories that many of the products that made or make up our material world were created, including nylon, the wool-like acrylic fibre

Orlon, the wash-and-wear polyester Dacron, fire-resistant Nomex, the synthetic rubber Neoprene, super-strong Kevlar, stain-resistant Teflon and stretchy Lycra. The company maintains an extensive archive covering all their their fibres, and the research I carried out there provided the material for the account that follows, and the background for a larger and ongoing project involving ethnography as well as archival investigation (2004a and in preparation, also 2004b).

Initially, Dupont entered the man-made fibre field at the end of the First World War by buying the American rights to a cellulose fibre – 'artificial silk' – that had first been developed in France. Dupont's interest in the fibre had been aroused by the fact that it involved nitrocellulose technology in which the company was well versed since the first product it had manufactured was gunpowder, and it had also noted that imports of artificial silk from Europe had grown steadily throughout the war when natural silk from the Far East was not available. Dupont opened factories to produce the fibre, and expected it would be a relatively straightforward matter to sell it to the New England textile mills that dominated the American cloth-producing trade at the time. However, when Dupont salesmen went out on the road with the new product, which they called 'Fibersilk', they encountered immediate opposition from the mill managers who declared synthetic fibres to be a 'fly-by-night novelty', and castigated Dupont's salesmen for 'wasting their precious time talking about something that was artificial and therefore ridiculous'.[5] Dupont soon found that the production of new man-made fibres also necessitated the production of meaning. Although imported artificial silk sold well and was widely used, mainly for underwear and hosiery, the company discovered that it was regarded by the public as a cheap and often shoddy substitute for natural silk, a 'budget' choice without any cachet – associations that were not attractive to a company whose products had always been synonymous with quality. Having been attracted to man-made fibres by the simple synergy of compatibility with its other chemical products and potential profits, the company now found itself confronted by culture in the form of embedded ideas about the new materials on the part of the mills and of the public. More challenging still, this was a different kind of public.

Dupont's entry into man made fibres coincided with the emergence of a new group of consumers. As the official history of the firm put it:

> The decade of the 1920's was featured by the dramatic mass emergence of many interesting phenomena, including the radio, the motion picture and women. Most, including women, had been around for some time: only now did the scene suddenly swarm with them. (Dupont 1952: 91)

Or rather, only now had women become independent consumers in significant numbers. Women in the 1920s, Dupont noted, were increasingly entering the business world, even ousting male stenographers. Women gained the vote, drove automobiles, wore ever-shorter skirts that showed off their hosiery, replaced boned corsets with rubberized girdles, and abandoned heavy underwear for filmy lingerie. Movies set the fashions, generating a demand for cheaper, more modish clothing and accessories. In the home, women wanted new appliances such as refrigerators, which were changing food buying patterns and creating demands for new kinds of packaging. Not only were women beginning to earn their own money; they increasingly took on the role of purchasing agents for the whole family. In fact, Dupont concluded, 'now that women had the asking power, there was almost no end to the good things women demanded of industry and especially its chemical branch' (Dupont 1952: 91).

Dupont soon found that the French fibre was extremely difficult to work with. Instead of continuing with a flawed product in the face of opposition from mills and the public, the company decided to find out what women wanted, and then use its laboratories and engineering technology to develop their own fibre to order. Turning to the fledging field of market research, Dupont funded a national study to poll 10,000 women on what they wanted from artificial silk. What women wanted, the survey revealed, was not another silk, but completely new kinds of outwear materials that were resistant to soiling, easy to clean and care for, that held their shape, were durable but also soft, were comfortable in warm weather, smart in appearance and reasonably priced. No single natural fibre had these qualities.

These expressed preferences reflected the emergent postwar lifestyle in which unparalleled leisure and mobility led to a demand for easy living, easy shopping and easy care. Yet despite these nascent social trends and expressed preferences, Dupont found that in practice the majority of manufacturers and consumers remained resistant to the idea of artificial fabrics and fibres generally. Acceptance was given a boost in 1924 when Dupont and other producers agreed to give artificial silk a new generic name – 'rayon' – from 'ray' for its sheen and 'on' to suggest a fibre, as in cotton (Rutledge 1966). This enabled consumers to think of rayon as a fibre in its own right, and not as an inferior version of another, natural fibre, and it also helped to overcome the mills' opposition. As a Dupont salesman recalled 'naturally the old time cotton mills thought anything "artificial" was blasphemy in the textile trade, and it wasn't until the term "rayon" was coined that we were able to make any dent on the market'.[6] Even a new name was not enough. The company discovered that in order to be successful it had to do more than make a new fibre and sell it to the mills. It had to promote a new way of living and of thinking about cloth to the consumers and the retailers who served them.

Dupont's artificial silk survey set the pattern for what became a fundamental part of their textile business. The company built up a textile marketing department unparalleled in the trade, embracing market research, advertising, promotion, publicity and retail services. Formal market research involved commissioning surveys 'to tell us how we are doing, what people really want, and where we should put more effort'.[7] It differed from advertising in that it came from the consumers rather than being directed at them. Findings went to the research and technical departments, to inform ongoing refinements of the fibres. For as long as they produced it, Dupont never 'finished' with a fibre; the laboratories were constantly working on improvements and new applications in response to changing needs. New fibres were introduced to the manufacturers and the public in intensive promotional campaigns that promoted the idea of the fibres, their performance and the new modern lifestyle of which they were part, as well as actual garments made by particular manufacturers. The important point here is that although the type of garment was already familiar to consumers, garments made of the new fibres had entirely innovative properties: the fibre and fabric, rather than the style, influenced everyday life. There were pictures in magazines of women golfing in figure-hugging non-sagging knitted sweaters or getting out of cars in skirts with no wrinkles, and men bounding down the gangways of airplanes in uncreased suits. Salesmen threw themselves fully clothed into swimming pools to show how well suits made of the new fibres weathered the experience. There were in-store demonstrations, fashion shows, trade fair exhibitions, sponsorship of events, talks at women's clubs by Dupont representatives, and promotions on radio and in the new medium, television. Each time a new fibre was introduced, Dupont had to go through the same process. In the company's words,

> Back in the 1950's and 1960's, the sale of man-made fibres had to be built in part on describing the advantages of these new fibres not only to the industry but also to the consumer. Consider such common apparel as sweaters which can be washed without shrinkage, undergarments needing no ironing, skirts and trousers with permanent pleats and creases, and outwear staying fresh-looking despite high humidity... None of these had any meaning before the advent of nylon, Dacron and Orlon.[8]

Yet despite market research and extensive publicity, the success of new fibres was by no means instant or guaranteed. For example, ease of washing and after care were among the most important features of an ideal fabric as revealed by the artificial silk survey undertaken in the 1920s, yet in the 1950s, when Dupont finally introduced wash and wear Dacron, intensive promotion was still required. A stalwart of Dupont's wash and wear promotion initiative was the manager of the information services for the Textile Fibers department. His hobby was collecting old-time household equipment, especially antique flat-irons which, he said, symbolized the tedious task that traditionally had been women's most disliked household chore. He used his flat-irons as props in presentations he gave to women's groups across the country on the theme of '*Your Mothers and Grandmothers Never Had It So Good*', highlighting the way that Dupont had pioneered the development of man-made fibres that freed women from arduous ironing board drudgery. 'There has been a complete transition from the once inflexible routine of wash on Monday, iron on Tuesday and maybe work furiously on Wednesday to finish the job' he would say, going on to extol the virtues of Dupont's easy care fibre that could be put through an automatic washer and dryer and emerge in less than an hour, ready to wear. At an appropriate point, he would step behind a screen that had been provided, change into a lounging robe, and then toss his wash and wear suit into the washer and dryer included among his props, continuing to talk while the suit was being laundered. Later, he changed back into the freshly washed suit and finished his lecture, the whole operation taking about forty minutes.[9] The audience, he reported, found it 'fascinating'. The idea of educating the consumer was nothing new; most of the literature that surrounds the British Great Exhibition of 1851 and the foundation of London's Victoria and Albert Museum were prompted by such ambitions. But these were highly patrician images of didactic persuasion. The real innovation was the investment in a far more interactive relationship that was as much based upon being educated by consumers as educating them, and was one of many new attempts to engage in this kind of collaborative meaning making. (Compare, for example, the party-plan techniques developed for Tupperware (Clarke 1999).

Also new were the intensity and speed of social change. As incomes rose, ever more people enjoyed better homes and cars, better living and, Dupont realised, a new culture. As a company representative observed, 'Time to enjoy these possessions became an all-important commodity, free time over and above the job and the household chores, and that is what we are selling. Our fibers in the last analysis mean more free time' (Keller 1955: 128). In order to promote their fibres, Dupont had to promote 'modern living'. By selling culture in order to sell cloth, the company was literally helping to create the fabric of a new society, and was being shaped by it in return. However, the process was, and is, far from straightforward.

Conclusion

The example of wash and wear illustrates a number of features of man-made fibres as material culture. First, there is the way they highlight the dynamic of history and illuminate social change. The long lead time, some thirty years in this case, between the first consumer survey and the launch of the product, means that consumer needs and values may have changed by the time the fibre appears. The newly enfranchised and independent American woman of the 1920s was very different to the conventional, domestically-orientated woman of the mid-1950s. It is difficult to imagine having to encourage women in the first group to give up the drudgery of ironing, in the way that was necessary three decades later. The initial conservatism with which wash and wear fibre was regarded in the 1950s is an indication of the way in which cloth, with its associations of 'cleanliness', 'order', and the performance of ritualistic labour, is linked to deep cultural values and ideas about social roles. These changed again in the 1970s when wash and wear, having gained acceptance, fell out of favour, a victim of a fundamental shift in social values, attitudes and practices that returned natural fibres to popularity. Now, in 2005, when fibre producers are trying to promote technically advanced textiles, it is wash and wear that has become the standard of conservatism. 'New fibres?' the head of production of a leading British fashion chain aimed at women aged sixteen to twenty-five said to me, 'It doesn't matter what these new fibres can do. "Can I put it in the washing machine and will it come out the same as when it went in" is all our customers care about'. This also points to the second thing that distinguishes man-made fibres, fabrics and clothing from the naturals – they are *performance* fibres, not fibres whose primary appeal depends on 'style' or 'look'. Man-made fibres are not inert, they have been created to *do*. They are the materializations of expressed cultural values, the realizations of culturally approved action, but their success or failure is tied to a historically specific mutually constitutive process between producer and consumer, production and consumption in which neither producer nor consumer is dominant. As Sahlins (1976: 185) put it, although it may appear to producers as a quest for profit and to the consumer as an acquisition of useful goods, it is basically a symbolic process:

> this view of production as the substantialization of a cultural logic should prohibit us from speaking naively of the generation of demand by supply, as though the social product were the conspiracy of a few decision makers able to impose an ideology of fashion through the deceits of advertising. Nor need one indulge in the converse mystification of capitalist product as a response to consumers wants. (Sahlins 1976: 184)

Third, the use of commercial and marketing records presents a very different and more complex picture than that arising from advertisements. The difficulties encountered, and periodic failures of fibres give as much, if not more, insight into cultural dynamics as accounts of successes alone. The special qualities of man-made fibres give special insights into the workings of the complex, capitalist commodified world in which we live and, at the same time, present the opportunity for more philosophical reflections. Agency is built into man-made fibres, but this agency can only operate in specific cultural contexts – are 'smart' fibres truly sapient in their own right? And is the agency they have greater than that which was put into them? More work in this field is needed to advance both kinds of understanding. Not merely of academic interest, the congruence of commerce and culture will determine whether these new fibres will successfully reach a mass market.

The material presented here has been largely historical, but this has been necessary in order to establish the way in which the industry works, something which is not immediately apparent if investigations are confined to the present. As Sahlins (1994: 37) puts it, ethnography with time and transformation built into it is a distinct way of knowing the anthropological object, with a possibility of changing the way in which culture is thought. I have concentrated on clothes and fibres, in order to restore cloth – the missing half – to the overall fashion equation, and to highlight the importance of man-made fibres generally. Indeed, after a long period when clothing and style dominated the field, the pendulum of interest is swinging the other way, with the most interesting developments coming from new fibres, both because of their technical capabilities (see Braddock and O'Mahoney 1999) and appearance. As a study commissioned by Dupont to mark the millennium notes, 'The spheres of chemistry and high fashion are drawing ever closer together, redefining the boundaries of what is wearable' (Wolf and Schlachter 2000: xxvi). It has long been recognized in anthropology that the most illuminating studies, such as Bean's (1989) work on Gandhi and *khadi*, involve both cloth and clothing, and that interrelationship is the next area that studies at home must explore. Küchler and Were (2003: 5) discuss the ways in which 'cloth and clothing are used in the Pacific as powerful surfaces that have contributed to new ways of thinking and being'; the same can be said of new fibres in our society, but here I would argue that the power is not limited to surfaces. The clothing aspect of new fibres greatly enriches the potential in the field. For example, the migration of fibres from one kind of garment to another, used in very different ways because of cultural impetuses, tells a much more complex story than simple changes of style. I am currently engaged in an ongoing study of the fibre Lycra, and the clothing and cultural uses to which it has been put. Perhaps no other single fibre illustrates the dynamics introduced here. Invented by E.I. du Pont de Nemours (Dupont) and launched in 1959 after some twenty years in development and an investment of $10 million (US), it is now recognized as the world's eighth[10] top textile brand and continues to evolve along with its consumers. It is hoped that this forthcoming study and the work presented here will help to further develop the study of contemporary cloth and clothing as material culture, bringing to an end a period in which, whatever we as anthropologists do in other societies, we live at home in a material world that is largely unexamined.

Notes

1. Source: *Textiles Intelligence* press release, January 23, 2003. *Technical Fiber Innovation May Be the Key to Survival for Companies in High Cost Countries.* www.textilesintelligence.com

2. Practices such as genetic modification and intensive breeding of plants, for example to produce coloured cotton that does not require dyeing, do not affect the substance of the argument, although it does point to the increasing need to modify our understanding of materiality.
3. In November 2003, finalized April 2004, Dupont's Textile and Interiors division, renamed Invista, was sold to Koch Industries Inco.
4. Agulnick, Seth 2002. *After a Bountiful History, Innovations Slow*. June 30, 2002, www.delawareonline.com/newsjournal/business
5. *Fiber Facts* (a Dupont company magazine) 10 May 1965.
6. *Fiber Facts* 10 May 1965:10.
7. Fiber Facts, 10 May 1965:11.
8. *The 1970's: General Summary*. Dupont Archive, Acc 2215, Box 77, File: Technological Information.
9. Dupont 1959. Dupont Archive, Textile Fiber Product Information 84.259, B1
10. The others starting with the first are Levi's, Nike, Adidas, Reebok, Chanel, Benetton, Armani, Wrangler and Hugo Boss. Source: Interbrand.

References

Bannerjee, Mukulika and Miller, Daniel 2003 *The Indian Sari*. Oxford and New York: Berg.

Barthes, Roland 1985 *The Fashion System*. London: Jonathan Cape.

Bean, Susan 1989 'Gandhi and *Khadi,* the Fabric of Indian Independence'. In Annette B. Weiner and Jane Schneider (eds), *Cloth and Human Experience*. Washington DC and London: Smithsonian Institution Press, pp. 356–79.

Benstock, Shari and Ferriss, Suzanne (eds) 1994 *On Fashion*. New Brunswick, NJ: Rutgers University Press.

Braddock, Sarah E. and O'Mahoney, Marie 1999 *Techno Textiles: Revolutionary Fabrics for Fashion and Design*. London: Thames and Hudson.

Braham, Peter 1997 'Fashion: Unpacking a Cultural Production'. In Paul du Gay (ed.), *Production of Culture/Cultures of Production*. London, Thousand Oaks and New Delhi: Sage Publications, pp. 119–76.

Breward, Christopher 1995 *The Culture of Fashion: A New History of Fashionable Dress*. Manchester and New York: Manchester University Press.

—— 1998 'Cultures, Identities, Histories: Fashioning a Cultural Approach to Dress'. *Fashion Theory,* 2(4): 301–14.

—— 1999 *The Hidden Consumer: Masculinities, Fashion and City Life 1860–1914*. Manchester and New York: Manchester University Press.

Bruzzi, Stella and Gibson, Pamela Church (eds) 2000 *Fashion Cultures: Theories, Explanation and Analysis*. London and New York: Routledge.

Buchli, Victor (ed.) 2002 *A Material Culture Reader.* Oxford and New York: Berg.

Campbell, Colin 1995 'The Sociology of Consumption'. In D. Miller (ed.), *Acknowledging Consumption: A Review of New Studies.* London and New York: Routledge, pp. 96–126.

—— 1996 'The Meaning of Objects and the Meaning of Actions: The Sociology of Consumption and Theories of Clothing'. *Journal of Material Culture,* 1(1): 93–106.

Clarke, Alison 1999 *Tupperware: The Promise of Plastic in 1950's America.* Washington DC and London: Smithsonian Institution Press.

Craik, Jennifer 1994 *The Face of Fashion: Cultural Studies in Fashion.* London and New York: Routledge.

Dalby, Liza 2001 *Kimono.* London: Vintage Books/Random House.

Du Gay, Paul and Pryke, Michael (eds) 2002 *Cultural Economy: Cultural Analysis and Commercial Life.* London, Thousand Oaks and New Delhi: Sage Publications.

Dupont Company 1952 *Dupont: The Autobiography of an American Enterprise.* Wilmington, Delaware: E.I. du Pont de Nemours and Company.

Entwistle, Joanne 2000a *The Fashioned Body.* Cambridge: Polity Press.

—— 2000b 'Fashion and the Fleshy Body: Dress as Embodied Practice'. *Fashion Theory,* 4(3): 323–48.

—— and Wilson, Elizabeth 1998 'The Body Clothed'. In *Addressing the Century – 100 Years of Art and Fashion* (Exhibition Catalogue) Hayward Gallery, London and Kunstmuseum Wolfsberg, pp. 106–11.

—— (eds) 2001 *Body Dressing.* Oxford and London: Berg.

Handley, Susannah 1999 *Nylon: The Manmade Fashion Revolution.* London: Bloomsbury.

Hansen, Karen Tranberg 2004 'The World in Dress: Anthropological Perspectives on Clothing, Fashion and Culture'. Annual Review of Anthropology, 33: 369–92.

Hebdige, Dick 1978 *Subculture: The Meaning of Style.* London and New York: Routledge.

—— 1988 *Hiding in the Light.* London and New York: Routledge.

Hendrikson, Hilde (ed.) 1996 *Clothing and Difference: Embodied Identities in Colonial and Post-colonial Africa.* Durham, NC and London: Duke University Press.

Hodkinson, Paul 2002 *Goth: Identity, Style and Subculture.* Oxford and New York: Berg.

Hollander, Anne 1978 *Seeing Through Clothes.* New York: Viking.

Ingold, Tim 2000 'Making Culture and Weaving the World'. In Rupert Graves-Brown, (ed.) *Matter, Materiality and Modern Culture.* London and New York: Routledge, pp. 50–71.

Jackson, Peter, Lowe, Michelle, Miller, Daniel and Mort, Frank (eds) 2000 *Commercial Cultures: Economies, Practices, Spaces.* Oxford and New York: Berg.

Keller, Manfred 1955. 'The Story of Living Fibers', in General Foods Corporation (ed.) *The Power of an Idea.* Portland, Maine, The Bond Wheelwright Co, pp. 121–43.

Kroeber, A.L. 1919 'On the Principle of Order in Civilization as Exemplified in Changes in Fashion'. *American Anthropologist* (new series), 21: 262–3.

Küchler, Susanne 2003 'Rethinking Textile: The Advent of the "Smart" Fiber Surface'. *Textile: The Journal of Cloth and Culture*, 1(3): 262–73.

—— and Were, Graeme 2003 'Clothing and Innovation: A Pacific Perspective'. *Anthropology Today*, 19(2): 3–5.

Kunzle, David 1982. *Fashion and Fetishism: A Social History of Corsets, Tight-Lacing and Other Forms of Body-Sculpture.* Totowa, NJ: Rowman and Littlefield.

Leitch, Vincent B. 1996 'Costly Compensations: Postmodern Fashion, Politics, Identity'. *Modern Fiction Studies*, 42(Spring 1996): 111–28.

Marchand, Roland 1985 *Advertising the American Dream.* Berkeley, Los Angeles and London: University of California Press.

—— 1998 *Creating the Corporate Soul: The Rise of Public Relations and Corporate Imagery in American Big Business.* Berkeley, Los Angeles and London: The University of California Press.

Marcus, George E. 1998 *Ethnography Through Thick and Thin.* Princeton, NJ: Princeton University Press.

—— 1999 'Critical Anthropology Now: An Introduction'. In George E. Marcus (ed.) *Critical Anthropology Now.* Santa Fe, NM: School of American Research Press, pp. 3–28.

McRobbie, Angela 1991 *Feminism and Youth Culture.* London: Macmillan.

—— 1994 *Postmodernism and Popular Culture.* London: Routledge.

—— 1998 *British Fashion Design: Rag Trade or Image Industry.* London and New York: Routledge.

Miller, Daniel 1997 *Capitalism: An Ethnographic Approach.* Oxford and New York: Berg.

Mintz, Sidney 1986 *Sweetness and Power: The Place of Sugar in Modern History.* New York: Viking.

Moore, Sally Falk 1994 'The Ethnography of the Present and the Analysis of Process'. In Robert Borofsky (ed.) *Assessing Cultural Anthropology.* New York and London: McGraw-Hill, pp. 375–6.

Nixon, Sean 1996 *Hard Looks: Masculinities, Spectatorship and Contemporary Consumption.* London: UCL Press.

Noble, David F. 1977 *America by Design: Science, Technology and the Rise of Corporate Capitalism.* New York: Alfred A. Knopf.

O'Barr, William M. 1994 *Culture and the Ad: Exploring Otherness in the World of Advertising*. Boulder and London: Westview Press.

O'Connor, Kaori 2004a 'Lycra, Babyboomers and the Immaterial Culture of the New Midlife: A Study of Commerce and Culture'. PhD dissertation, University College London. (A book drawn from this thesis is currently in preparation.)

—— 2004b 'Material Culture, Capitalism and Social Change at Home'. *Anthropology Matters*. November 2004, in press.

Ortner, Sherry B. 1999 'Generation X: Anthropology in a Media-Saturated World'. In George E. Marcus (ed.) *Critical Anthropology Now: Unexpected Contexts, Shifting Constituencies, Changing Agendas*. Santa Fe, NM: School of American Research Press, pp. 55–88.

Pastoreau, Michel 2001 *The Devil's Cloth*. New York: Columbia University Press.

Palmer, Alexandra 1997 'New Directions: Fashion History Research in North America and England'. *Fashion Theory*, 1(3): 297–312.

Renne, Elisha P. 1995 *Cloth That Does Not Die: The Meaning of Cloth in Bunu Social Life*. Seattle and London: University of Washington Press.

Richardson, Jane and Kroeber, A.L. 1940 'Three Centuries of Women's Dress Fashions: A Quantitative Analysis'. *University of California Anthropological Record* 5(2): 111–54.

Rubinstein, Ruth P. 1995 *Dress Codes: Meanings and Messages in American Culture*. Boulder, San Francisco and Oxford: Westview Press.

Rutledge, Charles H. 1966 *Milestones in the Du Pont Company's Textile Fibers History and Some Important Industry Dates*. Wilmington, Delaware: Textile Fibers Department, E.I. du Pont de Nemours and Co.

Sahlins, Marshall D. 1974 *Stone Age Economics*. London: Tavistock Publications.

—— 1976 *Culture and Practical Reason*. Chicago: University of Chicago Press.

—— 1994 'Goodbye to Triste Tropes: Ethnography in the Context of Modern World History'. In Robert Borofsky (ed.) *Assessing Cultural Anthropology*. London and New York: McGraw-Hill, pp. 377–95.

Schneider, Jane 1994 'In and Out of Polyester: Desire, Disdain and Global Fibre Competitions'. *Anthropology Today*, 10(4): 2–10.

Showalter, Elaine 2001 'Fade to Greige'. *London Review of Books* 23(1). www.lrb.co.uk/v23/n./show_01.html

Steele, Valerie 1996 *Fetish: Fashion, Sex and Power*. Oxford and New York: Oxford University Press.

—— 2001 *The Corset: A Cultural History*. New Haven and London: Yale University Press.

Strasser, Susan 2000 *Never Done: A History of American Housework*. New York: Owl Books/Henry Holt and Company.

Summers, Leigh 2001 *Bound to Please: A History of the Victorian Corset.* Oxford and New York: Berg.

Warwick, Alexandra and Cavallaro, Dani 1998 *Fashioning the Frame: Boundaries, Dress and the Body.* Oxford and New York: Berg.

Weiner, Annette B. and Schneider, Jane (eds) 1989 *Cloth and Human Experience.* Washington DC and London: Smithsonian Institution Press.

Wilson, Elizabeth 1895. *Adorned in Dreams: Fashion and Modernity.* London: Virago Press.

Wolf, Roberta and Schlachter, Trudy 2000 *Millennium Mode: Fashion Forecasts from 40 Top Designers.* New York: Rizzoli.

–4–

Aesthetics, Ethics and Politics of the Turkish Headscarf

Özlem Sandıkcı and *Güliz Ger*

In the last decade, an urban Islamic consumptionscape, in part opposing and in part imitating the secular consumption practices, has emerged in Turkey. Islamic-style clothing stores and fashion shows, fitness and beauty centres targeted specifically at modern Islamist[1] women have become commonplace. In this paper, we focus on one of the most publicly visible insignia of the Islamic consumption culture, the headscarf, and explore fashion, aesthetic and taste dynamics that underlie the practice of head covering. Through an analysis of styles of tying, patterns, colours, fabrics, sizes, shapes, designs, brands and usage of scarves, we aim to not only map out the 'symbolic potentiality' of the headscarf 'through its material properties' (Schneider and Weiner 1989), but also complicate the relation between religion, fashion and modernity.

Although present in other religions too, the practice of head covering today, whether it is in the form of scarf, veil or chador, has become synonymous with the exoticized and often vilified Islamic identity. Some regard head covering as a signifier of oppression and seclusion of women in Islamic societies, others see it as a symbol of resistance and liberation. However, while much is written on the identity politics of the headscarf, there is almost no attempt to understand its aesthetic and material dimensions (for an exception see Balasescu 2003). The effort put into selection, arrangement and securing of the headscarf and its material properties peculiarly vanish in the discussions of the Islamic headscarf. Focusing only on the political implications of the head covering strips away the material aspects of the scarf, granting it a purely symbolic existence, and, willingly or unwillingly, overlooks the aesthetic tensions embodied in this piece of cloth. We believe that through following these tensions we can map out the relationship between a material object and the self, and understand how the headscarf and head covering practices embody the struggle between remaining faithful to the Koranic principles on religiously appropriate dressing and constructing a fashionable, beautiful and modern appearance.

Turkey is a predominantly Muslim yet secular society and, traditionally, head covering has been associated with mostly rural or elderly religiously observant women. However, beginning in the mid 1980s, the practice began to transform from a traditional (read as spiritual and rural) to a political act. There were several reasons for the emergence of the headscarf as a symbol of political Islam. Under the neo-liberal Özal government that came into power in 1983, attitudes toward Islam began to change, signalling a departure from the strict secularism that was established by Atatürk in 1924. *Tarikats* (religious orders) became active again and several private Islamic educational institutions and companies backed by substantial funding from abroad were set up. As Islamic actors gained more visibility in the public sphere, the polarization between the secularists[2] and the Islamists intensified. By the 1990s, the distinction between traditional modest religiosity and politically threatening Islam was increasingly focused upon the issue of women's head covering. While many elderly faithful women and peasants covered their heads using *başörtüsü* (a scarf that covers only and loosely the head), it was primarily the young, urban and educated women who wore the *türban* (a large scarf that tightly covers the head, ears, the neck and the bosom). In the early 1990s, the Turkish military, governments and secularist elites perceived the *türban* as an indisputable symbol of religious militancy and a threat to secularism, one of the founding principles of the Turkish Republic. The strict enforcement of the ban on religious-inspired clothing in schools and public offices led to frequent clashes between the turbaned women, protesting in front of the universities and public institutions, and the police, raising political Islam's public presence (Göle 1997).

However, while the 1990s marked the increasing politicization of Islam and the polarization between secularists and Islamists, it also witnessed the emergence of an Islamic consumption culture (Kılıçbay and Binark 2002; Sandıkcı and Ger 2001, 2002). With the accumulation of wealth among certain segments of the politically active religious population, an Islamist bourgeoisie with a taste for conspicuous consumption began to emerge. The initial uniformity of attire, characterized by the large scarf and the accompanying loose-fitting long overcoat, gradually transformed into a heterogeneity of dressing styles, signalling the increasing fashion consciousness especially among the upper-class, urban, well-educated, young Islamist women. Textile companies catering to the Islamists developed rapidly. Several shops, most of which carry Arabic religious names, began to offer a wide array of headscarves, overcoats and other clothing items to their customers. Adopting fashion marketing tools, some of these companies aggressively publicize their clothing lines through fashion shows, catalogues, and television and newspaper advertisements (Navaro-Yashin 2002). Although the *türban* continues to operate as a symbol of political Islam (Mandel 1989), it also circulates as an object of material culture, subject to various consumption and production dynamics.

With these concerns in mind, our study is an ethnographic investigation of the contemporary urban head covering practices in Turkey, with a focus on the relationship between faith and fashion. Our interest lies on the middle- and upper-middle-class, urban, educated Islamist women covered by their own will, who exhibit, and sometimes openly admit, their interest in fashion and being fashionable. Data collected from several sources since 2000 inform our analysis. These include in-depth interviews with Islamist women living in Ankara and Istanbul, interviews with owners and personnel of Islamic-style clothing stores, observations at various sites that Islamist women attend, such as Islamic fashion shows, shopping centres and hotels, and a visual archive that consists of pictures taken by us as well as pictures circulating in the media, advertisements and company catalogues.

Religiously Appropriate Dressing: Subjectivity and Multiplicity

There are two passages in the Koran that address proper behaviour between men and women who mix outside kinship bonds, including ways of clothing and adornment:

> Say to the believing men that they should lower their gaze and guard their modesty. This will be most conductive to their purity. Verily, God is aware of what you do.
> And say to the believing women that they should lower their gaze and guard their modesty; that they should not display their beauty and ornaments except what ordinarily appear thereof; that they should draw their veils over their bosoms and should not display their beauty to any but their husbands, their fathers ... (and certain other members of the household). Let them not stamp their feet so as to reveal what they hide of their adornments. O believers, turn unto God all of you so that you may succeed. (Koran, 24:30, 31)

> Women, in advanced years, who do not hope for marriage, incur no sin if they discard their garments, provided that they do not aim at a showy display of their charm. But, it is better for them to abstain from this. God is All-hearing All-knowing. (Koran, 24:60)

According to the interpretations of Muslim theologians and intellectuals, the modesty emphasized in these passages encompasses all aspects of life and calls for decency, humility and moderation in speech, attitude, dress and total behaviour. Modesty prevents human beings from indulging in indecency, vanity and obscenity, and therefore should be adopted by both males and females.

However, while the Islamic rule of dressing modestly applies to men and women, *tesettür* – religiously appropriate modest dressing – has come to connote especially female clothing. The underlying assumption is that it is easier for women to arouse the sexual feeling of a man than the other way around, and therefore, women should cover up those parts of their anatomy that can draw the male gaze. As Makhlouf puts it 'the modesty code rests on two contradictory assumptions: that woman is weak and needs to be protected from threats to her honour, and that she has strong sexual impulses which threaten the honour of males and the integration of the group... The veil is a double shield, protecting the woman against external offences of society and protecting society against the inherent evil of woman' (1979: 38). Because women are instructed to not appear attractive, sexy and seductive, dress is likened to a 'house' that maintains privacy and keeps men and their desires away (ISAV 1991: 36). A woman clothed according to *tesettür* is regarded as keeping her dignity, honour and chastity, safeguarding herself from being the subject of gossip, protecting herself from molestation and harm. Although violating *tesettür* is not one of the 'great sins,' it is usually considered to be one of God's commands (ISAV 1991: 24).

In addition to modesty, there are two other tenets of Islam that pertain to clothing and adornment. First, a Muslim is expected to be well groomed and neat, have a beautiful and pleasant appearance, and dress artfully and aesthetically, using decoration and adornment, including perfume (ISAV 1991). Yet, clothing material and dressing manners that stimulate arrogance and vanity are forbidden. Second, waste, in clothing and other consumption, should be avoided. Luxury and excess are seen to be wasteful, and Muslims are instructed to refrain from showiness and waste. Clothing is expected to be functional (e.g. to protect against weather conditions and be suitable for job conditions) and ensure cleanliness, health and hygiene.

However, while modesty, pleasant appearance and avoidance of waste broadly establish the nature of Islamic dress, different interpretations of proper clothing coexist. Far from being a monolithic practice, head covering in particular and dressing in general are domains that are subject to tensions, contestations and negotiations. Theologians, intellectuals and feminists often engage in heated debates over what constitutes proper female Muslim clothing. Television channels, radio stations and publishing houses, owned by different religious orders, broadcast divergent views. Clothing stores and fashion designers introduce new styles and items that expand the heterogeneity in attire. All of these factors help women negotiate and justify different interpretations and practices of *tesettür*.

Its political connotation notwithstanding, the actual practice of *tesettür* ultimately becomes a subjective experience, shaped by various personal and social factors as well as the scriptural meanings and extensions. While there is a consensus that the main idea behind *tesettür* is to not to attract male attention, what does or does not attract attention remains questionable. While some believe that loose-fitting, long garments that do not reveal body contours are the proper style, others go for pants and tighter and shorter jackets, which are deemed more suitable for the lifestyle of a working woman. Some resist bright colours; others pick scarves that best match their skin colour. Some reject putting on make-up to avoid arousing carnal feelings; others adopt it as part of their daily grooming ritual. At the end, as many of our informants' practices suggest, 'everyone shapes their own *tesettür.*'

Meral, for example, a forty-four year old housewife with three children who covered thirteen years ago of her own free will, explained to us how she was influenced by her religious teacher, who thought that everybody had her own interpretation of *tesettür*. Meral believes that women are created as tempting creatures and hence they should dress according to *tesettür* in order to minimize temptation:

> When I first began covering, a religious teacher told me that everybody had her own *tesettür*. I liked this a lot. Someone wears bikini, but she cannot flaunt. That's her *tesettür*, she said. She said some couldn't wear bikini. Some cannot wear swimsuit at all. Some can wear short sleeved [tops]; others wear sleeveless [tops]. She said everybody has her own style of *tesettür*. But what is spoken in Islam as *tesettür* is what can normally be exposed like hands, face and feet, and the rest should be covered. More correctly, *tesettür* is in fact not to attract attention... That's what I understand from my readings. I mean *tesettür* is actually not to attract attention. Because woman is a creature that always tempts the man. What is expected of *tesettür* is not to attract his attention even more. Hair is something that makes someone look nicer, more beautiful; *tesettür* is because of this.

Similarly, Ceyda, a twenty-seven year old chemist, married with one child, emphasizes that one covers because of her belief in God and *tesettür* helps her to live modestly as instructed by God. Modesty requires one to refrain from drawing carnal attention. In her mind neither the black chador nor the tight pants worn by many young Islamist women fulfil the requirements of *tesettür*. Although due to different reasons, both dressing styles appear distinctive and, hence, attract attention:

> For me this [*tesettür*] is an order of Allah. Like fasting during Ramadan it is an order, not something you want to do. I mean one is not covered because of her husband, her family. She covers because she believes in Allah. *Tesettür* means not to attract attention. I think both black chador and tight pants are noticeable. They attract attention. One should not draw attention of the other sex. *Tesettür* is about being an ordinary person.

Many women who decide to cover go through a process of acquiring information about appropriate religious dressing style. They consult people whom they regard as knowledgeable about Islam, read the Koran, the Hadith (recommendations of the Prophet) and other books, and follow the debates on the media. Their own understandings and practices of *tesettür* form depending on the sources they seek advice from and their personal interpretation of what they learn. Serap is a fifty-nine year old widow who runs her late husband's company together with her children. She is a highly devoted Muslim who chose to cover at the age of thirty-three after a dream she had. She told us that she read a lot in order to find what the appropriate style of covering is, but could not locate any specific prescription about it. She complains about women who wear very long overcoats or the black chador. Rejecting keenly any single description of *tesettür*, she emphasizes that the only requirement is not to expose the body parts and draw attention:

> Actually, in Islam, there is nothing about [covering] style. I examined this a lot. First, there is nothing like chador at all. I don't know who invented this. I have been attending to [Koran] interpretation courses for years, trying to learn the Koran. There is nothing, there is no chador... There is nothing like 'you shall wear this or that.' Everybody is coming up with something. Some are wearing those very long overcoats. There is nothing like that! I mean it says something like you should not wear things that excessively expose body counters and attract attention.

Overall, there is a consensus that *tesettür* refers to modest dressing that does not attract male gaze. However, what is 'modest' and 'not sexually attractive' appears as highly variable and negotiated. As the meaning of *tesettür* pluralizes, aesthetic judgements, taste dispositions, and cultural and financial capital assume greater significance in the actual head covering practices of the Islamist women. On the one hand, the lack of consensus on what is proper *tesettür* provides freedom to women to express their own taste and understanding; on the other hand it creates tension, as they need to juggle between being distinctive yet not wasteful and being beautiful yet not ostentatious. Achieving a beautiful and faithful look requires a creative and resourceful negotiation of the subjective meanings, social influences and the fashion dynamics.

Fashion Dynamics and Social Influences

Up until the mid 1990s, headscarves were produced in small workshops, using serigraphic techniques. With increasing demand, factories utilizing advanced printing and manufacturing technologies gradually replaced the workshops. While the Turkish market is dominated by local production carried under either Turkish brand names or licensed foreign brands, headscarves are also imported from Europe, China and India. As in fashion in general, production of scarves follows a seasonal pattern. Generally, there are two creations per year, one for winter and one for summer. Some companies, however, may offer new collections in shorter periods, every three to four months, increasing the variety of offerings. Apart from seasonal designs, there are also classic models, which are offered throughout the year. Consistent with the cyclical pattern of fashion in general, design and colour of scarves change from year to year. Typically, if floral patterns dominate one year, geometrical designs follow the next year. After creating a motif, the designers prepare at least five or six varieties of it and send it to sample production. The samples are then tested and the best ones are chosen for mass production. The manufacturers prepare catalogues of their collections and send them to retailers pre-season. In addition to catalogues, the collections are marketed through fashion shows and design competitions. For example, a local producer Aker awards prizes to designs that win in its annual competitions. They then use its award-winning status as a selling point by marking the scarf with a 'Best Design Award Winner' label.

Fashion increases the variety of the scarves and, inevitably, influences which styles of tying and which colours, shapes and designs become more or less popular at a given time. Our informants stress that they enjoy the availability of numerous colours and patterns while acknowledging that there was a limited variety in the past. They also enjoy that there are now designers catering specifically to their needs. While some informants find it difficult to admit that there are fashions in scarves, trends keep changing:

> *Sema*: Scarves vary depending on fashion. Now there are these foulards with intertwined threads, trimmed with long fringes. Last year there were scarves made from thicker fabrics. The year before last, there were these designs, whatever they were called, batik? Now there are these *Asmalı Konak* (foulards fashioned after the scarves worn by the characters of a popular television show). Or the tulles, never existed before. More people use them this year. So, from year to year, from season to season, it changes. Whatever the fashion is, a scarf type is introduced accordingly... We no longer use the large square scarves... Young women prefer the foulards nowadays; older women still wear the large square ones.

In addition to the rectangular shawl-type foulards (Fig. 4.1a,b) that Sema prefers, the small square scarves (Fig. 4.2) are also fashionable. The foulards and the small square scarves create a very different and, according to our informants, modern look. These are distinct both from the classical/traditional style of tying (Fig. 4.3), prominent among rural women and some older urban women who are not affiliated with political Islam, and the once-prevalent large tying style (Fig. 4.4a,b), which covers more of the bosom and the back and is now practised only by older and/or conservative women. Furthermore, while a small scarf tucked into a shirt or a turtle neck sweater, or a foulard compose a sporty look, asymmetric arrangements (Fig. 4.5a,b,c) form fancy looks. Fashion also changes the preferred patterns, colours and materials. We noted that the currently trendy designs are Burberry, chequered, small floral or large almost abstract floral, and leopard.

Figure 4.1a Rectangular foulard

Figure 4.1b Rectangular foulard

Figure 4.2 Small square scarf

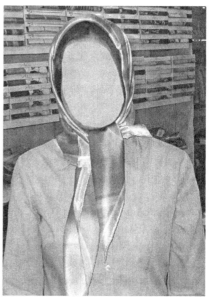

Figure 4.3 Traditional scarf

The Turkish Headscarf

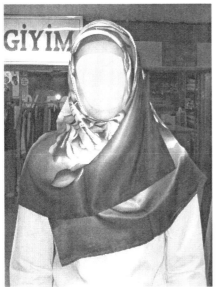

Figure 4.4a Large scarf   **Figure 4.4b** Large scarf

Fuchsia, brown and camel appear as popular colours, while 'crinkle' (crumpled thin fabric), chiffon, and a combination of velvet and tulle are trendy fabrics. For special occasions, elegant looking layered scarves with counter toned transparent tulle or netted outer fabric or the more glamorous glittery or bejewelled materials with fancy brooches (Fig. 4.5a) adorn the heads of many fashionably dressed covered women. While women claim that choice of colours and styles is a personal matter, we see more trendy scarves on the streets, and producers maintain that fashionable colours and patterns sell more; for example, we are told that many women have been asking for fuchsia scarves.

    Shop windows, mannequins and sales personnel play important roles in informing women about the fashionable colours, patterns and new trendy ways of tying. Many of the customers visit the stores without an exact idea of what kind of scarf they want to buy, and ask the advice of the sales clerks, hoping that they will have the experience and taste to help them pick the scarf that will look best on them. Once the acceptable price range is determined, sales clerks assess the facial features of the customer, namely the skin colour and the shape of the face. Depending on its form and size, the scarf can be tied in different styles, which can make the face look larger or thinner. We observed that the square scarf makes the face look rounder and chubbier and is preferred by women who have elongated and small faces, while the rectangular foulard makes the face look longer, thinner and smaller and is preferred by women who have bigger and rounder faces. Advice

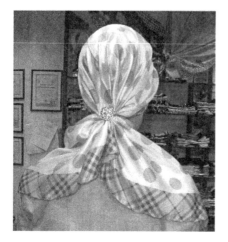

Figure 4.5a Foulard with brooch

Figure 4.5b Asymmetric style

Figure 4.5c Asymmetric style

on the colour of the scarf, on the other hand, depends on the skin complexion. Typically, darker colour scarves are recommended to women with fair complexion, and lighter colour scarves to those with darker complexion:

> They ask 'do you have a scarf that would look pretty on my face'? The most difficult question.... Of course dark colours look good on light coloured skin and light colours on darker skin. So we recommend light colours for customers with darker skins and

dark colours for lighter skins. ... Then there is also the shape of the face. For example, I don't prefer the rectangular scarves as these cover the sides of the cheeks completely. Since my face is thin, it makes my face appear even thinner.

The sales clerks also provide guidance on the match between the scarf and the colour of the outfit that it will be used with. For example, if the outfit is plain coloured, scarves with striking colours and patterns, which make an attractive contrast, are preferred. Indeed, achieving colour harmony in the overall attire emerges as a common concern for our informants. Surprisingly, in parallel to the fetishism of hair for an uncovered woman, the headscarf assumes almost a fetish status and becomes the focal point of gaze directed toward covered women. If the scarf is intelligently coordinated with the rest of the dress, it increases the beauty and attractiveness of the wearer; if not, however expensive it might be, it fails to create a distinctive look. Given the importance of colour harmony, many women complain about the difficulty of finding scarves that will go with their clothes. They claim that forming a wardrobe of matching clothes and scarves is more costly for covered than uncovered women who can 'go out in a pair of jeans and a T-shirt'. They argue that it takes a lot more time to search for and is more difficult to find *tesettür* clothes that are beautiful and fashionable. Some admit that they spent hours to find the right scarf:

> *Sema*: What scarf should I wear to match this outfit? Sometimes I think about this for hours. What colour, what design should I use? What combination can I create? It is more difficult for covered women [than uncovered women] to dress. Especially now. That was not the case in the past when one could put on any skirt, an overcoat, any scarf and walk out.

In addition to the production-side factors, popular culture and the political milieu influence the fashion dynamics. Television series often operate as a source or inspiration for headscarf trends. For example, Sema and many other informants refer to a highly popular television show, *Asmalı Konak,* broadcasted in the 2002–3 season and the headscarves that came to be known as *Asmalı Konak* or as *Sümbül Hanım* scarves (Fig. 4.1b), as they are named after one of the leading characters of the series. These are rectangular scarves with tassel made out of a thin and transparent material, and they are typically worn during summer with a bonnet underneath. The sales clerks we interviewed mentioned that *Asmalı Konak* scarves have become very fashionable and many customers come in asking for them.

Political figures also serve as role models and pioneers of fashion: various politically active Islamist women's scarves and, since 2003, the Prime Minister's wife's scarves have become fashionable. The political milieu influences fashion in a very unexpected way too: the ban on wearing the scarf in public spaces appears to have led to less conspicuous and what is considered to be more modern styles, such as the smaller scarves that are tucked inside the collar. However, although this tying style may have been initially triggered by the prohibition, it appears that it is being spread by the desire not to appear repelling to the uncovered public. Transmitting an appealing look becomes important given the negative and threatening image of the covered women among the strictly secular sections of the population. Many covered women suffer from ridicule or even insults from non-covered women due their appearance, and become stereotyped as 'ugly' and 'backward'. One of our informants recalls a traumatic experience she had years ago when she was scorned because of her attire:

> *Ece*: One day, several years ago, I wore something I liked very much, something I thought was very becoming. But as I was walking on the street a middle-aged woman said something to me, something like 'how comically dressed you are, how you still wear these!' I was at work that day and I looked at the mirror throughout the day. I wondered what the problem in my outfit was, what was crude and ugly, searching for something in my clothes or scarf that was wrong.

A modern and attractive look not only helps the covered woman appear less repelling to the uncovered public, it also serves the Islamists' political aims: by appearing attractive, a covered woman acts as a role model for other Muslim women and inspires them to cover themselves.

While fashion, popular culture and the political milieu shape overall trends, there are also other factors that guide the selection of a particular headscarf. Many covered women socialize in the Islamic public sphere. They attend the all-female recreational clubs run by the municipality[3] and other Islamic resorts. They observe popular designs and colours, and chat about the scarves and tying styles they see. Friends go shopping together, talk about the scarves they see on the shop windows, and help each other choose scarves. Like Balasescu's (2003) observation of upper-class Tehranian women, many of our informants indicate that they talk with each other about the brands of the scarves and whether to leave the brand name visible or hidden in the folds of the scarf.

Such social and political dynamics, embedded within fashion, escalate the attention to aesthetics. While the inescapable significance of fashion and what may seem to be an undue focus on outer appearance disturb some women, many justify fashionable aesthetic practices by resorting to the prevailing discourse that Islam commands people to be clean, well groomed and pleasant looking. Thus, they feel that by paying attention to their appearances, they fulfil one of God's orders. However, in practice achieving a beautiful yet not sexually attractive look is a complex task that requires a lot of beauty work. Substantial thinking, effort and time go into the arrangement of the scarf.

The Turkish Headscarf

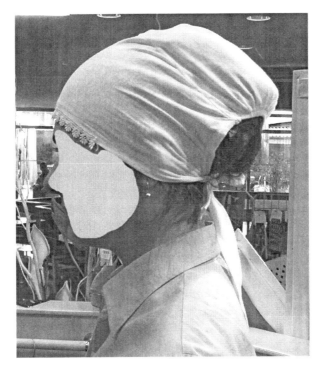

Figure 4.6 Inner bonnet

Beauty Work

Once the 'right' scarf is selected, which also requires considerable work, the woman faces the intricate process of tying it. Not only the scarf itself but also various accessories figure in the construction of the desired look. Before putting on the scarf, first either an inner bonnet (Fig. 4.6), made from cotton, Lycra or woollen knits, or a cotton muslin kerchief, *tülbent*, is worn. Allegedly, the inner bonnet serves two functions. First, it holds the hair together and provides a base upon which the scarf can be pinned down. This enables the scarf to stay on properly without slipping and losing its shapely position due to movement or wind. Second, when the scarf is made out of a thin and transparent fabric, the inner bonnet conceals the hair. The scarf, then, can be wrapped in different ways depending upon its shape – that is, whether it is a square scarf or a rectangular foulard. After a frontal fixing under the chin, the scarf can be tied in the back, one or both of the edges can remain in the front or be thrown to the back, or the edges can be left hanging or tucked inside the collar of the dress.

Women spend considerable effort and time to have the scarf appear *düzgün* (straight, shapely, smooth, rounded and symmetrical). As a saleswoman remarked 'while [the customers] try [the scarf] in the store, they pay the greatest attention to having it stay on *düzgün;* they spend hours in front of the mirror checking if it is *düzgün* or not.' If the scarf is not arranged properly and securely, it can slip during the day and lose its shape. The greatest time is spent on silk and silk chiffon scarves, which slip and require redoing every four to five hours. In order refrain from the inconvenience of retying the scarf, women pay great attention to arranging it *düzgün* at the beginning:

> *Emine*: I don't undo my scarf during the day, until I go home, even if I go home at midnight. I tie it properly with care in the morning so that it stays that way all day long. If I retie it all the time, that's not convenient. If you don't use a pin, scarves are slippery, you have to go to the restroom, find a mirror and straighten it and tie it again all the time. Sometimes you are outside. I use a pin so that it stays put for many hours.

Various accessories are used to have the scarf appear *düzgün* in the front and at the back. Despite their alleged functionality, many women use the inner bonnets or the cotton muslin kerchiefs as a means to make the rear top of the scarf stay raised. Women who have long hair first form a hair bun and then wear the inner bonnet. If the hair is short or thin, a muslin kerchief is wrapped around the head to add volume (instead of tying it like a bandana); or *topuzlu bone* – the bonnet with a bun – is used. These are bonnets with a pad stitched into the rear end. The bun of hair or padding elevates the back of the head, which according to many women make the head and the face appear beautiful and the scarf fold shapely and smoothly (Fig. 4.5b). For the front top, typically, a scarf band is used. A scarf band is a thin rectangular sheet placed right above the forehead to give to the front of the scarf a raised, rounded and symmetrical appearance. Such paraphernalia can be purchased ready-made or constructed at home, for example, by simply cutting an X-ray film or stitching a cloth band with a thin strip of cardboard or sponge inside. Some women prefer to leave the edge of the inner bonnet or the scarf band visible on the forehead. In this case, depending on aesthetic preferences, either a complementary or a contrasting effect between the colours of the scarf and the colours of the bonnets/bands can be created. Finally, pins are used to secure the sections of the scarf under the chin, at the back, or on top of the head so that the scarf does not slip and keeps its arranged form. These fastening accessories come in a large variety, including simple long pins with a large head, safety pins, as well as more decorative clips, buckles, clasps, or brooches.

In addition to the care given to a *düzgün*-looking scarf, our informants pay attention to the colours and patterns that the folds of a tied scarf reveal. Deciding on which colours and motifs should appear in the front, above the forehead, and on the neck, the side(s) and the back becomes yet another aesthetic challenge. Designers produce scarves with contrasting and complementing plain-coloured

The Turkish Headscarf

and patterned parts such that they can be worn interchangeably, revealing different parts of the scarf around different parts of the head to create different effects. For example, the scarf can be folded in such a way that the plain colour section remains on top of the head and the patterns appear on the front of the neck or on one shoulder.

The time and effort spent on arranging the scarf is greatest for women who are 'new to covering'. Using a larger number of accessories, such as the bonnets and the scarf bands, and trying different tying styles increase the preparation time, until one gains experience with a new model. There is a learning process, an acquisition of a cultural capital in learning to tie in different styles. This also enhances the instructive role of fashion and social influences we discussed in the previous section.

Another aspect of the beauty work is the details of taking care of the scarves: washing, choosing a shampoo (which is similar to choosing a hair shampoo), ironing and storing:

> *Sema*: Washing the scarf is very important, it requires extra care. You should not wash it in a washing machine. I wash them by hand, using a shampoo, never a detergent, in cold or lukewarm water, gently, without rubbing so that the colours will not fade away or loose their lustre and the scarf will not wrinkle or loose its shape. Soap can leave marks. I lay them flat to dry and then iron them. I keep the scarves I use less frequently in a drawer, but I hang my daily scarves, the ones that I wear more frequently stay on hangers so that they don't crease, thus I don't have to iron them again.

Whether in choosing the right scarf, arranging it in a *düzgün* manner, or caring for it, our informants engage in a complicated task. The time and effort expended on daily head covering practice and the significance of the beautification evoke the 'hair project' that women undertake (Haug et al. 1983). Just like the hair, the scarf conceals parts of the body or emphasizes them. Furthermore, it draws attention to the head. The scarf work not only entails the selection of colour, shape and design but also the general arrangement of the head. The process we described above is similar to choosing the right shampoo, the size, colour and style of hair, as well as the hair grooming rituals that McCracken (1988) discusses. It seems paradoxical that in the attempt to cover the seductive and provocative hair, the scarf and the scarf project come to replace the hair and the hair project, respectively.

Juggling over Ethics and Aesthetics

Overall, our analysis indicates that a major concern for our informants is to be well groomed, adorned and beautiful. Yet, this concern might have been considered as conflicting with two tenets of Islam: avoidance of waste and sexual attention.

The often-heard statement 'everybody shapes their own *tesettür*' seems to provide the grounds for heterogeneous head covering practices and the justifications for resolving the tensions between the religious principles and the seemingly contradictory actions.

Islam preaches that one should refrain from waste, luxury and overindulgence in material possessions. In accordance with these messages, many of our informants state that purchasing an expensive scarf is wasteful and contradicts the requirements of being a faithful person. However, while their discourses clearly indicate a negative attitude toward behaving wastefully, their actual practices are often in conflict with this attitude. Our informants state that they own between twelve and sixty headscarves and mention others who own several drawers full. The pursuit of colour harmony with a new outfit, the search for a fancy scarf for a wedding, and changing fashion trends make them buy new scarves, bonnets and brooches. Many admit they are willing to pay high prices[4] for premium brands of scarves and imported Italian clips unless constrained by affordability. The enthusiasm for headscarves, however, does not necessarily connote materialism and waste to them. On the one hand, they believe that covered women suffer from many social and political stigmas; enduring such difficulties provides a moral satisfaction in fulfilling the religious duties and also serves to offset any doubt of being wasteful. On the other hand, they justify the large numbers of scarves and accessories they own, the high amounts of money they pay for the brand name scarves they buy, and their beautification endeavours by referring to the Islamic injunction to have a pleasant appearance.

It is true that Islam commands people to be clean, well groomed and pleasant looking. Yet, the practice of this tenet is laden with tensions. Faithful women are not supposed to attract attention; they are supposed to avoid the male gaze. However, many do appear highly attractive. The debates underlining the contradiction between the principle and the actual practice frequently appear both in the secular and the religious media. While our informants acknowledge that having a pleasant appearance is important, they assert that this is carried out to fulfil God's orders and not to draw sexual attention. Thus, they justify the attention they pay to their appearance as following one of the principles of Islam. Furthermore, they believe that by appearing nicely a covered woman acts as a role model for other Muslim women and inspires them to dress according to *tesettür*, a behaviour that is perceived as highly respectable and admirable in their social milieu.

The concept of a pleasant appearance, however, is also highly subjective and negotiated. Our informants repeatedly use two terms when they talk about their actual head covering practices. First, they stress that the scarf should look *düzgün*. As we discussed above, although the effort put into arranging the scarf in a *düzgün* way appears to be functionally driven – that is, the scarf remains shapely for a long period of time without the need of retying – in practice, it is motivated more by the desire to appear beautiful and fashionable. Second, they mention being *rahat*. The word *rahat* connotes multiple meanings: feeling at ease, safe, secure, convenient, and without anxiety, disturbance, annoyance. The informants all agree that wearing a scarf is comfortable as it protects the head against rain and sun. Furthermore, they imply that being *rahat* is related to a sense of peace as the headscarf helps a woman to fulfil the religious duties and guards her from the male gaze. One interpretation of such peace is that 'the formal or public aligning of oneself with Islam' brings an inner ease and resolution, by 'providing a sense of community ... [and] ... protection from male harassment' (Ahmed 1992: 223). Each of the women we spoke with feels *rahat* in their own ways – they prefer different colours, designs, sizes, shapes and tying styles. However, even when they claim that head covering is a personal practice, which is not shaped by fashion dynamics and social influences, and that they choose the scarf and the tying style that they feel most *rahat* with, their actual practices suggest the opposite. As we discussed, trendy colours and patterns sell more and the currently popular tying styles and the fashionably coloured and patterned scarves appear more frequently on the streets.

Like Haug et al.'s (1983) discussion of hair, the scarf emerges as a symbol of potency in association with beauty. The scarf parades the political atmosphere, like the tightly gathered hairstyle of German National Socialism or the Afro of the African-American 'Black is Beautiful' movement. The politically charged socialization of covering the hair mirrors the life-long socialization of wearing the hair. Hence, like the female hair, the female hair cover, reflects women's struggle with ethics, politics and aesthetics.

Tying the Knot

If covering the hair and the neck serves only the religious injunction to avoid the sexual gaze of men as the Islamists claim, or signifies a threat to the republic, as the secularists claim, any kerchief should do. But instead, we observe a wide variety of fabrics, shapes, brands and tying styles. Women spent a lot of time, money and effort on choosing scarves and putting them on. They juggle for a chic, comfortable yet religiously proper head covering style. Choosing a scarf to buy or wear on a particular day entails much deliberation and arranging the scarf may involve an intricate and long process. These and other practices that we discuss above manifest the significance of daily beautification and a sense of aesthetics that is not always consistent with what would be expected of a narrowly conceived purely religious or political practice.

A prevailing discourse among the more fashion-conscious covered women is that dressing according to *tesettür* can and should be beautiful. These women are well aware that physical appearance helps creating a distinction, and in today's society where people are judged more with their material possessions than their personality, one is treated according to how she looks. The emphasis on appearance indicates not only the changes in what religious covering means but at a deeper level the quest for being 'modern'.

The turbaned woman circulates as either the oppressed or the liberated Other, but one who is always excluded from modernity. Encoded in the Islamic dress code, for many who are critical of it, is oppressive hierarchies and male domination (Ahmed 1992; Mernissi 1991; Yeğenoğlu 1998). In contrast, those who are sympathetic to it, read in the headscarf resistance to Western dominance, materialism and consumerism (El Guindi 1999a,b). The opposition between Islam and Western consumerism remains so strong that Turner confidently claims, 'consumerism offers or promises a range of possible lifestyles which compete with, and in many cases, contradict the uniform lifestyle demanded by Islamic fundamentalism' (1994: 90).

However, the actual head covering practices of urban, upper-class, educated women in Turkey that we observed contest the stereotypical discourses and images about covered women, complicating the tension between Islam and consumerism. Indeed, we argue that, far from being a fixed signifier of oppression or resistance, the headscarf in contemporary Turkey operates as an 'unstable sign' (Nava 1997), a cultural codifier of the tensions and promises of modernity. The headscarf connotes a political posture but also 'rank' and 'identity'. Urban, upper-class covered women are not categorically excluded from the spaces of modernity, as many claim, but rather become the subjects as well as the objects of modernization.

The emergence of fashion as a cultural mode of modernity has been linked with the emergence of the modern individual, progress and a break from traditions (Simmel 1904; Wilson 1985). The absence of even the potential of the headscarf as an aesthetic object rests on an assumption that Balasescu convincingly argues against. An assumption that: 'Since veiling is a practice that does not belong to the 'Western' space, and since fashion ... historically belongs to the West, the veil cannot be fashion' (2003: 47). The headscarf ruptures this linear and structural reading of the relationship between Western fashion and modernity, complicating the notion that there is no space for fashion and modernity in Islam.

Our analysis indicates that for some covered women head covering is anything but a traditional practice and the aesthetics of the headscarf is at least as important as its religious and political dimensions. In fact, the selection and wearing of headscarves entail an elaborate process that requires invocation of cultural and economic capitals. Our informants repeatedly speak of their desire to be and look beautiful, a yearning that underlies their struggle for being individual, distinctive, fashionable and modern, yet faithful. Fashion operates through change and variety, and calls for repeat purchase. Islam exhorts believers to refrain from waste. Those who pay high prices for brand name scarves argue that high quality assures lasting usage and, thus, avoidance of waste. Yet, as fashion changes large numbers of scarves remain unused in the drawers. The proliferation of colours, fabrics and patterns, which used to be limited until recently, and the marketing of fashionable headscarves enable taste and individuality operate simultaneously as means of justification and distinction. Fashion depends on exhibition; Muslim theologians assert that Islam defines beautiful as the moral and the graceful without exhibition. But as much as fashion connotes fragmentation, religious covering entails plurality in interpretation, which enables women to adopt different looks that may be admired or condemned.

These tensions indicate that the Islamic headscarf does not categorically make the wearer 'non-modern'. On the contrary, they point towards different expressions of modernity, which are subject to the logic of fashion and capitalist production. Like Balasescu's (2003) observations regarding Iran, we see in the invocation of fashion among the urban covered Turkish women, the claim to modern identity. In addition to fashion, various other dynamics also contribute to this construction of modern identity. Both the actual practices and the discourses of our informants indicate the personalized nature of *tesettür*. This modern emphasis on individuality finds support in Islam. Muslim intellectuals, citing evidence from the Koran, argue that Islam supports a pluralism of the human community (Esposito 2003: 94–6). While fashion proliferates styles, the beauty work establishes the self as a modern subject with free choice. The beauty work around the scarf gives the subject the sense of a self-constructing person, who can take control of her own body and image. Thus, personalization and body work together create a sense of modern agency that is free to choose and shape. As modern self-managing subjects, covered women act in order to feel as an ethical, in this case, a religious person, legitimating their practices using the ethics or ideologies of capitalist modernity as well as religion. That is, they deal with the ethical-aesthetic-political tensions that underlie the practice of head covering as Foucault's (1986, 1988) modern subjects.

Overall, fashion, personalization, beauty work and techniques of the self manifest the existence of a modern identity that is constructed mainly through imagery. Susan Sontag claims that 'a society becomes 'modern' when one of its chief activities is producing and consuming images' (1972: 153). If this is true, the relation between the headscarf and modernity does not suggest negation but new possibilities.

However, there are limits on these possibilities. The constraints on the freedom of modern subjects and the context of modern subjectivities as theorized by Foucault (1984) are also present here. Like the hair project (Haug et al. 1983), head covering practice is not merely a subjective matter. The connections to the domination of market capitalism and its discourses of modernity, individuality and independence, propagated by tools such as marketing, advertising, fashion and media, are noticeable in the accounts of these informants. Head covering is also a politically charged practice: it is shaped by the changing implementation of legal regulations; it is an assertion of difference from the secularists; it is diffusionist, aiming to spread the practice of covering; which many believe still covertly serves the male dominant social order. While the women who cover by choice feel a sense of empowerment provided by the choices and personalization they make, the practice itself reinforces the assumption held by some of the interpreters of Islam that women arouse temptation and threaten male honour. While women view covering as a conscious personal choice in search of a modern Islamic identity of an elite status, male control over female sexuality and presence in the public space has primacy over women's autonomy and control over their bodies (White 2002). This gender politics is not only pertinent to Islam; it is pertinent to fashion in general.

The political symbolism of the headscarf is prevailing and strong. However, its material and aesthetic dimensions are as significant as its symbolism in complicating the relationship between religion, fashion and modernity. The head covering practice of the urban, middle/upper-middle income covered women is characterized by diversity; but it is also characterized by tensions and negotiations. These women spend a lot of time, money and effort to achieve their desired look, and use the headscarf as a means for projecting their aesthetic judgments, religious interpretations, and social positions. What appears initially as a contradiction emerges as a creative and skilful negotiation of the principles of Islam and the ideals of beauty and fashion. Paradoxically, the headscarf offers women possibilities as well as limitations in constructing a modern identity.

Notes

1. We use the term 'Islamist' to refer to those who are politically religious to distinguish it from secular Muslims who are believers without an affiliation to political Islam.
2. Secularists include both practising or non-practising Muslims and non-believers.
3. Many of the municipalities in Ankara and Istanbul are governed by mayors who are the members of the Islamist Party.
4. The up-market brand name scarves can cost up to 85 euros.

References

Ahmed, Leila 1992 *Women and Gender in Islam*. New Haven: Yale University Press.
Balasescu, Alexandru 2003 'Tehran Chic: Islamic Headscarves, Fashion Designers, and New Geographies of Modernity'. *Fashion Theory*, 7(1): 39–56.
El Guindi, Fadwa 1999a *Veil: Modesty, Privacy and Resistance*. London: Berg.
—— 1999b 'Veiling Resistance,' *Fashion Theory*, 3(1): 51–80.
Esposito, John L. 2003 'Islam and Civil Society'. In John L. Esposito and François Burgat (eds) *Modernizing Islam*. New Brunswick, NJ: Rutgers University Press, pp. 69–102.
Foucault, Michel 1984 'On the Genealogy of Ethics' (interview). In Paul Rabinow (ed.) *The Foucault Reader*. New York: Pantheon, pp. 340–72.
Foucault, Michel 1986 *The Care of the Self, The History of Sexuality, Volume 3*. New York: Random House.
—— 1988 'Technologies of the Self'. In Luther H. Martin, Huck Gutman and Patrick H. Hutton (eds) *Technologies of the Self: A seminar with Foucault*. London: Tavistock, pp. 16–49.
Göle, Nilüfer 1997 'The Gendered Nature of the Public Sphere'. *Public Culture*, 10(1): 61–81.
Haug, Frigga et al. 1983 *Female Sexualization: A Collective Work of Memory*. Trans. Erica Carter. London: Verso.
ISAV (Islami İlimler Araştırma Vakfı Yayınları) 1991 *Islam'da Kılık-Kıyafet ve Örtünme* [Clothes and Covering in Islam]. 3rd edition, Istanbul: Islami İlimler Araştırma Vakfı Yayınları.
Kılıçbay, Barış and Binark, Mutlu 2002 'Consumer Culture, Islam and the Politics of Lifestyle: Fashion for Veiling in Contemporary Turkey'. *European Journal of Communication*, 17(4): 495–511.
Makhlouf, C. 1979 *Changing Veils: Women and Modernization in North Yemen*. London: Croom Helm.
Mandel, Ruth 1989 'Turkish Headscarves and the "Foreigner Problem": Constructing Difference Through Emblems of Identity'. *New German Critique*, 46(Winter): 27–46.
McCracken, Grant 1988 *Culture and Consumption*. Bloomington: Indiana University Press.
Mernissi, Fatma 1991 *The Veil and the Male Elite: A Feminist Interpretation of Women's Rights in Islam*. Trans. M.J. Lakeland. New York: Addison-Wesley.
Navaro-Yahin, Yael 2002 'The Market for Identities: Secularism, Islamism, Commodities'. In Deniz Kandiyoti and Ayşe Saktanber (eds) *Fragments of Culture: The Everyday of Modern Turkey*. London: I.B. Tauris, pp. 221–53.

Nava, Mica 1997 'Modernity's Disavowal: Women, The City and the Department Store'. In Pasi Falk and Colin Campbell (eds) *The Shopping Experience*. Thousand Oaks: Sage.

Sandıkcı, Özlem and Ger, Güliz 2002 'In-Between Modernities and Postmodernities: Investigating Turkish Consumptionscape'. *Advances in Consumer Research*, 29, Salt Lake City, UT: Association for Consumer Research.

—— 2001 'Fundamental Fashions: The Cultural Politics of the Turban and the Levi's'. *Advances in Consumer Research*, 28: 146–50.

Schneider, Jane and Weiner, Annette B. 1989 'Introduction'. In Annette B. Weiner and Jane Schneider (eds) *Cloth and Human Experience*. Washington: Smithsonian Institution Press, pp. 1–29.

Simmel, Georg 1904 'Fashion'. *International Quarterly*, 10 (October): 130–55.

Sontag, Susan 1972 *On Photography*. Harmondsworth: Penguin Books.

Turner, Brian 1994 *Orientalism, Postmodernism and Globalism*. London and New York: Routledge.

Yeğenoğlu, Melda 1998 *Colonial Fantasies: Toward a Feminist Reading of Orientalism*. Cambridge: Cambridge University Press.

White, Jenny 2002 'The Islamist Paradox'. In Deniz Kandiyoti and Ayşe Saktanber (eds) *Fragments of Culture: The Everyday of Modern Turkey*. London: I.B. Tauris, pp. 191–220.

Wilson, Elizabeth 1985 *Adorned in Dreams: Fashion and Modernity*. London: Virago.

–5–

Cloth That Lies: The Secrets of Recycling in India
Lucy Norris

There has long been perceived to be a divide between scholars of clothing, dress history and contemporary fashion on the one hand, and work on the economic and social conditions of the production and consumption of cloth on the other (Taylor 2002). While the former are often accused of fetishizing the object through obsessive description without due regard for a wider social context (Fine and Leopold 1993), the latter conceal a mysterious lacuna with regard to the materiality of the thing itself, and an unwillingness to acknowledge the importance of the ephemerality of fashions (Styles 1998). Although a few anthropological studies of cloth have begun to bridge this divide (e.g. Weiner and Schneider 1989), in both studies of cloth and clothing the main emphasis has always been on the way cloth is turned into clothing, effecting a subsequent separation between the two. In effect this implies the dissolution of our interest in the materiality of cloth as it gives way to our interest in the sociality of clothing.

What has been largely neglected is the inverse transformation. It is not that people do not recognize that clothing is often transformed back to fibre and rags, but it is assumed that that constitutes the end of our concern for the social life of clothing. However, there is a largely unacknowledged and invisible world in which this secondary transformation becomes productive, not just of various forms of social relations, but also of massive cultural flows that create new connectivities that are typical of the way the world is being constantly reconstructed (Latour 1993; Appadurai 1996). What is almost completely absent from these accounts is the centrality of the materiality of cloth itself and the propensities of fibre and textile to become the medium by which these flows and their consequences are realized.

Historical research in India has helped highlight the way many attributes of cloth itself, which we either ignore or fail to acknowledge, have been central to the perception and subsequent use of cloth as an agent in South Asia (Bayly 1986). For example, the ability of cloth to become the transformative medium that absorbs the essence of a venerated older person and is wrapped around a new born baby as a protection. There is the means through which colour and fibre are used to construct a polarity, at one end of which stands the bride, shimmering in her bright red and gold silks and at the other end the widow in her pale cottons. Then there is the dynamism of the acquisition of clothing, in which a person's very substance is made evident in the density and scale of her wardrobe of accumulated fabrics, often gifted at important events during her life. This in turn echoes the ideal distancing from materiality through separation and loss that gives the elevation required by renunciation appropriate to later life.

All of this is familiar, perhaps even classic, anthropological territory, but during fieldwork in New Delhi and the Punjab, I was exposed to very different images of transformation. *These* images are of huge piles of cast-off clothing from both India and the West, in markets, streets and warehouses. No longer desired as beloved envelopes of the self that once projected multivalent images of belonging and difference, these discards are peeled away from the body, as a snake sheds its skin, through routine practices of detachment and riddance. I argue that in the process recounted below, it is not the form and fashion of the clothing that is of value, but rather the phenomenal, perceptual qualities of fibres, textures, colour and pattern. These attributes of cloth can be conceived as 'qualisigns', referring to Munn's use of the Piercian term, that is, 'icons that exhibit something other than themselves *in themselves*' (1986: 74). They can possess characteristics of both passive decay, for example fragility, impermanence and vulnerability, and at the same time of active regeneration and reconstitution through their ability to be reconstituted in new configurations of material form and surface design. It is these material and hence perceptual qualities of cloth that can be released and set free from the structures and strictures of clothing.

Garments that once constituted the permeable layers connecting inner self to outer sociality have many trajectories once they no longer hold a value in the wardrobe. In India, old clothing is dealt with in similar ways to those that have been documented in the West and elsewhere. It may be hoarded as family heirlooms, emblems of group identity (Weiner 1992; Tarlo 1996), or individual mementoes (Stallybrass 1993; Stewart 1993), handed on to younger family members, given to servants (Lemire 1991), or reused and recycled creatively within the home as an expression of love and thrift (Greenfield 1986; Seriff 1996). All these options conserve the connection between cloth and the body, valuing the signs of such former presences, and often utilizing them to create both intimacy and hierarchy. The last resort might be simply to throw clothing away in the rubbish bin, but this is a fate which never befalls it in India.

One further option remains: their recommodification. The previous inhabitants of this category of clothing have realized the full value of these material qualities through using culturally appropriate systems of exchange. In the West, this largely means giving them to charity organizations who then resell them on the global market, resulting in the feeling of having done something altruistic as well as ridding oneself of the unwanted burden of former selves. In India, middle-class housewives barter them for shiny steel cooking utensils, a highly valued resource within the woman's domestic economy. In both cases, what is created through riddance is exchange value, or 'getting something for nothing'. The unwanted clothing thus slips from being transient in value (declining) to rubbish, from where it can be rescued and reinvested with value, on the way to becoming more durable in value once more (Thompson 1979).

These discards constitute a vast resource in India, both imported from abroad via international dealers and produced locally through the bartering system. Mountains of trash wait to be transformed into treasure. Container loads of rags are shipped in from all around the developed world, and relocated in massive warehouses across northern India, but remain invisible to all except those who work within them. These constitute the raw material from which new, 'Indian' products will be manufactured. Nearby in local markets in small towns and major cities are found equally massive heaps of unwanted Indian clothing, saris, *shalwar kamiz* and suiting here being sorted, selected and offered for sale. From this mass of material, dealers and fabricators create new products and niche markets through entrepreneurial recycling, producing clothing for the local poor and fashionable street gear for Westerners. These images are much less familiar than the typical bridal scene, or the image of the spiritual absorbency of the sacred thread, but actually they are in their own way a potent form of interconnected change that is transformative both of people, of India and increasingly of international connections. I now want to elaborate on these two examples of a kind of bilateral symmetry in trade, by showing how understanding them requires much more attention to the specific materialities involved.

The Recycling of Indian Clothing

I have described the commodification of Indian clothing elsewhere in more detail (Norris 2004) and its subsequent recycling by entrepreneurial dealers (Norris 2005). Here I will only briefly sum up the main dynamics of the process in order to make the comparison with the importing of used clothing from abroad. Periodically, middle- and upper-class Indian women sort though their clothing, and put to one side garments that they wish to divest. Good quality clothes are usually passed on to younger family members, while worn clothes are handed on to maids and servants in carefully prescribed amounts, but women are reluctant to hand over items that are considered 'too good for the maid'. Especially in urban middle-class households, there is now an increasing surplus of unwanted stuff, which will not wear out, and for which more traditional routes of reuse and disposal cannot accommodate. These clothes represent an emotional, economic and social investment and are never just thrown out. Their commodification begins with Indian housewives bartering their families' old clothing for stainless steel kitchen pots on the doorstep. Such pots are favoured by women across India, and are often artistically arranged on kitchen shelves; indeed, they are one of the main components of a woman's dowry, along with her trousseau and other domestic goods.

The women dealers who carry out this trade are members of the Waghri caste, known as itinerant traders (Fig. 5.1). Classified by British Colonial officials as criminals and untouchables, they are still looked down upon, and householders warn that they are 'casing the joint' for return visits by their husbands. Implying that the Waghri men are all thieves and worse, they are making an obvious identification of person with the rubbish goods in which they trade. These dealers are the mainstay of a flourishing informal economy which removes the waste from the threshold of the household and takes it out into society to be reprocessed into desirable products; in Indian cosmology, they are classified as polluted because their trade, and hence dangerous to members of middle-class households.

After a lengthy period of exhaustive haggling on the doorstep the deal is sealed. Pieces of disintegrating cloth have been turned into shiny new metal pots, a translation of form into a more durable, desirable product, equally, if not better, able to represent and reflect a woman's sense of identity and values. The Waghri women carry away overflowing bundles slung across their backs, returning to their homes in a suburb of northern Delhi. Nearly 40,000 people in the extended neighbourhood live in families that are involved in the trade in some fashion. Every lane is festooned with used garments, in the process of being washed, mended, stockpiled and sorted ready for resale and transformation, yet the suburb remains hidden from the middle-class city-dweller from whom the clothing has been harvested. Indeed, it is this invisibility that allows for such radical translations of form and the overturning of previous regimes of value.

Every morning before dawn, a huge market attracts thousands of buyers and sellers. Rows of women sit behind piles of clothing, calling out their wares to the circulating buyers. These are more usually men, who buy selected types of clothing for niche markets. Some dealers specialize in cotton saris and dhotis, which are torn into squares, and amassed until bulk shipments can be made to factories around the world for use as machine wipers. Others specialize in old army uniforms, blue jeans, men's shirts and shoes. The value of women's clothing is largely defined according to fabric quality, decorative features and hence suitability for wear by the poor. However, in an inversion of middle-class values, a new-looking synthetic *shalwar kamiz* will fetch more than an older cotton version, as ease of laundering and low maintenance is more important. These clothes are usually pressed and folded, and sold at weekly markets. The market acts as a centrifugal force for processing waste – in the search for a new retail niche, traders

The Secrets of Recycling in India

Figure 5.1 Waghri women spread their kitchen wares out on the ground to tempt passing women into bartering their old clothes in return.

will buy in the cities and then travel out through the satellite towns and villages, bringing new fashions and a variety of garments with them.

The highest profits are to be made from silky saris. Here middlemen accumulate saris with decorative borders and ends to be sold on to dealers who transform them into international products. Saris are cut into small pieces avoiding tears and stains and made into patchwork cushions, hangings and bedspreads. Other manufacturers specialize in making clothing such as sundresses, skirts, trousers, hot pants and short halter-neck tops, often copying designs from clothing worn by foreigners. These are then sold on to tourists, and both buyers and sellers interact to create up-to-the minute fashions in major budget travellers destinations across India. Some of these travellers engage in selling them abroad, importing quantities of them for sale in markets and festivals across Europe, America, Japan and Australia. In a few cases, Western entrepreneurs have joined forces with the makers, subsidizing small manufacturing units and creating a consolidated supply chain of goods. These developments reveal the increasing economic rewards to be made from such transformation of cheap resources. But it has been taken one step further by the popularity of Indian furnishings in the West. Some major high-street retailers have started selling 'sari cushions' and so on, but in order to retain a regular supply of unblemished goods, these products are made to imitate their recycled originals, and now use new, clean fabric.

Lucy Norris

The Recycling of Imported Clothing

The Importers

I now turn to the particular trade in used Western clothing imported into India, for it provides an extraordinary example of the various, often invisible, means through which value is maximized in the market. The dynamics of this trade as described below are illustrated in Figure 5.2. The global trade in second-hand clothing has been highlighted by Tranberg Hansen's study of *Salaula* in Zambia (2000), in which she documents in detail the mechanisms through which used clothing is sold in the international market. In the West, cast-off knitted jumpers and coats originally donated to charities are often unsuitable for sale within those countries. Rigorous sorting procedures at depots such as 'Wastesavers' in Yorkshire, England, are designed to ensure that the value of a particular garment is maximized for the charity who collects them, sifting out retro-fashions and high quality classic items for resale in specialist shops, and unwearable garments to be sold as machine wipers and filling material. Those items that are deemed unsuitable for sale in Western charity shops are sold to independent recycling companies, who then grade and sort them by fibre content, before baling them and selling them abroad by the container load.

Used clothing is therefore traded internationally as a commodity, originating in Western countries such as the USA, Canada, Europe, Australia and Japan.[1] These recycling companies are the direct descendants of the eighteenth- and nineteenth-century 'Rag and Bone' men, now trading in huge volumes in global markets. These clothes are often sold on as garments, prized as quality clothing of Western origin and therefore different, new and potentially fashionable (e.g. Hansen 1994), or to provide basic bodily protection for the poor. Governments can treat them as an addition to an impoverished economy unable to afford new clothing (e.g. Pakistan, Bangladesh), or as a threat to indigenous industries, imposing various levels of protectionist import restrictions or outright bans (e.g. Kenya, India).[2]

The importation of used clothing for resale in India is legally restricted to those holding an import licence from the Ministry of Commerce.[3] In the summer of 2000 those used clothing imports that were approved were subject to a 200 per cent import tax, unless it could be proved that they had been imported by a recognized charity for free distribution to the needy. As there is considerable demand for cheap second-hand Western clothing in India and a flourishing black market, especially in men's clothes and woollens, the Indian Customs officials have to determine whether an application to import clothing for charitable purposes is indeed bona fide. Some smaller organizations have been found to be acting corruptly, using charitable organizations as a front with profits siphoned off by high-level officials. But policing such trade is difficult; a customs official at the Inland Container Depot in Delhi frequently exercised his own moral judgement

The Secrets of Recycling in India

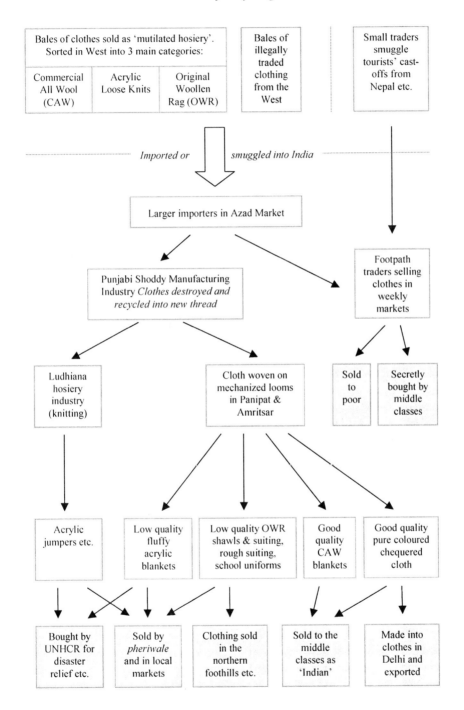

Figure 5.2 Recycling imported Western clothing in India.

in deciding which container loads of clothing might be genuinely charitable. He had recently permitted a container load of European women's clothing to go to Assam, as it was well known that women in the tea plantations wore skirts and blouses unlike those in other regions of India. A deputation from a Sri Lankan Buddhist Police organization was similarly allowed to send clothing to Tibetan refugees in Dharamsala, but a Swami who left as I entered the room had just been refused permission to send imported women's clothing to Bihar – as culturally inappropriate garments, the official knew that they were more likely to be diverted to the black market once the dispensation was issued. The inland depot in Delhi allowed approximately only twelve container loads of clothing per year.

What is of interest to this chapter is an alternative option, whereby used woollen clothing can also be legally sold as a fibre commodity in the form of 'rags'. Imported rags are a permitted commodity that attracted a tariff of only 40 per cent. India has insufficient wool to meet her needs, and woollen rags are allowed to fuel the recycling industry known as 'shoddy' manufacturing, now located in the Punjab. In order to try and control illegal imports of wearable garments, the Indian government (among others) insists that all used clothing is slashed by large machines wielding fiendishly sharp rotating blades before packaging for export by the West, creating a product generically known as 'mutilated hosiery'.

These clothes are then exported either in vacuum-packed plastic wrapped in bales of approximately 350 kg, or loose bales of 500 or 1000 kg. About fifty to sixty 350 kg, or forty-five 500 kg bales fit into the average 40-foot long shipping container, making each one weigh between 18 and 22 metric tonnes. The key area for tariff trickery and the maximizing of profit lies in passing off imported containers of wearable used clothes as 'mutilated hosiery' to customs officials at the docks, thereby avoiding the need for impossible-to-obtain licenses and high tariffs.

The official told a cautionary tale of trying too hard to tackle the problem. In Kolkata in the late 1990s, a backlog of 400 containers had accumulated, all garments illegally declared as 'mutilated hosiery'. The garments were vacuum packed, so that as customs officials checked bales by cutting them open, the contents expanded and they occupied greater and greater amounts of space. This put off a full-scale check on all imports. Even though the usable clothing discovered was impounded, an amnesty had to be declared to allow the dealers to remove their vastly enlarged commodity, which was physically clogging up the warehouses and docksides. Clothing's very nature seems to lend itself to such secretive, underhand transformations during its processing. Although cloth's vulnerability permits it to be slashed, when squashed into layers of flat textile in a bale, the shape and potential of garments are hidden and the cuts remain invisible. The clothes constantly threaten to suddenly spill out from their vacuum-packed environment and reveal themselves as impostors, still whole and ready to be slipped on once more.

The Secrets of Recycling in India

Second-hand clothing tends to move in and out of various markets, which operate on both sides of the law, and it is difficult to be sure of exact quantities, values and trajectories as they are traded. As imports are legal in all the countries bordering India but not in India itself, cross-border smuggling is also a real problem, and many of the smaller dealers' families originate in Nepal and Dharamsala, north India, where Tibetan refugees stockpile clothing given to them by Western tourists for later resale in India. These independent dealers operate on the basis of extended family networks, where key members establish bases in large cities such as Delhi and younger members are used to expand the markets in which they sell. Many informants also mentioned the practice of diverting charitable aid relief destined for Bangladesh through to India; one claimed that the whole illegal trade began on the Bangladeshi and Thai borders.

The main business centre for dealing in old clothing in Delhi is Azad market, established after Independence largely to deal with auctioning off government surplus, and lines of shops still sell off uniforms, boots, equipment, tyres, tents and the ubiquitous red and blue striped floor mats. Many importers claimed the highest profit to be obtained from imported used textiles is from buying clothing of reasonable quality and selling it on as garments; they are adamant that such clothing is needed by the poor, who cannot afford to buy new Indian clothing, thus adding a positive moral dimension to their illegal trade. It seems there is never enough used Indian clothing in the market and its quality is very low by the time it has been thrown out. According to them, an apparent 'craze' for foreign things is much less of a consideration than abject poverty, and demand is high. However, at the local suburban weekly markets where such clothing is sold to customers, no attempt is made to remove the brightly coloured paper thrift store labels attached to most of the clothing in the USA and Canada. The exotic origin of the clothes was important to their marketing, although few would be able to read the labels – one trader enthusiastically sang out 'foreign' every minute or two to attract buyers.

In Azad market, many, if not most, importers are undoubtedly operating in the black market, although some claim to be solely rag importers. In a rabbit warren of cupboard offices in an old covered market, businessmen sit surrounded by phones and towers of plastic covered bales of clothing, small boys keeping up a constant flow of *chai,* sweet milky tea. Smaller bales, neatly strapped, have their origins emblazoned across them: 'CANN-AMM Best in Used American/Canadian clothing', complete with flags and national colours. These dealers use such bales as samples, maintaining huge *godowns* (warehouses) in the city outskirts. Networks extend across India (Kolkata, Chennai, Mumbai), and through to the UK and the USA; many Indians living in the West are increasingly acting as agents in the old clothing trade, and along the US Eastern Seaboard many of the traditionally Jewish firms are now owned or operated by Indians.

It is clear that in this underhand trade the importers and dealers are often outsiders, of diverse origins and traditions, and the trade appears to develop as new waves of economic migrants enter the business. As a trade dealing in polluted waste, it is shunned by the higher Hindu castes, yet offers an opportune starting point for those with little to invest. There is a minimal crossover with the dealers in used Indian clothing, and the systems of collecting, processing and importing second-hand clothing and waste products remain separate from the resale of Indian clothing or the export of products made from saris. The main trade in imported clothing on a largescale is in the hands of Punjabi Sikhs and former refugees from Partition, and more recently the Tibetans and Nepalese.

Many dealers in Azad market make a good profit by buying up rags in vast quantities. Until 1988–9, only mill owners (as the end users) could import rags, but a policy was then introduced of issuing 'Open General Licenses', so middlemen can now operate legally and profitably. Approximately 90 per cent of woollen rags are imported via Kolkata, the rest through Chennai and Mumbai. A pair of Sikh brothers, for example, works in the family firm in Azad market, importing 'mutilated hosiery' from the USA. They buy up bales of rags at 25 to 50 cents/kg CIF (Cost, Insurance and Freight), then have to pay 40 per cent import duty on them. They make only 2–3 Rs/kg profit, but turnover is very high. They import between 100 and 150 containers a year, and send them straight from the Mumbai docks to the recycling factories. Occasionally one of the brothers travels to the USA, but mainly they use agents and family contacts.

The Punjabi Shoddy Manufacturing Industry

Textile recycling originated in the Yorkshire Dales at the turn of the nineteenth century with the development of the 'pulling process' whereby woollen fibres can be reclaimed by shredding textiles and turned into 'shoddy' yarn. This yarn is then respun and subsequently used for weaving or knitting. This description outlines the potential products of multiple recycling in the UK:

> A woollen jumper which lasts seven years can be recycled into a woollen coating fabric, which can be made into an overcoat that is good for perhaps ten more years. The discarded overcoat can then go on to become a blanket, which can again yield service for ten years. The blanket can then be recycled as filling for furniture or bedding or perhaps as the insulation or soundproofing in a motor car. So a wool fibre, starting life on the back of a sheep, can have a useful life of 50 years before nothing more can be done with it. (Smosarski 1995: 113–14)

Demand for recycled fibres has reduced in the UK since the 1960s, 'due to the development of lighter-weight waterproof fabrics, the need for fewer military

The Secrets of Recycling in India

uniforms since abolition of National Service, and the increased use of inferior synthetics'.[4] Yet countries such as India utilize the technology to make up for a lack of indigenous raw materials and an inability to purchase new wool internationally at affordable prices. The export of used Western clothing for the shoddy industry is arguably an international trade in waste products, but those involved deny this definition and conceive of it differently. The 'Basel Convention on the Control of Trans-boundary Movements of Hazardous Waste and Their Disposal' (United Nations Environmental Programme) regulates the export of toxic waste to developing countries, and calls for its environmentally sound management.[5] It classifies second-hand textiles as waste, but allows their export as they are on a special 'Green List'. Textile recyclers in the mid 1990s were indignant that their products were classed as waste at all, seeing them as an environmentally friendly resource for the world's poor and needy.[6]

One shoddy manufacturer, whose mill had been in business for nearly sixty years, explained that India began buying shoddy yarn from Italy in the 1950s and 1960s.[7] In 1958, the first second-hand machines were imported from Milan to Mumbai, and India began producing her own shoddy wool. In the 1970s labour unrest and increased management costs led to heavy expenses, and the factories closed down. Business shifted to the Punjabi plains, and was established firmly in Amritsar and latter Panipat in 1975. A few hours drive north of Delhi, Panipat is now the major centre for the recycling of mutilated hosiery in India, with 100 to 300 mills processing shoddy from old clothing, and associated industries in Amritsar and Ludhiana.

As I was passed through networks of importers, agents, dealers, manufacturers and distributors during fieldwork, it became apparent that both the complexity of the system, based on blood ties and personal contacts, and the expansive entrepreneurial spirit of the individual players creates a complicated web of business relationships. Each dealer appeared eager to take risks and to develop opportunities, securing the best deals in obtaining the raw materials and developing saleable products. Thus major importers one year became buyers from other importers the next, mills were set up by brothers, uncles and cousins to pool resources or diversify products, and relatives were sent abroad to secure the supply chain as agents for others on a commission basis.

Processing the Raw Materials

The processes of manufacturing shoddy yarn are to a large extent determined by the actual garments available, their fibre content, and ultimately the technological requirements for their transformation.

Three main grades of 'woollen' clothing are imported into India:[8]

1. 'Commercial All Wool' (CAW). 70–80% wool hosiery, i.e. jumpers, scarves and hats. [50c/kg].
2. 'Acrylic Loose Knits'. 100% synthetic hosiery, i.e. jumpers. [32c/kg].
3. 'Original Woollen Rag' (OWR). 70–80% wool cloth, i.e. old coats. [21c/kg].

When buying clothing in the international market place, the reputation of the source companies in the West is very important in judging the probable fibre quality and colour of the bales' contents. Good companies in the West are known to employ careful sorters and graders: they have a first and a second grading, and do not mix fibres. The names of firms such as 'Allied', 'International' (Texas) and 'H.B.' (Bradford, UK) act as brands that guarantee quality; for example 'H.B.' is known for the best quality English wool coats and jumpers, which cost more than the Canadian equivalents.

One dealer explained that buyers favoured clothes from the USA and UK as they were generally new and 'bright' shades, whereas German clothing tended to be poorer quality and 'dull' shades. 'Bright' means intense, such as royal blue, while 'dull' can refer to pastel shades as well as greys, browns and olive greens.[9] The purity of colour in the used clothing is extremely important; the fibres are not re-dyed, and the purer and brighter the colours obtainable in the raw material, the more valuable the end product. However, the Original Woollen Rag from northern hemisphere winter coats is overwhelmingly comprised of dark greys, browns, greens and blacks, in checks, tweeds and so on, with only a few groups of bright shades. Manufacturers with old equipment can make a profit by using these materials, but the end products are unsurprisingly sludgy colours and receive the lowest market rates.

As the bales are cut open on the warehouse floors (Fig. 5.3), this mutilated hosiery is sorted further into a range of 'colour families', e.g. peacock, *rani* (hot pink), *mehendi* (henna), American beauty (a bright red shade), saffron and checked. Larger colour families were next sorted into sub-groups of light pastel, dark and bright shades; the more rigorous the colour sorting, the purer the eventual result. In addition were the 'fancy' groups, multicoloured checks and tweeds that were the one exception, occasionally being re-dyed black once sorted. The huge piles of clothing were then stripped of all their non-woollen fibre components by women workers: labels, buttons, zips, press studs, leather patches and trimmings, shoulder pads and linings. Buttons were burnt off, while mainly synthetic coat and jacket linings were removed and bought by the local *kabariwale* (rubbish men) and periodically carted away on overflowing trucks. Approximately 90 per cent of Commercial All Wool is recovered, with only 10 per cent burnt or sold as *katran* (rags). The clothing is then cut into pieces about 50 cm square by the same women, who sit on the floor using traditional vegetable cutters (Fig. 5.4).

The Secrets of Recycling in India

Figure 5.3 A bale of old clothes from the UK waits to be sorted at the factory in Panipat

Interestingly, the one by-product for which there is no use are the garment labels, which are perhaps the most obvious evidence of the transformation of values that is taking place. Once advertising a brand name that was vital to the value of the original garment, this information is now worthless, or in fact detracts from the re-evaluation process. These labels provide the material evidence for the history of the twentieth-century trans-national trade in new clothing, charting the course of fibre sources, designs, manufacture and retail across the globe. But as grubby exuviae snipped from a garment collar they bear witness to the archaeology of wardrobe turn-outs, as seen from the archaic typefaces, logos and colonial terms

Figure 5.4 Once the clothing has been sorted by colour, women cut it up into small squares

such as 'Manufactured in the British Crown Colony of Hong Kong' which have lingered for decades in Western closets. Also found are scrappy paper labels from garments that failed to attract a potential buyer in American thrift shops, which reveal the over-optimistic second-hand value given in dollars and cents.

The clothes are then broken down into a tangled mess of fibres and soaked overnight in a solution to which is added bettering oil, to enable them to pass through the machinery better and stop static electricity building up. The fibres are teased, carded and spun into new thread: the antiquated machinery used is itself recycled from Italy, while the threads are wound onto spools made from old newspapers. The purer the wool content in used clothing and the longer the fibre staple, the better quality it is and a stronger, finer thread can be produced by recycling. The oldest recycling machines can only produce poor quality, thick, heavy wool products with a short staple, hence returning a lower profit on the finished goods, while newer machinery can producer a finer yarn. Woollen yarn is classified into 'counts': the higher the count, the finer the yarn; the quality of the end product therefore depends upon both the raw material and the technology available.

Different production methods and end products are centred in different areas, although not exclusively. Panipat manufacturers can achieve only an 8½ to 10 count thread as their machines are the oldest, in Ludhiana they make 10, 12 and 14 count threads, in Amritsar 12 to 13 count.[10] Panipat is largely known for its cheap shoddy blankets and shawls made from Original Woollen Rag, Ludhiana is a centre for synthetic hosiery and knits products from recycled Acrylic Loose Knits, while Amritsar weaves better quality woollen cloth from Commercial All Wool to be made up into clothing.

Panipat: Blankets and Shawls

Companies in Panipat have been manufacturing blankets for the poor for the last 100 years, but only using shoddy thread since the 1970s. The lowest grades of recycled threads are hand-woven into blankets on upright looms. Ten blankets are woven at a time, then cut afterwards. The woven cloth is then wet with water, and rolled in 'milling' machines and dried: the pile is then raised through steam treatment, the steam generated by boilers stoked with rice husks. The resulting blankets are semi-felted and 'fluffy'.

These blankets are of low quality, in plain and simple monochrome and not expected to last. The plainest, one season blankets are purchased by Aid agencies such as the UNHCR and the Indian government for disaster relief, and sent to Orissa, Bangladesh, and further afield to Africa. Each one costs approximately Rs 60.[11] Ironically, the clothing given to charity in the West may be helping to keep refugees and disaster victims warm, but through a circuitous route few would imagine, via the recycling of their constituent fibres (see also Hansen 2000).

Catering for the very lowest end of the market, another mill produced very poor quality men's shawls, *lohi*, in a range of grimy camel colours, from Original Woollen Rag (in this case usually old coats). Costing about Rs 80 each, they measured about 54 inches by 90 inches. The same firm wove bolts of cloth from which were cut clothing such as blazers, jackets and types of winter tunics, *phiren*, all favoured in the mountainous northern states of Uttar Pradesh, Kashmir and so on. All of these products, the blankets, shawls and clothing, were thick and gritty to the touch, with a greasy texture and unpleasant smell. It suddenly became clear that at no stage, from being ejected from the Westerner's wardrobe, via travelling across the globe, being shredded and rewoven, were these garments ever washed; the human dirt and environmental pollution encountered along the way literally clung to their very fibres. The mill owners were sure that the poor Himalayans who bought them would never notice; in any case, they could never afford pure virgin wool.

Using better quality yarn, brightly coloured shades (often fluorescent) can be woven alongside darker ones, in bold stripes and chequered designs made locally on computers. These are exported to Russia and other developing countries, or sold in India, each fetching between Rs 100 and 150. Some shopkeepers order in bulk and distribute them via *pheriwale*. These are travelling salesmen who buy up a bale or two of thirty to thirty-five blankets from the shop, and take ten or fifteen around with them every day, going door-to-door. They make perhaps Rs 10 profit on each one.

I purchased a single blanket made from Original Woollen Rag for Rs 250; its plastic wrapper had 'Product of India' proudly emblazoned across it. Another smaller baby's blanket in fluffed acrylic-wool mix similarly declared itself to be 'Indian'; it had a vase with flowers across it, a common design found across the northern Indian (Fig. 5.5). Less obviously grimy and gritty to the touch, both still possessed a certain greasiness and whiff of mechanical oil about them, yet

Figure 5.5 A baby's blanket woven from recycled thread and sold in Indian markets

it is unlikely that a middle-class consumer would ever realize how they were actually made, and would have no idea of the origin of the materials: the product has been completely 'Indianized'. In fact, it has been suggested that such smells could, ironically, be reminiscent of dry cleaning fluid, a signal of the opposite condition of cleanliness and purity.[12] The higher the fibre quality and colour purity, the more elaborate the designs; the best blankets made from Commercial All Wool can be sold for Rs 400 to 500 each, but these tend to be made in Amritsar. One manufacturer estimated that only 1 per cent of the population would be able to afford blankets made from pure virgin wool from Australia or New Zealand, which retail at over Rs 1,000.

The middle classes profess it to be unthinkable to purchase second-hand cloth openly in the market unless one is very poor.[13] Yet unknown to them, some of the better quality 'new' products on sale are, paradoxically, profoundly old and truly dirty. For the very fibres of many apparently new blankets and woollen goods are, in fact, recycled from imported woollen clothing, a fact that is completely concealed. The successful recycling of such material to a wider market requires traders to navigate such customers' value systems skilfully through various strategies of transformation and marketing. While other recycled goods are admired as evidence of thrift or artistic creativity since being taken up by the West (Cerny and Seriff 1996; Coote, Morton and Nicholson 2000) the origins of these textiles are all but invisible to the eye.

Ludhiana: Knitted Hosiery

Ludhiana is a centre for the manufacture of knitted synthetics; most of the raw materials used are new, but there are some smaller manufacturers using recycled shoddy to make clothing. The end product is equally reliant on the available technology, the quality of yarn required and the price of new versus shoddy thread on the international market.

The hand-knitting machines in smaller units use two threads at once and require mixed wool/synthetic threads to strengthen the garment. Adding 10 per cent of polyester thread also adds a softness and lustre to the jumper – makers were keen to show the 'sparkle' it added to the otherwise drab thread. But manufacturing costs must be carefully controlled, and polyester thread is usually much more expensive. However, when the international price of crude oil sank to $10 a barrel, the price of polyester yarn suddenly fell, reaching rock bottom in 1999. Shoddy was only a little less, and could not compete unless prices for mutilated rags also fell. The world market in mutilated hosiery is therefore linked to the international oil market: the value of an old sweater linked to international politics through materials and technology.

Jumpers were also never washed and had the same greasy, gritty feel to them as the Panipat blankets. The cheapest combination of colours is 'air force' and 'light grey'. More expensive colours are those that have been dyed darker to hide imperfections: black, maroon, red, navy and coffee. The garment designs were copied from larger manufacturers who in turn got their inspiration from fashion shows and magazines. The jumpers were of such poor quality that only 5 to 10 per cent were used within India, while 70 per cent was exported to Bangladesh and the Middle East for re-export.

Amritsar: Woollen Suiting

The woollen cloth produced in Amritsar is altogether finer in quality, and all the mills are competing in the international export trade with the West rather than the world's poorest markets. Amritsar tends to have newer machinery, but above all, it is claimed, the softest water. Several manufacturers claimed that this is one of the most important reasons why Panipat makes such poor quality cloth that it is impossible to export it. The only international competition for the Amritsar businessmen comes from Korea, who entered the market in the mid-1990s, and more recently China. Some of the mill owners were trying to break into the international market for virgin wool products, hoping to change the global impression of Indian woollen products as inferior. By investing in newer technology, they only now needed to import wool from Australia and New Zealand to achieve the same standards as Italy.

But the majority of mills produce high quality shoddy suiting, which is then sent to Delhi to be made up into clothing. One unit had a carding machine from Belgium, which produced 12 to 14 count threads. This was then woven into suiting on four Polish looms, which used punch cards to create tweed designs. The selvedges were decorated with phrases, slogans and brand names of modernity rather than the manufacturer's name:[14] 'Millennium 2000', 'Heritage Club' and, in tribute to Rupert Murdoch's pan-Asian satellite TV channel, 'Star Plus'. It is clear that simple categories of 'new' and 'recycled' bear no relation to the extremely complex strategies employed by manufacturers, traders and retailers to transform 'waste' textile materials of all kinds into saleable 'new' commodities.

At Diamond Woollen Mills, a wide range of colourful checks and 'tartans' were manufactured. Their cloth was sold to Delhi garment manufacturers to fulfil export orders; the colours and designs were often determined by the buyers from abroad. The company made 10,000 metres per month, working twenty-four hours a day in shifts to satisfy demand. Unlike cheaper products, the cloth was washed with detergent during the finishing process, and had lost the unpleasant pungency of other examples. This cloth is in fact made into clothing that is then exported back to the West as fashion garments. Coming full circle, one manufacturer told me he had been amazed when, on a business trip to London, he had seen a red tartan jacket for sale in Oxford Street made from 100 per cent Indian shoddy cloth.

Conclusion

The recycling of imported Western clothing in India shares many of the characteristics of strategies utilized in the recycling of Indian clothes. Knowledge about, and preservation of, signs of the previous individual owner is not given a positive value, in fact signs of the body have to be removed, but in an unusually brutal manner (Gregson and Crewe 2000). The manufacture of extremely cheap blankets and jumpers from shoddy for the very poor and disaster victims reflects an economy of technology that adds value to cast-out garments, giving them a new lease of life for a year or two at best. However, in order to manufacture a product attractive to the middle classes, it is again necessary to conceal the second-hand, foreign origin of the material, destroying it completely and throwing away the very labels and fashion trimmings that gave the garment its value in the West. This effacement of former lives creates a new exchange value located in the shoddy fibres; once stamped with a 'Product of India' strap-line, the blanket has a new value as desirable commodity. The two extremes encompass the approaches needed to add value to 'rubbish' for different consumers: one focuses on the foreign origins of cloth, whilst the other denies it completely.

These examples reveal the hidden, often subversive flow of goods between India and the developed world, characterized by disintegration, disposal and destruction on the one hand, and by reclamation, reintegration and renewal on the other. The materiality of cloth is essential for this translation of form, for it is in ambiguities of its material properties, its colour, its strength and fragility, its capacity to absorb, to reflect, to be cut and restitched that its transformative value lies. It is by variously utilizing qualities such as colour, fibre characteristics, pattern, sheen and texture, while being rid of the form of the clothing, its wear, tear, holes and stains that translations occur.

These facets of materiality enable cloth to hold the relationality of people and things within their very fibres, and are not dependent on the circumstances of a garment's cut, style or subservience to the vagaries of fashion. Such qualities are also the necessary prerequisites for the creation of exchange value through destruction and the renewal of perceptions of self, identity and sociality at all levels. Clothing is acknowledged to be an essential part of the construction of an image of the self for projection outwards to the social world, and a locus of embodied meaning through the social relations in which its production and consumption are implicated. However, in my work I argue that the shedding of unwanted garments permits a renewal of self and personhood whilst creating a new resource for exchange. At the level of the person, this destruction results in the shattering of the image of self held within those fibres, a form of iconoclasm at odds with iconic notions of identity described in many studies of clothing and ascribed to certain fashions, cuts and styles. The manipulation of the market through the transformation of such fibres results in constantly shifting sets of relationships between entrepreneurs, who rely on invisibility and secrecy to produce a valued new product from the heaps of unwanted stuff that they surreptitiously collect. And as the value with which they are able to reinscribe cloth increases, so does their own social worth.

Similarly, at the level of the nation state, such interconnected transformations stand in contrast to stereotypical images of either India's cheap export garments or highly prized hand-woven silk saris, or of the black market, perceived to be overflowing with second-hand goods imported from the developed world. Despite the models of nationhood and international relationships constructed through formal trade deals such as the Basle Convention, which operate around the concept of political entities and geographical boundaries, the investigation into the materiality of the used clothing trade reveals a complex pattern of ravelling and unravelling relationships, an intricate network of social relations formed, broken and patched up alongside the cloth in which they deal, ever ready to respond to challenges in the market to create new hybrid products whose origins remain deeply obscured.

Notes

1. In the UK, of personal and household textiles (post-consumer waste), 43% becomes second-hand clothing, 12% wiping cloths, 22% filling materials, 7% for fibre reclamation, 9% are re-used second-hand shoes and 7% is rejected as waste (*Textile Recycling Association* August 1996).
2. A position supported by the International Textile, Garment and Leather Worker's Federation., who campaign on behalf of Bengali workers amongst many others, especially in Africa. See http://www.itglwf.org (accessed 27th February 2004).
3. Information regarding legal requirements, import tax and customs was obtained through an interview with an anti-smuggling official in Customs at the Inland container Depot in Delhi. Additional material, often conflicting in detail, derives from about a dozen interviews with old clothes importers and 'shoddy' manufacturers. Details were correct at time of fieldwork in summer

2000 but have been altered subsequently during the wider processes of Indian economic liberalisation and changes in GATT Regulations.
4. *Textiles & The Environment – Recycling* EIU/Special Report 1991.
5. See http://www.basel.int/pub/basics.html#intro. (accessed 20.02.03). This is the official website of the Secretariat of the Basel Convention, United Nations Environment Programme (UNEP). Although hazardous waste was originally defined as waste 'toxic, poisonous, explosive, corrosive, flammable, ecotoxic and infectious', a later amendment agreed to ban, by 31 December 1997, the export of wastes intended for recovery and recycling (Decision II/12).
6. *Materials Recycling Week*, 10 February 1995.
7. In 1974, Ginsburg was told by a dealer in Deptford that the shoddy trade had previously shifted from Yorkshire to Italy (1980, fn. 67).
8. Prices as of March 2000, in US cents per kilogram after Customs, Insurance and Freight (CIF) at Mumbai docks.
9. Buyers cannot choose colours, and are reliant on what they find in the bales. If certain shades are fashionable in India, such as camel was in 1999, the recyclers cannot provide them in any quantity; their poor clientele have to take what comes. Yet the huge scale of the trade results in a wide array of colours mixed in bales, so bulk buying allows for a degree of control over the design of end products.
10. In Bradford, England it is 16–20, and the highest quality still comes from Italy, at 20 count.
11. During 1999–2000, £1 was equivalent to approximately 65–67 Indian Rupees (Rs).
12. Mukulika Banerjee, pers. comm.
13. It is highly likely that some middle-class informants did in fact buy imported used clothing in secret; the concept that such underhand behaviour existed was firmly established.
14. The edge of a fabric that is woven so that it will not fray or unravel. Selvedges usually display the name of the manufacturer, sometimes the name of the design, the fibre content or the country of origin.

References

Appadurai, Arjun 1996 *Modernity at Large. Cultural Dimensions of Globalization.* Minneapolis, London: University of Minnesota Press.
Bayly, C.A. 1986 'The Origins of *Swadeshi* (Home Industry): Cloth and Indian Society, 1700–1930.' In Arjun Appadurai (ed.) 1986 *The Social Life of Things: Commodities in Cultural Perspective.* Cambridge: Cambridge University Press, pp. 285–321.

Cerny, Charlene and Suzanne Seriff (eds) 1996 *Recycled Re-seen: Folk Art from the Global Scrap Heap*. New York: Harry Abrahams Inc. (Catalogue to exhibition originating at the Museum of International Folk Art, Santa Fe, NM.)

Coote, Jeremy, Morton, Chris and Nicholson, Julia 2000 *Transformations: The Art of Recycling*. Pitt Rivers Museum, University of Oxford.

Fine, B. and Leopold, E. 1993 *The World of Consumption*. London: Routledge.

Ginsburg, M. 1980 'Rags to Riches: The Second-hand Clothes Trade 1700–1978'. *Costume*, 14: 121–35.

Greenfield, V. 1986 *Making Do or Making Art: A Study of American Recycling*. Ann Arbor, Michigan: UMI Research Press.

Gregson, Nicky, Brooks, Kate and Crewe, Louise 2000 'Narratives of Consumption and the Body in the Space of the Charity/Shop'. In Peter Jackson, Michelle Lowe, Daniel Miller & Frank Mort (eds) *Commercial Cultures: economies, practices, spaces*. Oxford: Berg, pp. 101–21.

Hansen, Karen Tranberg 1994 'Dealing with Used Clothing: *Salaula* and the Construction of Identity in Zambia's Third Republic'. *Public Culture* 6: 503–23.

—— 2000 *Salaula: The World of Secondhand Clothing and Zambia*. Chicago, London: University of Chicago Press.

Latour, Bruno 1993 *We Have Never Been Modern*. London: Prentice Hall.

Lemire, Beverly 1991 *Fashion's favourite. The cotton trade and the consumer in Britain, 1660–1800*. Pasold Studies in Textile History, 9. Oxford: Oxford University Press.

Munn, Nancy D. 1986 *The Fame of Gawa. A symbolic study of value transformation in a Massim (Paua New Guinea) Society*. Cambridge: Cambridge University Press.

Norris, Lucy 2004 'Shedding skins: the materiality of divestment in India'. *Journal of Material Culture*, 9(1): 59–71.

—— 2005 'Creative entrepreneurs: the recycling of second-hand Indian clothing'. In A. Palmer and H. Clark (eds) *Old Clothes, New Looks: Second Hand Fashion*. Oxford, New York: Berg.

Seriff, Suzanne 1996 'Folk Art from the Global Scrap Heap: The place of irony in the politics of poverty'. In Cerny & Seriff, pp. 9–29.

Smosarski, G. 1995 *Materials Recycling*. London: Financial Times Management Report, Penison Professional.

Stallybrass, Peter 1993 'Worn Worlds: Clothes, Mourning and the Life of Things'. *The Yale Review*, 81(2): 35–50.

Stewart, Susan 1993 *On Longing. Narratives of the Miniature, the Gigantic, the Souvenir, the Collection*. Durham, NC & London: Duke University Press.

Styles, John 1998 'Dress in history: reflections on a contested terrain'. *Fashion Theory* 2(4): 381–89.

Tarlo, Emma 1996 *Clothing Matters: Dress and Identity in India*. London: C. Hurst & Co.
Taylor, Lou 2002 *The Study of Dress History*. Manchester: Manchester University Press.
Thompson, M. 1979 *Rubbish Theory: The Creation and Destruction of Value*. Oxford: Oxford University Press.
Weiner, A. 1992 *Inalienable Possessions*. Berkeley: University of California Press.
Weiner, Annette B. & Schneider, Jane (eds) 1989 *Cloth and Human Experience*. Smithsonian series in Ethnographic Enquiry. Werner-Grenn Foundation for Anthropological Research.

–6–

From Thrift to Fashion: Materiality and Aesthetics in Dress Practices in Zambia
Karen Tranberg Hansen

Inviting us to focus on materiality as a surface that constitutes social relations and states of being, Daniel Miller (1994, see also introduction to this volume) is taking reigning anthropological paradigms to task for explaining away the material significance of clothing. To this scholarly 'disappearance act' might be added the media 'cover story' that is particularly pertinent to my research topic, the international second-hand clothing trade and Africa. When showcasing second-hand clothing, such media accounts are in fact discussing something else.

The international second-hand clothing trade has a long history, yet its changing cultural and economic nexus has not been the subject of much substantive work either at the point of collection or at the point of consumption. Social science scholarship, including dress studies and anthropology, has barely lent these garments an eye although second-hand clothes have been around in much of Africa since the early colonial period. If at all they have paid passing attention to the flourishing second-hand clothing markets in many African cities, Western observers have seen the dress practices such markets are giving rise to as a faded and worn imitation of the West.

Without access to print-media reporting from the last two decades, I would never have been able to trace the recent shifts in this trade, at its source in the West, and its end-point in Zambia (Hansen 2000). Yet the news story rarely changed. It blames everyone: private individuals in the West who donate clothing to charitable groups, the not-for-profit organizations who resell the major part of their huge donated clothing stock to middlemen, and the commercial textile recyclers, graders, exporters and importers who are earning their living from marketing clothing that initially was donated. And at the receiving end in poor countries like Zambia, ordinary people are blamed for buying imported secondhand clothing instead of supporting domestic textile and garment industries.

In a couple of recent media accounts that focus on Zambia for example, second-hand clothing imports become a window on the neo-liberal market ills that are argued to be 'killing' the local industry (*Washington Post* 2002), or a metaphor for the adverse economic development effects that the World Bank, the International

Monetary Fund and 'America' generally are having on the lives of local people (Bloemen 2001). The single most striking observation about such accounts is their total lack of curiosity about the clothes themselves and how consumers deal with them. In effect, the clothes have become entirely incidental. Aside from their utilitarian value for money, what in fact accounts for the attractions of imported second-hand clothing?

Being dressed well in Zambia is a sign of both well-being and desires. I suggest that a focus on the materialities entailed in dress practice will help to reveal some of the popular appeal of second-hand clothing to urban consumers in Zambia. The chapter briefly describes how the West's discarded clothing becomes fashion in a process that expresses a vibrant aesthetic sensibility in its cultivation of appearances that make people take notice, with admiration or opprobrium as the case may be. Consumers' concern with the quality, construction, care and style potentials of garments places materiality at the center of their clothing savvy, the critical skill that I call 'clothing competence'.

In their engagements with the West's used clothing, consumers in Zambia reconstruct these garments as 'new' or 'fresh' and transform them by notions of taste and selection to fit the embodied dress norms of a local clothing universe. It is by crafting themselves through dress that Zambian wearers of secondhand clothing achieve the look they call 'the latest', that fluid appearance of change and novelty that we tend to associate with fashion. But if the effect of such appearances rarely is precise or explicit but rather fluid and volatile, appearance is itself not arbitrary. Rather it is the product of a set of clearly identifiable, interacting practices the effects of which converge in the moment of display. Behind the commanding appearances of 'the latest' lie a series of practices that entail competence in dealing with garment fabrics, strategy and rehearsal in the ways in which people dress. Materiality is part and parcel of that process.

Dressing, and dressing up, is both an end and a means in Zambia. Crafting oneself through dress provides that space between the performed and the desired that we may term fashion even for the case of second-hand dress. Joanne Finkelstein, whom I am paraphrasing for this constructive insight, acknowledges that our first inclination is to think of fashion as instantaneous and volatile, that is, really fleeting and evanescent. Yet she argues 'the constancy of circulation, whether in ideas or material goods, indicates that the actual function of fashion is to give the appearance of change and novelty without actually precipitating any ruptures of the status quo' (1998: 5–6). Like Finkelstein, Gilles Lipovetsky also sees permanence as one of fashion's most significant features through 'its logic of inconsistency, its great organizational and aesthetic mutations' (1994: 4). While preoccupations with the dressed body are of long standing in Zambia, specifically styled garments come and go. The preoccupation with the dressed body is an aesthetic sensibility that implicates discerning skills from a variety of sources in creating an overall look that results in pride, pleasure and experiences of feeling good.

In the pages that follow, I first provide brief background notes on second-hand clothing markets in Zambia. Then I explore how fashion works out in some specific cases. I begin with examples of young men's dress preferences, turning to adult working women's preoccupation with dress in public settings for a detailed analysis of the crafting process. I argue that the meanings of 'new' or 'fresh' and 'the latest' do not inhere in the garments themselves but are constructed anew in each context. While the crafting of 'the latest' hinges both on the material properties of garments and identifiable 'techniques of the body' (Mauss 1973) that I alluded to above, the process also has an affecting hold that makes heads turn. When this occurs, the problematic reference to the Western origin of these clothes has long vanished.

Secondhand Clothing Markets in Zambia

Zambia is one of the world's least developed countries. This was not always the case, but the economy has been on a downward slide since the mid-1970s. Between 1980 and 1994, Zambia received numerous structural adjustment loans from the World Bank and its sister agency, the International Monetary Fund. Today Zambians are poorer, on a per capita basis, than they were at independence from British colonial rule in 1964 (UNDP 2001). Yet the enormous crossover appeal of secondhand clothing cannot be explained merely in terms of its affordability to poor people but above all by reference to the importance people attribute to dress and appearance. Past and present, people in Zambia have been eager to cut a fine figure. The anthropologists who conducted research on urban life in the late colonial period were struck by African preoccupations with the dressed body (e.g. Mitchell and Epstein 1959; Powdermaker 1962; Wilson 1941-2). Dressing in second-hand clothes was part of this active engagement with clothing when the economy was less depressed than it is today. In the 1940s and 1950s, such clothes were brought across the border from the Belgian Congo into Northern Rhodesia. Since the mid-1980s, secondhand clothing has been imported directly from the United States and Europe into Zambia. Importers truck container loads of second-hand clothes from ports in South Africa, Mozambique and Tanzania to Zambia's capital, Lusaka, where they wholesale bales whose contents in turn are retailed in local markets and distributed across the country.

Since the mid-1980s, imported secondhand clothing in Zambia has been referred to as *salaula*, which in the Bemba language means approximately 'selecting from a pile by rummaging' or for short, 'to pick'. The term describes vividly the process that takes place once a bale of imported second-hand clothing has been opened in the market and consumers select garments to satisfy both their clothing needs and their clothing desires. The shop window of Zambia's second-hand clothing trade, the big public markets, creates an atmosphere much like the West's shopping malls where consumers pursue almost unlimited desires with an abandon not possible in the formal stores, where they are often dealt with offhandedly or are pressured to purchase.

The value consumers in Zambia attribute to *salaula* is created through a process of recommodification that involves several phases. In the United States and Europe the sorting and compressing of second-hand clothing into bales in the clothing recycler's warehouse strip used garments of their prior social life. The decommissioned value of the West's unwanted but still wearable clothing is then reactivated on local terms in transactions between overseas suppliers and local importers. Through subsequent transformations the meanings shift in ways that help redefine used clothing into 'new' garments. These transformations begin in communications between exporters and importers and in onsite visits, continue at the wholesale outlet and in public markets, and they are made visible in how consumers put themselves together with *salaula*. In addition to these processes through which the register of meaning of clothing shifts, there are also physical and material changes involving alteration, mending and recycling.

On first sight, these *salaula* markets meet the non-local observer's eye as a chaotic mass of second-hand clothing hung up on flimsy wood contraptions, displayed on tables or dumped in piles on the ground. That view is deceptive. A variety of informal rules organize vending space and structure sales practices. Both vendors and customers know these practices. A prospective customer looking for a specific garment will go to a particular part of the market. The vendors of men's suits, for example, one of the most expensive items, tend to be located in a part of the outdoor market that is near to major thoroughfares such as a main road passable by automobiles. So are vendors of other high demand garments, such as women's skirts and blouses, and the best-selling item of all, at least in Zambia, baby clothes. There are spatial clusters of vendors selling shoes and, during the winter in the southern hemisphere, cold weather clothing. These spatial demarcations are not static as vendors sometimes change inventory.

The display on most second-hand clothing stands is carefully designed. High quality items are hung on clothes-hangers on makeshift walls. A clothes-line or a wooden stand may display a row of cotton dresses. Everything that meets the eye has been carefully selected with a view both to presentation and sales strategy. Lively discussions and price negotiations accompany sales. The piles on the ground include damaged items and garments that have been around for a while. Such items are sold 'on order', that is, several pieces at a discount, and they are often purchased by rural customers who take them to the villages to resell.

Near the high-end of the secondhand clothing display, and near the major roads of the market section cluster the 'boutiques'. Boutiques in these markets sell specially preselected items, coordinated to form matched outfits that are stylish. They tend to be operated by young vendors who 'pick', in the language of the market. Once other traders open second-hand clothing bales, the pickers descend on them, selecting garments they buy on the spot. Then they make up, for instance, women's two-piece ensembles, men's suits and leisure wear. Most of the boutique operators I met were young men who were very skilled at choosing quality stock with a fine eye for what might sell, a great sense of style and a flair for making stunning combinations. I also met boutique operators who were women. Some of them had tailoring skills and they sewed clothing to order from their own homes.

Consumers in Zambia go to secondhand clothing markets for many reasons. White-collar workers of both sexes in Lusaka's city centre often spend their lunch hour going through the second-hand clothing stalls, sometimes making purchases at whim. Others go to find just that right item to match a particular garment. Some women who tailor in their homes search the *salaula* markets for interesting buttons, belts and trim to accent garments. And some go to purchase garments with the intention to resell. But the vast majority shop from *salaula* for clothing for themselves and their families. They come into the city centre from residential areas like those in which I examined clothing consumption and where roughly two-thirds of all households supplied most of their members' clothing from *salaula*. Only the very tiny high-income group in Zambia has an effective choice in the clothing market. This group purchases clothing everywhere, including from second-hand clothing markets. For them, a visit to *salaula* markets is definitely a social outing.

Clothing Competence

Clothing consumption is hard work. A vital dimension of the demand side is cultural taste and style issues that come together in the creation a 'total look'. Concerns with fabric quality, texture and construction precede that creation, which in turn revolves around the anticipated dress needs of the specific situation. When shopping from secondhand clothing markets, consumers' preoccupation with creating particular appearances is inspired by styles and trends from across the world. *Salaula* fashions bring consumers into a bigger world: the world of awareness, of now.

Consumers draw on these influences in ways that are informed by local norms about bodies and dress. The desired clothing profile for both women and men is neat and tidy. It is a product of immaculate garment care and of wearing clothes in ways that are not considered to be too revealing. Even then, female and male garments are understood differently. The cultural norms about how to dress weigh down on women more heavily than on men, with the result that women feel restrained in their freedom to dress so as not to provoke men (Hansen 2004). Above all, women must cover their 'private parts', which in this region of Africa includes their thighs. This means that dress length, tightness and fabric transparency become issues when women interact with men and elders both at home and in public.

The desire for uniqueness, to stand out, while dressing the body on Zambian terms entails considerable skill in garment selection from the abundance of salaula, making discriminating decisions concerning quality, style and value for money, in garment coordination to fit specific occasions and contexts, and in the overall presentation and comportment of the dressed body to produce a 'total look'. As I demonstrate below, many consumers are extraordinarily savvy when it comes to clothing purchases aimed to produce particular effects. In order to highlight that shopping from salaula does not mean that anything goes, I have called this skill that is critical to the successful work of consumption *clothing competence*. The underlying sensibility in the preoccupation with clothing is a visual aesthetics that on first sight cultivates endless variation yet on closer analysis also is in the service of continuity.

Suit Aesthetics and Provocative Wear

Unlike young women who carefully monitor the way they dress in public, young men like to draw attention to themselves, in different ways to be sure, depending on their socio-economic circumstances and regional location in Zambia's declining economy. They actively seek to present a smart appearance that is both fashionable and neat. Young men's self-conscious preoccupation with suits and jeans illustrates different constructions of these attributes of dress.

Suits are worn widely across the civil service ranks and other white-collar jobs in Zambia. Formal suits index young urban men's desire to become adult, hold jobs and head households. Cutting a fine figure in a smart suit conveys something important about personal background, respectability and responsibility. In these views, suits are identified with patriarchal social power that is widespread throughout Zambia. Most of the young men in their late teens or early twenties in a secondary school in Lusaka who in 1995 described for me where they bought their clothes and how they liked to dress aspired to this dress practice and the ideal it conveys. 'Suits are the clothes I like most', explained Simon, 'because they make me look decent and soon I will be joining the society of workers.' Morgan, his classmate, described a pair of trousers and a jacket he recently had received: 'I was full of joy ... I like these clothes because a lot of people say that I look like a general manager and not only that, they also say that I look like a rich man.' And Moses' delight in a double-breasted jacket his father had given him is evident: 'I like jackets because they suit me like a second skin.'

Other classmates liked jeans, particularly because they are durable but also because 'they are in style now'. But wearing jeans had a flip side that too readily called forth the image of scruffy youths and street vendors, who in the popular view readily are associated with illegal activities. According to Moses, 'I hate wearing jeans because people may fail to distinguish between cigarette sellers and myself.' Lusaka's downtown streets are full of young male traders in all kinds of goods. They put much effort into being seen, and many of them dress in a striking manner.

If suits and jeans frame young urban men's desires for a better life, young men in rural areas have similar desires but are more circumscribed by the conditions in which they live. Secondary school students in Mansa, a provincial town in Luapula Province, explained this clearly. Joshua explained: 'Of all the clothes, I like strong ones which can serve me longer such as jeans. I like them because it is not easy for me to buy soap, and most of the time I do manual work in order to earn my living.' The suit figures in the desires of these young rural men mostly by its absence. Describing why the suit combination did not fit his situation, Nicholas explained: 'Such clothes can easily be torn and I think they are for office working people, so they don't suit me.' Yet he added as an afterthought, 'If I had a choice, I would really like to wear suits.'

Jeans are a must in the evolving street-vendor style. In addition to the style explanations I describe below, the preference of street vendors for denim has an obvious practical reason. Jeans, one of them explained, 'are durable; they are nice and easy to keep especially for bachelors like me who have no one to look after our clothes'. What the young vendors my assistant interviewed in 1997 did for their own pleasure was to dress up in public in variations on the baggy-jeans look. The layered look was in vogue that year as was knitted headwear and shoes with thick rubber soles, often worn without socks.

The secondary school students and the young street vendors purchased their clothes from a variety of sources. Some bought imported clothing from 'suitcase' traders who bring in garments from abroad, some went to the tailor for specific wear, and all of them scoured the *salaula* market for just the right items. As one of the street vendors explained, 'In *salaula* you will find things you can't believe how good they are.' When shopping for clothes, the young vendors looked for garments that will contribute to the overall creation of a particular style, in this case 'the big look', rather than for brand-name items. 'I wear the big look because it is fashion,' one of them said while another explained how he liked to 'move with time'. 'I don't like common clothes and imitations,' said yet another.

Making associations between specific articles of clothing and behaviour, young people construct an understanding of their world and how they inhabit it. Young male secondary students with high economic aspirations for themselves do not want to be mistaken for the school drop-outs turned street vendors. They desire suits. The vendors for their part wear clothes they equate with the power and success achieved by popular performers both in Africa and beyond. Putting themselves together with clothing the major part of which is from *salaula*, both groups of young people are dressing to explore who they are and whom they would like to become.

Strategy and Rehearsal

Clothing competence is a result of a variety of strategies consumers pursue in their work to achieve a particular look. Both material and aesthetic, these strategies include rehearsals that seek to anticipate the effects the dressed body may elicit in context.

To flesh this out I describe some examples of adult women's dress practice. Distinctions by spatial and temporal context are helpful here such as whether a woman is at home or at work, for example in an office setting, whether she is moving in public and for which purpose, for example shopping in an open air market in the city centre or a residential area, visiting a supermarket, or travelling by public transportation. There are special occasions as well that call for particular attire, among them, church attendance, funerals, kitchen parties and weddings.

Let us consider Mrs Miyanda, the schoolteacher I introduced in my book for a discussion of the hard work of consumption that is invested in a trip to one of Lusaka's largest *salaula* markets to shop for clothes for her children, a shirt for her husband and 'the latest' for herself (Hansen 2000: 194–6). She spent considerable time in the market, carefully scrutinizing quality both of fabric and tailoring, and style, wanting something that was both 'different' and 'unique'. The pink top she bought for herself, she immediately took to a tailor for alteration and embellishment with 'gold' buttons to look more like the tops in the style of the 'office wear' that then was popular among women working away from home.

While Mrs Miyanda's dress practice when working around the house is plain, involving almost any worn dress or skirt and blouse combination with a *chitenge* (colourful printed cloth) wrapper on top, her dress for other occasions is carefully assembled, and with a calculus to produce a particular effect; that 'total look' that makes people take note. Behind this dress practice is a daily rehearsal involving careful evaluation with her choice of clothing depending on how she wants to be seen, where, when and by whom.

The daily rehearsal of clothing combinations entails considerable attention to the physical care for clothes. The preferred clothing profile in Zambia is spick and span, requiring immaculate ensembles that have been carefully laundered and ironed. Because washing machines are beyond the purchasing power of teachers like Mrs Miyanda, all garments are washed by hand in cold water with strong detergents. Young girls, and boys, are taught from an early age to hand launder their own garments. As a result of clothes drying in sunlight and subsequent ironing, often with a charcoal-heated iron, vibrant colours quickly mute and fabrics weaken. Clothes are always ironed in order to prevent insect larvae hidden in seams from entering the body. Physical practices such as these contribute to the rapid turnover in the life of clothes.

Mrs Miyanda's desire for uniqueness produces considerable variation in how she dresses for work. Like most other women whose dress practice I observed closely Mrs Miyanda never wears 'the same' dress to work, at least according to her own account. She arranges and rearranges her garments. One ensemble is succeeded by another and so on, leaving the impression of infinite novelty and indeed of ephemerality as one outfit leaves space for another. But this process is a strategic gesture, a sleight of hand that showcases rapid turnover while indeed conservation/continuity prevails. In fact, Mrs Miyanda rotates her garments and makes new combinations of dresses and skirts. Her rotation might occasionally include garments of a cut and style that in the West might be considered to be evening dress. She also wears *chitenge* outfits to work, something that I rarely saw in the 1980s. And as an active member of the Seventh Day Adventist Church, she wears a church uniform for service on Saturdays, a blue dress with white trim, and a white headscarf.

The inclusion of Mrs Miyanda's evening dress and her *chitenge* outfits among the garments she wears to work testifies to the many lives that clothes go through in their involvement with their owner's changing circumstances. Going out of fashion hinges not primarily on the materiality of an outfit but rather on the eclipse of the moment of display. Once the demonstrative moment for display has passed, most garments continue their utilitarian lives. When she tires of garments as dress for school, Mrs Miyanda decommissions them from public settings to work around the house where they might be worn until they have exhausted their wear.

Demonstrative Display

The attraction of *salaula* to clothing-conscious Zambian consumers goes far beyond the price factor. Consumers want clothing that is not common. 'Clothes from *salaula* are not what other people wear,' one woman said to me when explaining why clothes from *salaula* are viewed as 'exclusive'. The clothing sensibility such statements convey hinges on social constructions of gendered and sexed bodies, comportment, personal grooming and presentation. It manifests itself in a visual aesthetic that is created in context. In short, this meaning/value/ sensibility does not inhere in the garments themselves but is attributed to them in social interaction.

My concerns with appearance and context are at the core of Joanne Entwistle's notion of dress as situated, embodied practice that people use 'to orientate themselves to the social order' (2000: 39). Influenced by Bourdieu's notion of habitus, she highlights how space helps to construe the meaning of dress at the same time as formally or informally enforced norms of dress may constitute the meaning of a particular place. Below, I bring these insights to bear on a specific event in which women's dressed bodies are at the centre of attention. It does not matter for my argument that the dress on which I focus was not second-hand, for of course new and second-hand clothes implicate each other in these processes.

When my friend Audrey attended her sister-in-law's kitchen party in one of Lusaka's high-income residential areas in August 2002, she wore a two-piece 'Indian' inspired outfit in blue-toned colors. Kitchen-parties are all-female events where relatives and friends, including expatriates, come together with presents to help the bride-to-be with utensils for her new home. They are modelled on a loose version, a fusion, of initiation ceremonies and bridal showers. There are drums, dance, food and drink, and above all, bodies dressed to be viewed.

Kitchen parties such as this one are veritable fashion runways on which elaborately styled *chitenge* outfits receive the most detailed valuation. When attending this event, Audrey had worn her blue-tone two-piece outfit before. It was quite clear that some guests at the party took note of her low-key dress presentation. Audrey was in the process of divorcing her husband for whose younger sister the kitchen party was held; she didn't even want to be there. Unlike Audrey, the bride-to-be's mother and a few other women guests experienced the thrill that arises from demonstrative display of clothes and accessories that they have never previously put together in this particular manner. These women proudly displayed the latest *chitenge* styles. Theirs was the sensation of the dressed body beautiful in that one glorious instant that will never be experienced in that way again. For that single moment we love, or as Audrey, hate what we wear.

As a place of activity, an interactive space, the kitchen party operates by a set of norms that guide acceptable dress and body presentation. The aesthetics of kitchen party dress, not only *chitenge*, is evaluated in a process that mobilizes lively discussions of both 'the latest' and 'proper' styles. One young woman who turned up at a kitchen party in 1995 in a *chitenge* outfit consisting of a short-sleeved *chitenge* top and loose bermuda shorts got so much flak from the mature women that she wore a *chitenge* cloth as a wrapper for the rest of the party. One of the worst commentaries I have heard was directed toward a heavy-set woman in her thirties who turned up at a 'Christian' kitchen party in 1997 in black tights and a T-shirt hugging her waist. Short and tight garments, displaying 'private parts' and 'body structures' for all to see are definitely not *comme il faut* at such events. The group of women who constitute the specialists and are 'in the know' of clothing competence take note, just as they did censoriously of Audrey's previously worn outfit at her sister-in-law's kitchen party.

Conclusion

Monitoring the way they dress in public, clothing-conscious Zambians pay considerable attention to the material possibilities of their garments, seeking to anticipate their desired effects. Young men eager to become adults desire suits because they convey notions of authority and independence that their everyday life in school and at home denies them. Young male street vendors dress in oversize jeans not only because they are durable and easy to care for but also because such garments are a part of a worldwide dress style turned fashionable by international performers. Mature women for their part continuously rework their wardrobes in daily efforts to dress differently. This process hinges on detailed physical care of garments and on crafting, that scrutiny of fabric, construction and colour that creates the appearance of a 'total look' that differs from outfits worn before. The success or failure of the production is difficult to anticipate. This is because there is an experiential dimension to dress that only emerges in the response of viewers of the event created by the wearing of this particular combination of clothes. What is more, the clothes also 'respond' in the sense that they fit well and feel right. This inter-activity is part of what makes dress an embodied experience (Entwistle 2000). Moses experienced his new jacket as a second skin enveloping his body to perfection. How the meaning and value of clothes in everyday dress, fashion, new and secondhand, are experienced has to do with context. This is because there is an experimental dimension to dress, both in wearing and viewing (Ash 1996), and this is why Audrey's previously worn two-piece outfit did not feel right and did not command admiring gazes from guests at the kitchen party.

The meaning and value of Zambian preoccupations with clothing does not inhere in garments themselves and does therefore not have much to do with whether clothes are second-hand or new. Experiences of dress, the evaluations viewers make of it, are not given or fixed but created anew in each context. Clothes are not worn passively but require people's active collaboration. Audrey can place her tired outfit in a different regime of value by shifting the context of its status, for example, from party dress to work wear to housedress. In their daily rehearsal for dressing and dressing up, women in Zambia try to anticipate the situations and contexts in which they will be finding themselves. Seeking to negotiate the specific moment of such situations, they may experience the thrill of enjoyment, or disapproval. In this affectual experience of dress, the distinction between used clothing and fashion that I referred to at the outset becomes irrelevant as do the problematic differentiation between Western and non-Western dress. The attraction of second-hand clothing to consumers in Zambia about which I inquired at the outset is now evident. Masked in Western media accounts of global inequities, imported second-hand clothes are not incidental accessories but active participants in transforming the lives of their new wearers.

Acknowledgements

This paper is based on research into second-hand clothing undertaken during the 1990s (Hansen 2000), and it also contains observations from research in progress I have been conducting in Zambia since 2001 on youth and urban social reproduction. An earlier version was presented at the conference, 'Making an Appearance: Fashion, Dress and Consumption', at the University of Queensland, Brisbane, Australia, 10–13 July 2003. The fashion performance argument has been previewed briefly elsewhere (Hansen 2003).

References

Ash, Juliet 1996 'Memory and Object'. In Pat Kirkham (ed.) *The Gendered Object*. Manchester: Manchester University Press, pp. 219–24.

Bloemen, Shanta 2001 *T-Shirt Travels: A Documentary on Secondhand Clothes And Third World Debt in Zambia*. New York: Grassroots Pictures. Video.

Entwistle, Joanne 2000 *The Fashioned Body: Fashion, Dress and Modern Social Theory*. Cambridge: Polity Press.

Finkelstein, Joanne 1998 *Fashion: An Introduction*. New York: New York University Press.

Hansen, Karen Tranberg 2000 *Salaula: The World of Secondhand Clothing and Zambia*. Chicago: University of Chicago Press.

—— 2003 'Fashioning: Zambian Moments'. *Journal of Material Culture*, 8(3): 301–9.

—— 2004 'Dressing Dangerously: Miniskirts, Gender Relations, and Sexuality in Zambia'. In Jean Allman (ed.) *Fashioning Power: Clothing, Politics, and African Identities*. Bloomington: Indiana University Press, pp. 166–85.

Lipovetsky, Gilles 1994 *The Empire of Fashion: Dressing Modern Democracy*. Princeton: Princeton University Press.

Mauss, Marcel 1973 'Techniques of the Body'. *Economy and Society*, 2(1): 70–89.

Miller, Daniel 1994 'Style and Ontology'. In Jonathan Friedman (ed.) *Consumption and Identity*. Chur: Harwood, pp. 71–96.

Mitchell, J. Clyde and Epstein, Arnold L. 1959 'Occupational Prestige and Social Status among Urban Africans in Northern Rhodesia'. *Africa*, 29: 22–39.

Powdermaker, Hortense 1962 *Copper Town; Changing Africa. The Human Condition on the Rhodesian Copperbelt*. New York: Harper and Row.

UNDP (United Nations Development Programme) 2001 *Zambia Human Development Report 1999/2000. Employment and Sustainable Livelihoods*. Ndola: Mission Press.

Washington Post 2002 'The Dumping Ground' (by Jon Jeter), April 22.
Wilson, Godfrey 1941–2 *An Essay on the Economics of Detribalization*, Vols. 1 and 2. Rhodes-Livingstone Papers, nos. 5 and 6.

–7–

Nga Aho Tipuna (Ancestral Threads): Maori Cloaks from New Zealand
Amiria Henare

Cloaks hand-woven from the fibres of *harakeke* (New Zealand flax or *Phormium tenax*) (Fig. 7.1) have been made and worn by Maori since after their ancestors arrived in New Zealand from Eastern Polynesia between AD 900 and 1200. Early ethnographic evidence describes the central role of these garments in social life, marking status, creating ritual spaces and protecting the wearer from the elements, from weapon blows, and against potent vital forces. Cloaks continue to play key roles in present-day Maori life, being worn at weddings, graduations and other ceremonies and draped over coffins at funerals, smoothing the passage between life stages. This chapter considers how cloaks or *kahu* are able to perform these roles, providing *aho* or threads that join layers of generational time, acting as tangible

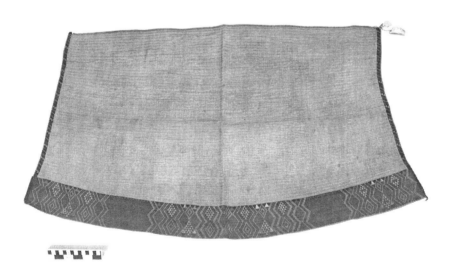

Figure 7.1 Finely woven *aronui* or *kaitaka* cloak, made in the nineteenth century, possibly for a child. 625 × 1107mm. University of Cambridge Museum of Archaeology and Anthropology. CUMAA Z6355.

and substantive links between ancestors or *tipuna* and their living descendants. Theoretically, understanding the enduring importance of such *taonga* or treasured artefacts involves revisiting debates on the 'invention' of tradition as well as more recent analyses that foreground the role of creativity in producing social relations. In light of current negotiations about the nature and control of cultural property in New Zealand, it also means taking seriously the idea that cloaks and the practice of weaving allow for ancestral presence; a way of conceiving of persons that seems either mystical or 'imagined' only when viewed in light of an ontological apartheid between persons and things.

In his article 'Owning Creativity' (2003a), James Leach draws a contrast between two ways of valuing culture and tradition. On the one hand is the tendency to objectify culture as 'heritage' or 'cultural property', typified in policy directives and discussions emanating from organizations like UNESCO. These discourses treat aspects of culture as 'thing-like', Leach notes, and value 'objects, identity, heritage, and customs in a package which make cultural groups look like individuals to whom certain rights are attached' (2003a: 124). On the other hand he identifies the valuation of culture as *kastom* among the Reite, a Nekgini-speaking people in Papua New Guinea. Unusually among those who have written about Melanesian *kastom* in recent years (e.g. Keesing and Tonkinson 1982; Thomas and Jolly 1992; Harrison 2000), Leach emphasizes less what *kastom* might have in common with notions of cultural property than its difference from this particular mode of objectification.[1] He defines *kastom* as a notion 'that appeal[s] to the inherent and ongoing creativity of human engagement with the world', and as fundamentally distinct from conceptions that value culture 'as tradition and heritage, embodied by objects or sites' (2003a: 125). *Kastom*, he argues, is 'the power to make relationships through imposing form and eliciting response', as opposed to 'the kinds of effectiveness that are envisaged to be a part of controlling cultural property' (2003a: 132).

In elaborating this distinction, Leach extends his argument to debates about the ownership and control of *taonga* or treasured artefacts, among Maori in New Zealand. Citing the work of Paul Tapsell, on the return of an ancestral cloak to his kin group from a museum, Leach suggests that claims made by Maori for the return of such items are inspired less by a desire to 'own' the thing in a legalistic sense, than by the need to regain power over its relational potential. What counts for Maori, Leach implies, is not the 'possession' of the object *qua* object, but its ability to generate relationships through ongoing cycles of circulation and return. As he puts it elsewhere, citing Wagner (1975) 'it is not in fact the objects that are the goal' (2003a: 131).

Cut to New Zealand, where a claim that asserts *tino rangatiratanga* (exclusive and comprehensive rights[2]) over Maori knowledge, natural resources and cultural objects as *taonga* and as forms of intellectual and cultural property is currently before the Waitangi Tribunal (a quasi-judicial body assessing claims for the restitution of resources expropriated through colonization). This wide-reaching claim, known colloquially as 'Wai 262', specifically concerns native flora and fauna and indigenous knowledge relating thereto, moveable cultural heritage objects, physical cultural objects in general and traditional knowledge pertaining to cultural, medicinal, artistic, spiritual and technological spheres. The basis of the claim, made by members of six *iwi* or tribes on behalf of all Maori, is that all of these things are *taonga*, treasured ancestral possessions, rights over which are protected in the Treaty of Waitangi (through which New Zealand was established as a British colony, and the basis for the Tribunal's jurisdiction). Lodged in 1991, Wai 262 has attracted much recent attention as a significant factor delaying the reform of laws governing the ownership and transactability of intellectual property in New Zealand.

Here we have a case in which Maori people have identified aspects of their culture – including knowledge – as *taonga*, precious things at risk of alienation. Given this emphasis, it is perhaps tempting to look at the claim and conclude that Maori have objectified their culture and adopted UNESCO-speak simply because of their post-colonial situation. They cannot but use the language of property law to protect their culture, it might be argued, because it is the only one the dominant Euro-western culture understands. Worse, it might be surmised that through a long period of intermarriage and colonial occupation, Maori minds have been colonized such that they now see the world through European eyes, their unique vantage point having been lost along with much of the rest of their patrimony. Yet to take this view, I would argue, is to buy into precisely the kinds of assumptions Leach cautions us to avoid. To proffer such explanations would be to perceive an inherent lack or incompleteness on the part of contemporary Maori, a tragic inauthenticity that can only be remedied by a return to an age of cultural purity, before the arrival of Europeans.

Leach, as I have said, diagnoses the problem in terms of a contrast between incommensurable assumptions about the nature of social life – an ontological disparity, if you will. Indeed, one might mistake his distinction, between the valuation of culture in object form and that grounded in its relational efficacy, as a contrast between objectification and process.[3] In shifting focus from resemblances between *kastom* and cultural property, to the ways in which they diverge, he places perhaps too much emphasis on the objectifying tendencies of UNESCO-speak, and not enough on those evident in *kastom*. Such an emphasis seems to throw Maori deployment of the language of cultural property into relief as the displacement of one set of assumptions by another (objectification in place of process), or its strategic mobilization for political ends. Yet what he is talking about, in fact, is different modes of objectification. Whereas *kastom* values creativity, he notes, cultural property privileges continuity and integrity, and they thus operate according to different registers of significance and effect. Both, however, produce objects, in the form of persons and artefacts (or rather person–artefacts), among other things. His point is that these things only look like 'objects' to those who regard their relation with 'subjects' in oppositional terms (that is people other than Reite, to whom they appear as subjects in their own right). Like Maori *taonga*, which may be ancestors, therefore, Reite *kastom* is not just an abstract notion, but rather consists in and through efficacious person–things. Moreover this *kastom*, like *taonga*, arises from a creativity that is explicitly *continuous*, though unlike in the Maori case, its continuity is not particularly conceived as operating across generational time.

What I want to propose here then, building on Leach's insights, is that Maori assertions of a continuous cultural tradition are not incompatible with the valuation of creativity, unless understood in terms of a contrast between social relations as process and their ability to take on object form. In the case of *taonga*, at least, there appears no necessary distinction between the value placed on the relational potential of these 'objects' (both material and conceptual) and their ability to instantiate ancestral power, in fact these aspects appear to create the conditions for each others' existence – you can't have social relations without *taonga*, nor *taonga* without social relations, which is precisely why rights over them are so jealously guarded (it is perfectly true that Maori value highly 'the power to make relationships'). This is not to say that distinguishing between *taonga* as process and as objects might not be useful, merely that the distinction does not always appear significant in Maori (or Nekgini, one might say). The principle analytic virtue of such a contrast is perhaps to highlight the capacity of *taonga*, like people, to *instantiate* relations within the general flux of creativity – to concentrate them and bring them into focus in particular ways. Where the power to make relationships is contested, furthermore, there may be similarly good reasons to emphasize the object-status of *taonga* over their relational potential.

Here I want to examine some of these issues with reference to *whatu* or Maori weaving, which is among the *taonga* that Wai 262 seeks to protect. Beginning with an introduction to the historical circumstances in which this practice arose and my own (rather limited) experience of doing it, I look at how weaving and the cloaks thus produced (also identified as *taonga*) perform important roles in ensuring continuities in Maori social life – of what it is to be Maori – that are in no way incompatible with cultural creativity. Whereas recent studies of Maori artistic practice, like those of Melanesian *kastom*, have emphasized how art forms have adapted and changed in response to shifting socio-political contexts (e.g. Neich 2001; Sissons 1998; Thomas 1999), this paper emphasizes what has remained continuous, taking seriously the assertion that weaving, along with other practices and forms, is a *taonga tuku iho*, a treasure handed down (from ancestors) (Hakiwai 1996: 53–4). Rather than accepting the view that historical contingencies have effected an irrevocable disjuncture within Maoridom – a shift from 'unselfconscious' to 'politicized' modes of reproduction, or, in other words, from culture that is simply 'lived' to that which is 'invented' or 'creatively imagined' – I will argue instead that Maori weaving quite literally provides continuous threads or pathways between layers of generational time that constitute tangible and substantive links between ancestors and their living descendants.

But first, a brief disclaimer. In pursuing this line of argument I do not mean to promote what Alfred Gell has called a species of 'material culture mysticism' (1998: 21), nor do I wish to partake in the kind of anthropocentric neo-animism that, as Peter Pels (1998) has argued, characterizes Appadurai's seminal *Social Life of Things* (1986) and variations thereon. Instead of emphasizing the primordial mystique of ancestral potency, or its socially constructed aspects, in other words, I hope rather to deploy an expanded (Maori) concept of personhood to show how cloaks and weaving techniques allow for ancestral presence; a presence that seems either mystical or 'imagined' only in light of a fundamental separation between persons and things. The twist to this tale is that Maori (like many other people) often treat objects according to these dichotomies, that is, as basically 'inanimate'. At the same time, however, it is still often asserted that certain *taonga* are ancestors, that they bear the *mana* (personal standing) and *wairua* (spirit) of people who died many years before. Anthropologists have tended to 'make sense of' such statements in three ways: some acknowledge their own belief in ancestral potency, but struggle to write about it without succumbing to romanticism (e.g. O'Biso 1987 on the *Te Maori* exhibition); others effect a kind of suspension of belief or disbelief akin to Gell's 'methodological philistinism' (1992), simply recording what their informants say as something that does not require further analysis beyond the fact that it performs certain social functions. Still others have effectively (albeit unintentionally) undermined such claims by labelling them politically motivated, symptoms of (laudable) Maori resistance to their incorporation by modernity and global capitalism. I am unsatisfied with all three accounts. The first two tend to elide the fact that most Maori today live in cities, go to school, watch TV, listen to urban music and are generally part of what is glossed as 'modern society'. In so doing, these anthropological interpretations slide easily toward the nostalgic, the romantic, and the old salvage ethnography paradigm of writing it down 'before it's too late'.

The third anthropological response, which reduces claims of ancestral presence to politicized 'inventions', is exemplified by Allan Hanson, whose influential article 'The Making of the Maori: Culture Invention and Its Logic' was published in *American Anthropologist* in 1989. Hanson argued that contemporary Maori beliefs about the antiquity of particular cultural traditions are a function of anthropological romanticism allied to post-colonial indigenous political mobilization. This alliance of interests, he said, masked the fact that many so-called

Maori 'traditions' were actually 'invented' by anthropologists in the nineteenth and twentieth centuries. Hanson thus drew a contrast between culture as creativity on one hand and its objectification as 'tradition' on the other, a tendency he implied was not indigenous but rather adopted by Maori in the course of their engagements with Europeans. His article, syndicated in the *New York Times* (Wilford 1990) with favourable commentary from George Marcus, Clifford Geertz, Stanley Tambiah and Richard Handler, was attacked in New Zealand as yet another instrument of cultural imperialism and condemned as the uninformed musings of a visiting scholar. Hanson has continued to express surprise that his work should have been interpreted as an attack on Maori (e.g. 1991, 1997), yet, while I do not completely agree with his detractors, I find his response naive. The unacknowledged basis of his argument is that, (despite what they might think) Maori claims to the continuity of various traditions are not literally true – they are 'symbolic constructions' made for political ends – and he thus calls their authenticity into question. In assuming that ancestral presence (objectified as 'tradition', among other things) can only be 'invented' or 'creatively imagined' (as all culture is creatively produced), the task of the anthropologist is thus to account for why such claims are made by placing them into context (which in Hanson's analysis is reduced to post-colonial political activism). The task, in other words, is to highlight the difference between process (the cultural creativity that produced the claims) and content (the claimant's misguided faith in constructed objectifications). This clearly foregrounds rather than avoids the issue of authenticity, as it proffers a definitive answer to the question of belief – that the claims concerned do not correlate with historical evidence, and therefore cannot possibly be 'true'. As I think Gell had realized by the time he write his last book *Art and Agency* (1998), adopting this stance does not in fact bypass the question, but rather makes it impossible to take informants seriously. Needless to say, perhaps, I am attempting something rather different.

Whatu as a *taonga tuku iho*

According to Maori anthropologist Te Rangihiroa (Peter Buck), the production of textiles through *whatu* or finger weaving developed from basketry techniques brought to New Zealand from Eastern Polynesia by the ancestors of Maori people, whose arrival is generally placed between the tenth and thirteenth centuries AD (1926: xviii). Although it is called 'weaving', the technique actually involves a kind of twining (Fig. 7.2), in which single or double pairs of wefts are wrapped around each warp thread individually by hand (so-called 'true weaving' being that carried out on a loom). I was taught the techniques of *whatu* in 1996 by Hinemoa Harrison and Eddie Maxwell, leading practitioners of the art, and by Maureen Lander, an artist and lecturer in Maori art and material culture at the University of

Nga Aho Tipuna: *Maori cloaks from New Zealand*

Figure 7.2 *Whatu* or Maori finger-weaving. Photograph by Amiria Henare

Auckland. First we learned how to cut flax leaves from the plant so as to ensure its survival, then to split them into workable sections before slitting the 'skin' of the leaf and stripping out the fibre using the edge of a mussel shell. Once we had extracted the silky white fibre or *muka*, we were shown how to divide it into hanks to be *miro*'d on the thigh, thus producing a length of thread suitable for weaving. When we had made a sufficient number of threads, we were taught how to set up the *whenu* or warp threads in preparation to begin weaving. In *whatu*, each line of wefts is called an *aho*, a word which evokes the *aho tipuna*, the ancestral lineage linking the *papa* or generational layers in *whakapapa* (genealogies). To *kanoi* is to weave the main thread of a garment, and it is also to trace one's ancestry (Salmond 1997: 207). These and other linguistic parities suggest a homology between *whatu* and relations of descent, indicating that familiarity with the technique might offer 'conceptual purchase', as Küchler puts it (2002), when it comes to understanding Maori kinship and its terminology. Annette Weiner picked up on a similar theme in her book *Inalienable Possessions*, noting that 'the complex symbolism associated with ... cloaks refers specifically to women and human and cultural reproduction' (1992: 50). She goes on to detail how woven cloaks were instrumental in many of the rituals surrounding birth and death in early Maori society, using examples derived from the historical ethnographic literature, and it is to some of this material that I now turn.

Accounts of Maori life in New Zealand gathered by ethnographer Elsdon Best in the late nineteenth and early twentieth centuries indicate that the existence of a shared vocabulary to describe genealogical relations and techniques of cloth production is more than just coincidence. By the time Best conducted his researches among the Tuhoe tribe and neighbouring Maori kin groups, Europeans had been in the country for more than a hundred years, and many of the activities and traditions he recorded were falling out of use. Despite this Best was able to gather a wealth of information about old and still-current practices, aided by his informants who were often literate and educated in both English and Maori schools of learning. These men (and they were mostly men) provided Best with detailed accounts of Maori concepts, rituals and techniques, often in the form of letters written in Maori in answer to his innumerable and specific inquiries.

Among the ethnographer's wide-ranging interests were the rituals surrounding childbirth and death, through which the dangerous passages between states of being were navigated with the help of *tohunga* or priestly experts. Woven textiles often played key roles in these procedures, and some of Best's descriptions of rituals surrounding childbirth are of particular interest here. Drawing on at least two accounts, one from Te Whatahoro of Wairarapa (Best 1914) and another from an anonymous member of the same kin-group, the Ngati Kahungunu tribe (Best 1929), Best describes activities centred on the *whare kohanga* or 'nest-house', a shelter built especially for the delivery of children. When a woman of aristocratic lineage was in the early stages of labour, he notes, she would repair to this hut and remain there until the child's umbilical cord dropped off, whereupon the *tohi* ritual of baptism was conducted (detailed below). Some tribes referred to this hut as the *whare kohanga*, Best notes (1906: 16; 1924: 6), while others constructed a separate and additional shelter called a *whare kahu* for delivery, reserving the *whare kohanga* for post-partum recovery of mother and child. The *whare kahu* is of interest here, as its literal translation is 'foetus house', *kahu* referring to the amniotic sac surrounding the foetus. *Kahu* is also a generic name for garments, and is today (as it was then) applied particularly to woven cloaks.

In addition to the conceptual consonance between the languages of weaving and kinship, Best's writings offer a wealth of detail on the ubiquity of woven cloaks in rituals and activities pertaining to birth. Maori women, he notes, delivered on their knees, often with an old garment laid out between their legs to receive the child (1906: 18). Following parturition, the child might be presented to its relatives on the porch of the *whare kohanga* (according to some accounts), where it was laid on a cloak in its mother's lap (1914: 141) and honoured with gifts of *taonga* including further woven garments as well as greenstone or whalebone weapons. In other versions, the mother and child remained secluded with their attendants until the *tohi* or baptism ceremony, seeing only their closest family. The *tohi* was performed away from the *whare kohanga* in a sacred place near water, with varying degrees of elaboration according to the seniority of the child's *aho tipuna* or line of descent. *Tohunga* or priestly experts always officiated, however, and cloaks played a central role in the proceedings. After a suitable site was selected, the *paparoa* or place of honour for a high-born child and its parents was set up as follows, according to Best's Kahungunu informant:

> The assistant expert grasped [a fine woven] mat and spread it out so that the plaited border was at the margin of the water, or the banks of the stream. When the assistant had spread the mat he took certain native garments and spread them over the mat, so that the twisted hems on the collars were at the margin of the water. (1929: 248)

A complex ritual then ensued whereby the parents stepped onto the *paparoa* of cloaks, holding the child, and flanked by members of their immediate family including the child's maternal and paternal grandparents. The priest then took the child and immersed it up to its neck in water, chanting *karakia* or incantations to make the child grow fit and well, sometimes dedicating it to the arts of carving or warfare (if a boy), or in the case of a girl, to Hine-te-iwaiwa, the 'personification' as Best puts it, of both weaving and childbirth (1906: 19, 158; 1924: 7). The child was then returned to its parents who stepped off the *paparoa*, which was folded aside so that a hole could be dug in which the child's *pito* or umbilical cord was buried, thus substantiating its attachment to the land. The cloaks were then placed on the shoulders of the father, who wrapped them around the child in his arms in preparation for the *pure* ritual which took place back at the village. Here the garments were laid out in similar style but on the porch of the principal house of the settlement. The father stepped onto them once more, presenting the child to its extended kin group who would keen over it in an act of welcome. The child was then given further *taonga* as gifts, including woven garments, and was laid upon the cloaks on the porch while the parents joined in a ritual *hakari* or feast.

From the moment it came into the world, then, a high-born child was surrounded by woven textiles or *kahu*, which smoothed its passage in a number of ways from one phase of life into the next, acting as an *aho* or direct line between the realm of the ancestors and that of mortals. Cloaks were sometimes laid out to encompass and define sacred space, and at other times enveloped the child like the foetal membrane or *kahu* within which he had until recently dwelt. As Weiner notes (1992: 57) citing Best and others, such associations also arose at the other end of the life cycle, at the time of death. Here again the body was laid out upon cloaks or enshrouded in them and placed on the porch of the principal house of the village so that relatives could weep over it and present it with gifts (Best 1924: 54–5). In both cases, therefore, cloaks provided a pathway between the *papa* or layers of generational time.

The importance of cloaks in this connexion was reflected in strict ritual regulations governing the practice of weaving. In an article on the lore of the *whare pora* or craft of weaving, Best describes the procedure for initiation into this art. 'Prior to the commencement of the weaving', he wrote:

> the learner, sitting before the [weaving] frame or pegs, took a hank of dressed fibre in her hand and sat inactive as the expert recited a charm the object of which was to force the knowledge of the art of weaving into the mind of the learner, and render it permanent. As the expert finished his recitation the scholar leaned forward and bit the upper part of the right hand *turuturu*, or rod, just closing her teeth on it. She then proceeded to weave [the *aho tapu*,] the first cross thread. (1924: 513)

In the most recent comprehensive study of Maori weaving (1969), Hirini Moko Mead takes issue with Best's assertion that this ritual was designed to impart 'knowledge' to the young weaver. Knowledge, in the sense of the skills necessary to perform the task of weaving, he notes, was acquired through practice and technical training, not imputed into the acolyte by way of ritual magic. The true function of the ceremony, Mead argues, was to instil *mana* and confidence in the weaver, and (most intriguingly) to ensure that she would provide a clear pathway through which ancestral efficacy could flow into the work. Provided the rules of the *whare pora* are followed, Mead writes, citing Best, 'she can make no error':

> From this point onwards any errors she makes are ritual rather than technical. Even a technical error such as preparing a weft which is too short is regarded as a ritual error, that is an error committed by the gods to indicate a future calamity.

'The weaver', Mead concludes, 'is a passive vehicle through which fate operates' (1969: 171). The ritual, in other words, opens a pathway between layers of generational time, making the weaver a conduit for ancestral efficacy manifested in the substance of her weaving. Her actions are necessarily 'true' instantiations of ancestral power in that they are by definition *technically* correct, for they can only be *ritually* wrong (i.e. wrong at the hands of the ancestor). Like the bindings, feathers, threads and hairs used in other rituals, the *aho* or wefts are thus quite literally means through which ancestral efficacy enters the present – instantiations, rather than representations, of ancestral power. This, I hope, goes some way toward explaining how cloaks may be understood quite literally as *taonga tuku iho*, treasures handed down from ancestors.

Changing Times

From around 1900, when the Maori population was at its lowest ebb due to the effects of colonization, warfare and disease, concerted efforts were made by Maori leaders, notably members of the Young Maori Party, to reassert the *mana* of their people and inject new life and enthusiasm for their heritage through a wide-ranging programme of cultural and economic regeneration. One man in particular, the lawyer and MP Apirana Ngata, launched a series of projects focused on the building and refurbishment of meeting houses as centres for Maori communal life, a movement that entailed the revitalization of traditional art forms including carving, weaving and the performing arts. Ngata commissioned an ethnographic survey of his own kin group, the Ngati Porou, which was carried out by Elsdon Best and a team from the national museum, aided by Ngata's friend and Young Maori Party colleague, the young medical doctor Te Rangihiroa (Peter Buck), whose work on weaving I cited earlier. Buck was then carrying out a detailed study of the techniques of Maori basketry and textile manufacture, research that would ultimately lead to an illustrious anthropological career including a visiting professorship at Yale and the Directorship of Hawaii's Bishop Museum. The ethnographic evidence gathered on this and other fieldtrips was fed into Ngata's programme of cultural reinvigoration, and has ever since continued to provide a resource for Maori eager to master ancestral crafts (the films taken on these expeditions are in fact regarded as *taonga* in their own right). As part of my instruction in weaving at Auckland University, for example, we were shown clips of film footage in which Ngata and Buck are filmed weaving a *tukutuku* or rushwork panel for the interior of a meeting house.

A special government-funded school of Maori Arts and Crafts that still operates today was set up in Rotorua in 1927 at Ngata's initiative, and teachers were recruited to instruct young Maori in traditional arts. From the 1950s, following on from these initiatives, the Maori Women's Welfare League was active in promoting the teaching of *whatu* or cloak-weaving, which had been somewhat neglected in Ngata's programme, focused as it was on architectural and performing arts. Here weavers such as Rangimarie Hetet and her daughter Diggeress Te Kanawa were instrumental in spreading the knowledge and skills of weaving to a wider group of women, some of whom are now regarded as the leading practitioners in the field (Paki-Titi 1998). Writing in 1969, Hirini Mead noted that:

> At Te Kuiti flax fibre is still prepared by the method described by Governor King in November 1793. A cut is made across the blade of the flax and a mussel shell held in the right hand is pressed firmly against the strand and with one outward stroke the fibre is separated from the epidermal skin. (1969: 190–1)

This is just as I was taught in 1996. While he acknowledged that many of the old rituals were no longer practised, Mead observed:

> Implicit in the attitude of the weavers themselves and the reverence with which Maori admirers regard garments made with traditional materials by traditional methods is a set

of values which regards old methods as still being ritually correct and appropriate. Old techniques are seen as a link with the ancestral past. (1969: 191–2)

Despite dramatic changes in the context surrounding Maori weaving and the garments thus produced, therefore, cloaks and the techniques used to produce them have continued to act as tangible instantiations of ancestral efficacy.

Cloaks and Persons

In trying to engage with ways of being in which objects can be ancestors and relations can be things, it is useful to consider what is meant by the definition of a 'person'. Best was particularly drawn to such matters because of his interest in what he called the 'spiritual concepts of the Maori' (1900), the ontological and cosmological 'furniture' of the Maori world, ideas that continue to inform Maori practice and preoccupy anthropologists (Maori and otherwise) today. In an article published in the *Journal of the Polynesian Society* in 1900 and 1901, Best attempted to elucidate Maori ideas about 'what constitutes life, what vital essences man is endowed with, and what occurs at death, whether man perishes entirely as the breath leaves the body, or whether some spirit or essence then passes from the body to reappear and live on in another world' (1900: 173). He tried, in other words, to engage with Maori notions of personhood, and his observations, developed by later writers, offer further insights into the mechanisms through which cloaks or *kahu* might manifest ancestral power. His definitions are not only relevant to 'the old Maori world', but correspond closely to what contemporary authorities today define as definitive aspects of what it is to be Maori.

The key concepts so far as we are concerned are those of *wairua*, *mauri*, and the *hau* made famous in the writings of Marcel Mauss (who was in fact citing Tamati Ranapiri, another of Best's informants). These principles or efficacies are each characteristic not only of human beings but also of other aspects of the world, including what might be described as 'animate' and 'inanimate' things (Salmond 1985: 241). The *wairua* Best defines as 'the spirit of man', 'the shadowy self', 'an intelligent spirit or essence'. 'It is the *wairua* that leaves the body during sleep', he writes, 'thus the *wairua* can leave the body without injury thereto, though if one's *hau* be taken away the body perishes' (1900: 177). When one dreams, he noted, one's *wairua* 'is probably greeting the spirits (*wairua*) of other persons, possibly those of the dead, or is on the look-out for any danger which threatens its physical basis, that is to say – the body of the sleeper'. The *wairua* can move easily between the realms of the living and the ancestors, and thus acts as an *ara* or pathway between the two.

Best glosses *mauri* as 'the "breath of life," or spirit of life', and he notes that it 'is sometimes described as the soul' (1901: 2). More precisely, he notes that

'*Mauri* might be termed the spark of life, or the physical life principle', it is 'that which moves within us, as in sudden fright'. Unlike the *wairua*, it 'ceases to be at the death of the body' (1901: 3). *Mauri* is also a quality shared with other entities in the physical world, such as the land or a forest, yet while the human *mauri* is 'an activity, an immaterial element' that may be 'represented by a material object', it seems that in other cases a *mauri* can also *be* a material thing, like a stone or a piece of fern (1901: 4–5). As in the following quote from the contemporary weaver Erenora Puketapu Hetet (a granddaughter-in-law of Rangimarie Hetet), in such cases the object and its *mauri* might almost be regarded as one and the same:

> It is important to me as a weaver that I respect the *mauri* (life force) of what I am working with. Once I have taken it from where it belongs, I must give another dimension to its life force so that it is still a thing of beauty. This is the central idea, and it applies to all sorts of work. The materials are seen as having a life of their own, not simply as means to the worker's ends. (in Williams 2001: 108)

Hau, like *mauri*, is described by Best as 'the vital essence or life principle', which 'cannot leave its physical basis, the body' without causing death (1900: 189). As with *mauri* and *wairua*, it is a quality people share with non-human entities including 'inanimate objects' as well as aspects of the living environment such as trees and land (1900: 190–1; Salmond 1985: 241). According to Best, the *hau* of a child, like its *wairua*, is implanted by the father during coition (1900: 185), a statement that contradicts Weiner's claim that the elusive source of this principle – the metaphysical substance identified by Marcel Mauss as the 'spirit of the gift' – is in the woven garments made by women and used in the *tohi* ceremony (1992: 50, 55).

The important thing to note here is that cloaks and people alike, along with other *taonga*, may possess *wairua*, *mauri* and *hau*. With regard to these ubiquitous elements of personhood, at least, there is no clear ontological distinction between persons and things. This is not to say that Maori do not commonly distinguish between 'animate' and 'inanimate' objects – as I have already said, they do – but that a distinctively Maori set of assumptions endures that allows for the possibility of object–persons and person–things. Cloaks, therefore, like other *taonga* or treasured objects crafted by ancestors, are often named and are held to instantiate the efficacies of the people that made and used them. As Anne Salmond has put it: 'The alchemy of *taonga* [brings] about a fusion of men and ancestors and a collapse of distance in space-time ... the power of [such things can] give men absolute access to their ancestors' (1984: 120).

Maori anthropologist Paul Tapsell, whose work is cited by Leach, has developed this argument to demonstrate how an ancestral *taonga* of his kin group, the dogskin cloak named Te Kahumamae o Parerautuu (Parerautuu's cloak of pain) provides 'a genealogical pathway bridging the generations, which allows the descendants to ritually meet their ancestors, face to face' (1997: 335). In describing how he orchestrated the return of this cloak from the Auckland Museum to its descendants in 1993, Tapsell tells how researching the cloak's passage through space and time was 'like tracing a single *aho*, or thread in a cloak'. He goes on:

> The thread, like the flight of the *tui* [a native bird with a characteristic swooping flight], appears and then disappears ... in a repeating pattern that interlocks with other threads, or *taonga*, descending from one layer of *whakapapa* [or genealogy] to the next... Each *taonga* represents a single genealogical thread, stitching sky to earth, *atua* to mortals, ancestor to descendant, generation to generation... (1997: 335)

Tapsell was impelled to secure the cloak's return by one of his tribal elders who, reciting his own ancestral connection to the cloak, told how it had been woven by his ancestress Parerautuu, a high-born widow, to persuade an allied chief to avenge the slaughter of her menfolk in a battle that took place around 1800. Tapsell was able to confirm this provenance through historical research, and the Museum agreed to return it to its ancestral *marae* or meeting place in 1993. 'After her ceremonial return', Tapsell writes, describing his elder's reunion with the ancestor:

> I watched the tall old man quietly collapse to his knees in front of Parerautuu. With great reverence he leaned forward and completed the *hongi* with his great grandmother. A lifetime of energy abandoned him and tears rolled down his cheeks onto the cloak as his family helped lift him back to his feet. I found myself also filled with emotion as I realised ... the burden that at last had been lifted from Hari's aging shoulders. (1997: 343)

The cloak's *mauri* and the *wairua* of Parerautuu was felt by Tapsell and his kin in the form of *ihi*, *wehi* and *wana*, physical and emotional sensations provoked by close contact with their ancestress, the treasured *taonga*. In performing the *hongi* with the cloak, furthermore, the elder enacted an intermingling of his *hau* and that of the ancestress. Tapsell's account is instructive in that it demonstrates the persistent capacity of such treasured artefacts to collapse genealogical space-time, allowing ancestors to remain 'in touch with' their descendants. Nor is it an isolated example – other such experiences have been recorded in recent years, notably in connection with the Te Maori exhibition of *taonga* from New Zealand museums which toured the USA from 1984 (e.g. O'Biso 1987; Butts 1990).

Conclusion

In taking seriously the idea that *whatu* or Maori weaving and the cloaks thus produced are *taonga tuku iho* – treasures handed down from ancestors – I have attempted to take up a position from which different ways of conceiving relations between persons and things are possible. Now, of course, neither mothers delivering babies nor weavers necessarily engage in the kinds of elaborate rituals described by Best, yet the possibility remains among Maori that objects can be ancestors and aspects of people and relations may be instantiated in things. *Whatu* is still practised, Maori children are born, and cloaks continue to smooth the passage between one phase of life and the next. Over time the focus for the use of cloaks has shifted away from birth to rites of passage later in life, such as weddings and graduations, and to *tangihanga* or funeral gatherings, when cloaks are draped over the body in its coffin on the meeting house veranda, surrounded by family and photographs of ancestors. Yet in these forums cloaks continue to provide pathways between contemporary people and a dynamic yet ever present ancestral past by enacting genealogical relations in the present. Perhaps the best way to think of such relations in this sense is as the *kaupapa* or body of a cloak made up of continually interlacing *aho tipuna*, the ancestral and present-day threads of which at once run parallel and lie closely entwined. The weaver continues to work in a creative continuum that remains distinctively Maori, and other things as well.

Acknowledgements

I am grateful to Maureen Lander, James Leach, Marilyn Strathern and the anthropology departments of UCL and Goldsmiths University for their helpful comments and advice on various drafts of this paper.

Notes

1. Lissant Bolton (2003) is another scholar who has recently emphasized the distinctive nature of *kastom* as opposed to Euro-western (and particularly anthropological) notions of culture and tradition.
2. The precise meaning of this term has been extensively debated in academia and in the reports and proceedings of the Waitangi Tribunal (e.g. Orange 1987; Waitangi Tribunal 1987; Kawharu 1989). Here I refer to the gloss given by a Ministry of Economic Development (MED) discussion document concerning

the Wai 262 claim (MED 2002: 28). The claim itself defines *tino rangatiratanga* as incorporating a range of 'full and exclusive' rights and responsibilities.
3. Leach elsewhere explains why this is not a contrast he wishes to promote, noting that 'while process appears to threaten the notion of structure altogether, employing process as the anti-structure' (or anti-object, one might add) 'may only serve to reinforce the analytic necessity of describing what flexibility can be judged against' (2003b: 24).

References

Appadurai, Arjun 1986 *The Social Life of Things: Commodities in Cultural Perspective*. Cambridge: Cambridge University Press.

Best, Elsdon 1900 'Spiritual Concepts of the Maori (Part I)'. *Journal of the Polynesian Society*, 9: 173–99.

—— 1901 'Spiritual Concepts of the Maori (Part II)'. *Journal of the Polynesian Society*, 10: 1–20.

—— 1906 'The Lore of the Whare Kohanga: Notes on procreation among the Maori people of New Zealand' (Parts II & III). *Journal of the Polynesian Society*, 15: 1–26, 147–62.

—— 1914 'Ceremonial Performances pertaining to birth, as performed by the Maori of New Zealand'. *Journal of the Royal Anthropological Institute of Great Britain and Ireland*, 44: 127–62.

—— 1924 *The Maori*. Memoirs of the Polynesian Society Vol. V, Wellington: Board of Maori Ethnological Research.

—— 1929 'Maori Customs pertaining to birth and baptism'. *Journal of the Polynesian Society*, 38: 241–69.

Bolton, Lissant 2003 *Unfolding the Moon: Enacting Women's Kastom in Vanuatu*. Honolulu: University of Hawaii Press

Butts, David 1990 'Nga Tukemata: Nga Taonga o Ngati Kahungunu [The awakening: the treasures of Ngati Kahungunu]'. In P. Gathercole and David Lowenthal (eds) *The Politics of the Past*. London: Unwin Hyman

Gell, Alfred 1992 'The Technology of Enchantment and the Enchantment of Technology'. In J. Coote and A. Shelton (eds), *Anthropology, Art and Aesthetics*. Oxford: Oxford University Press.

—— 1998 *Art and Agency: An Anthropological Theory*. Oxford: Oxford University Press.

Hakiwai, Arapata 1996 'Maori Society Today: Welcome to Our World'. In D. Starzecka (ed.) *Maori Art and Culture*. London: British Museum Press.

Hanson, Allan 1989 'The Making of the Maori: Culture Invention and Its Logic'. *American Anthropologist*, 91: 890–901.

—— 1991 'Reply to Langdon, Levine, and Linnekin'. *American Anthropologist*, 93(2): 449–50.

—— 1997 'Empirical Anthropology, Postmodernism and the Invention of Tradition'. In M. Mauzé (ed.) *Present is Past: Some uses of Tradition in Native Societies*. Lanham: University Press of America.

Harrison, Simon 2000 'From Prestige Goods to Legacies: Property and the objectification of culture in Melanesia'. *Comparative Studies in Society and History*, 42: 662–79.

Kawharu, Hugh 1989 *Waitangi: Maori and Pakeha Perspectives of the Treaty of Waitangi*. Auckland: Oxford University Press.

Keesing, Roger and Tonkinson, R. (eds) 1982 'Reinventing Traditional Culture: The Politics of Kastom in Island Melanesia'. *Mankind* (special issue) 13(4).

Küchler, Susanne 2002 'Binding in the Pacific: Between Loops and Knots'. In V. Buchli (ed.) *The Material Culture Studies Reader*. Oxford: Berg.

Leach, James 2003a 'Owning Creativity: Cultural Property and the Efficacy of Custom on the Rai Coast of Papua New Guinea'. *Journal of Material Culture*, 8(2): 123–43.

—— 2003b *Creative Land: Place and Procreation on the Rai Coast of Papua New Guinea*. New York and Oxford: Berghahn.

Mead, Sidney (Hirini) M. 1969 *Traditional Maori Clothing: A Study of Technological and Functional Change*. Wellington: Reed.

Ministry of Economic Development 2002 *Bioprospecting in New Zealand: Discussing the Options* (discussion document). Wellington: Ministry of Economic Development.

Neich, Roger 2001 *Carved Histories: Rotorua Ngati Tarawhai Woodcarving*. Auckland: Auckland University Press.

O'Biso, Carol 1994 [1987] *First Light*. Auckland: Reed Books.

Orange, Claudia 1987 *The Treaty of Waitangi*. Wellington: Allen & Unwin.

Pels, Peter 1998 'The Spirit of Matter: On Fetish, Rarity, Fact and Fancy'. In P. Spyer (ed.) *Border Fetishisms: Material Objects in Unstable Spaces*. London: Routledge.

Paki-Titi, Rora 1998 *Rangimarie: Recollections of Her Life*. Wellington: Huia Publishers.

Salmond, Anne 1984 'Nga Huarahi o Te Ao Maori: Pathways in the Maori World'. In S.M. Mead (ed.) *Te Maori: Maori Art from New Zealand Collections*. Auckland: Heinemann.

—— 1985 'Maori Epistemologies'. In J. Overing (ed.) *Reason and Morality*, ASA Monograph Series No. 24, London: Tavistock.

—— 1997 *Between Worlds: Early Exchanges Between Maori and Europeans 1773–1815*. Auckland: Viking.

Sissons, Jeffrey 1998 'The Traditionalisation of the Maori Meeting House'. *Oceania*, 69(1): 36–46.

Tapsell, Paul 1997 'The Flight of Parerautu: An investigation of *Taonga* from a Tribal Perspective'. *Journal of the Polynesian Society*, 106: 323–74.

Te Rangihiroa (Peter Buck) 1926 *The Evolution of Maori Clothing*. Wellington: Board of Maori Ethnological Research.

Thomas, Nicholas 1999 *Possessions: Indigenous Art/Colonial Culture*. London: Thames & Hudson.

Thomas, Nicholas and Jolly, Margaret 1992 'Introduction'. *Oceania*, 62(4): 241–8.

Waitangi Tribunal 1987 *Report of the Waitangi Tribunal on the Orakei Claim (Wai-9)*. Wellington: Department of Justice.

Wagner, Roy 1975 *The Invention of Culture*. Englewood Cliffs, NJ: Prentice Hall.

Weiner, Annette B. 1992 *Inalienable Possessions: The Paradox of Keeping-While-Giving*. Berkeley: University of California Press.

Wilford, John Noble 1990 'Anthropology Seen as Father of Maori Lore'. *New York Times*, 20 February, p. C1 (continued on p. C2 as 'Was Lore of the Maoris invented by Anthropologists?').

Williams, David 2001 *Matauranga Maori and Taonga: The Nature and Extent of Treaty Rights held by Iwi and Hapu in Indigenous Flora and Fauna, Cultural Heritage Objects, Valued Traditional Knowledge*, Wellington: Waitangi Tribunal.

– 8 –

Relative Imagery: Patterns of Response to the Revival of Archaic Chiefly Dress in Fiji
Chloë Colchester

During the colonial era in Fiji, an archaic item of chiefly clothing made from barkcloth (*masi yarabalavu,* hereafter simply referred to as *masi* for the sake of brevity[1]) was revived. Although contemporary versions of this article of chiefly clothing are rarely worn during ceremonial activity in contemporary Fiji, they are still made for a variety of ceremonial occasions. Furthermore *how* it is used, presented and displayed indicates that it is still highly regarded as an item of archaic chiefly dress. As I argue below, the use of *masi* to mount petitions for assistance is a striking example of the way in which appeals to religiously powerful imagery may be intensified during periods of crisis, which in turn gives rise to the formalization of religious imagery (Gell 1998). Beliefs regarding the divine origin of pattern imagery mean that *masi* is not simply be regarded as a tool, but as a foundation, or a formative entity in itself, one whose ritualized presentation shapes future events, just as it shapes the perceptions of its users through the play of analogy and resemblance. For while the patterns on these items of clothing have been formalized, the manner in which the finished garments are made and presented is open to nuance. Thus *yarabalavu* presents an example of the way in which even highly controlled religious imagery carried on articles of chiefly clothing may bring the potential for new realizations into new historical contexts. The political struggles surrounding the presentation and display of these anachronistic chiefly garments in contemporary Fiji reveals the complex issues involved in a long-ongoing debate about the causal effects of *masi* and the consequence of ritual action that has persisted in Fiji for over a century.

  This paper draws on research into the impact of Protestantism on traditions of religious art in the Pacific. In what follows, many readers will recognize my debt to Webb Keane's masterly accounts of Sumbanese attempts to maintain traditional ritual forms while transforming their meanings in a manner that is consistent with Protestant practice and belief. In a series of papers he has drawn attention to Protestants' doomed attempts to 'consolidate a human subject who is independent from, and superordinate to, the world of mere dead matter' (Keane 2004). Yet while Keane's ethnographic work has focused on the way that male

Protestant converts use ritual oratory and forms of public speech to reconfigure the relations between objects and subjects, my concern here is with women in Fiji, who, given existing distinctions between men's and women's ritual activity, have little potential to use public speech as an instrument to guide or control the interpretation of ritual objects (Keane 1997, 1998). Therefore, the emphasis in this paper is on non-verbal interpretation, that is, on the way in which *masi yarabalavu* is enacted and displayed.

These observations need not be restricted to Fijian women. At the risk of overgeneralizing, ethnographies of language use in the Pacific islands have suggested that geography may explain why Pacific Islanders have developed few avenues for discussion or the verbal expression of overt criticism. Instead they have noted that the use of indirect speech as well as other, more mediated forms of expression is highly elaborated, and may have been further enhanced by the experience of missionary activity and colonial intrusion (Bolton 2003).

Fijians are often amused to find that Europeans are relatively blind to such non-verbal forms of expression. They say that Europeans have a 'great pen' in their minds. In this respect, the strident image presented an initial meeting with Natewa's *vunivalu*, Ratu Tevita Vakalalabure (who had trained for the ministry in the Seventh Day Adventist seminary prior to claiming leadership of Natewa, and later becoming a member of parliament, and a Fijian senator for the neoconservative, Soqosoqo vakavulewa ni taukei (SVT) Party was indicative. The senator was sitting on a throne-like chair upholstered in red plush velvet wearing a white tuxedo, and he was holding a stone in one hand like an orb. He informed me that it was once believed to have been one of the *vanua*'s ancestral deities. The earth monument that he had raised over his father's grave (who had become a champion shot-putter while serving in the Fijian auxiliary service in France during the First World War) was clearly visible through the door behind him. At the time I believed that he was mocking my typically 'anthropological' interest in barkcloth and other traditional, if not anachronistic, aspects of Fijian culture. However it has subsequently become clear to me that, although his pose was clearly tongue-in-cheek, it also demonstrated the quandary of charismatic leadership, now that factions within the village who claimed membership of archaic *matanitu* (chiefly confederacies) were marshalling their expertise in ceremonial protocol, their mastery in ritual form – including *masi* manufacture, and re-emphasizing the significance of the ancestral foundations (*yavu*) that justified their ancestral right to title.

As the recent coups have demonstrated, the Fijian chiefly hierarchy is in a state of flux at both regional and national levels. Independence (achieved in 1970) has meant that criteria for holding chiefly title that were suited to the period of colonial occupation are increasingly open to doubt (France 1969). In the mid-1990s, only fear of compromising title to land was preventing the regionalist colonial model of political organization and land tenure from being subject to formal legal review. Nevertheless, rivalry for chiefly title was intensifying. While it is true that the colonial system reinforced the pre-existing chiefly hierarchy in certain parts of Fiji (see for example, Toren 1988) this had not occurred everywhere. In the village of Natewa, the chiefly capital of the Natewa region (*tikina*), where I conducted fieldwork research into the manufacture and use of Fijian barkcloth (*masi*) between 1995 and 1997, post-colonial political instability was particularly evident. Here, descendants of the man who had been made *vunivalu* (paramount chief)[2] for largely pragmatic reasons during the colonial era, were facing fierce competition from the members of old, and even archaic, chiefly confederations (*matanitu*), some dating back as far as the sixteenth century (see Sayes 1982).

The potential consequences were profound, since it was the reconfiguration of the *vanua* (the conjunction of land, chief, people and supernatural beings into ritual polity; Nayacakalou 1975) into a colonial spiritual polity (based upon the association between a chiefly hierarchy and the colonial church) that had enabled a mixed community of peoples to be resettled into villages under the leadership of a new chiefly hierarchy. By the very fact of demarcating the *vanua* of Natewa as a geographic region rather than a ritual polity, embracing the land, ancestors and people, the colonial era had enabled these communities to assert their independence from the interference of the great chiefly confederations based in Bau and Somosomo.

Competition was not restricted to chiefly factions. Even *within* factions, family trees that had been composed to prove right to land during the colonial era were no longer seen as justifying right to chiefly title in the present. In opposition to the importance given to worldly authority in colonial and legal definitions of chiefship, an alternative, more religious sense of chiefship was being revived, which placed greater emphasis on the importance of other worldly authority. With this religious sense of chiefship went the sense of the importance and consequence of the human act. Since chiefs existed not only to the people whom they were addressing but also in the eye of God, being able to harness the appropriate means of address whether *tabua*, *yarabalavu*, or conversely, evidence of good conduct such as a newly refurbished church, was now required in order to make the protagonist a fitting instrument for divine intervention, and therefore a good chief.

In the mid-1990s, attempts to win divine support through such good works were evident in the surfeit of the number of initiatives being mounted in each of the villages in the region. Quite apart from the obligation to undertake ritual work on behalf of kin, as well as the escalating demands for church attendance, a seemingly endless number church-building schemes and other fund-raising projects – such as youth initiatives, farming initiatives, school fund-raisings and so on – competed for people's time and limited resources. No sooner had a project been ceremonially launched by one of the chiefs, with the members of other chiefly families pledging their support and commitment, than a rival enterprise was started by a competing faction to claim the cooperation of some of those involved. The high degree of in-marriage, which had become a distinguishing feature of the region during the colonial era when the pre-colonial system of marital alliance between chiefly families broke down, meant that each new project necessarily leached support from others. The surfeit of this activity meant that the chiefly village of Natewa was littered with the humiliating evidence of abandoned collaborative initiatives: a pile of handmade cement blocks that an old man had hoped might provide the foundations of a new and better church; the ruins of a newly made traditional Bauan *bure* (house), which had been burnt to the ground by a rival faction; a row of broken-down outboard engines belonging to a now defunct fishing cooperative.

The colonial structure of church and state was fragmenting under the strain of this activity. Regional projects were giving way to local initiatives, while local initiatives had to compete, in turn, with the increase in ritual activity at the level of each individual household. At the same time, the support for new church denominations (such as Assemblies of God and Seventh Day Adventists) was on the increase, and charismatic movements in both the more established Methodist and Catholic Churches were attracting the burgeoning population of Fijian youth. Thus, even at a local level, the head of the Methodist Women's Institute and the Village Headman were publicly humiliated by faltering support. The conflicting demands upon a number of the older women, in particular, was such that they had to be treated for exhaustion on a number of occasions, while younger members of the community spoke in private of their dreams of establishing their own farmsteads away from the village, in order to escape the incessant demands upon their time and resources.

Just as donations of cash or consumer goods have become a feature of life-cycle events, ritual work is now not only demanded at life-cycle ceremonies but also for modern initiatives and fund-raising events. *Cakacakavakavanua* or *cakacakavakavuvale* (literally 'ritual action in the manner of the land/polity, or 'ritual action in the manner of the household ancestors')[3] is divided according to gender. Men's activities included ritual speech making, the ritualized preparation and presentation and consumption of feasts and kava, while women's activities include the ritualized manufacture and presentation of women's ceremonial valuables, such as pandanus mats and indigenous barkcloth clothing. Both men and women's activities also embrace contemporary attitudes towards culturally appropriate behaviour which have appeared in the wake of conversion, and much ritual action is dedicated by prayer (Toren 1988).

Ritual action is an ongoing labour. For example, Fijian barkcloth (*masi*) is typically newly made for each ceremonial event from freshly felled paper mulberry saplings, and is intricately patterned with stencilled motifs in tree sap and earth in a manner that is suited to the occasion. Given the effort this demands it is not surprising that ritual work is described as *onga,* a burden, which weighs upon the Fijian population, absorbing time and effort. Nevertheless it is the kind of collaborative activity that rural Fijians excel at; it enables them to surpass themselves, and to gauge the strength and nature of their relationships with each other while reflecting upon the past. Ritual work produces impressive effects that no amount of Christian prayer can ever do: huge feasts; moving rhetoric; substantial displays and performances of cleverly patterned clothing. And, given that many members of rural communities are comparatively strapped for cash, it is something that they *can* contribute to fund-raising projects, and which therefore sustains the cooperative ethos.

Fund-raising provided occasions for each rival political faction to demonstrate the wealth of both traditional and modern resources at its beck and call. How much cooperation could faction 'A' call upon? How much cash could they levy from urban-based relatives working in town? To what extent could they demonstrate their control of chiefly channels and their mastery of chiefly protocol compared to faction 'B' or 'C'? To what extent would their oratory and displays of barkcloth demonstrate their grasp of traditional ritual forms of speech and imagery in a manner that would demonstrate their capacity to provide adequate leadership in the present? All these were relevant concerns. But more than this, depending upon the insight and skill of the protagonists involved, these events could also be the occasion of a telling performance, a new and surprising insight, which could renew participants' commitment to the faction involved. For political rivalry did not merely involve competition over the control of material but also moral resources: it had also become a battle of wits that involved the co-ordination of traditional practice and Christian belief.

The Controversy over Population Decline and the Revival of Masi

The distribution of centres of *masi* production, which once covered a great swathe of the archipelago to the south and east of Viti Levu, suggests that prior to the conversion to Christianity and the colonial occupation of the islands *masi* was once formally organized into an established chiefly confederacy, a ritual polity (*matanitu*) centred on the paramount chief, *vunivalu* on the island of Bau. As the anthropologist A.M. Hocart understood, the *masi* garments of these chiefs were believed to play a vital part in securing *mana,* the capacity to increase the fertility of the land and people. By virtue of investiture with cloth at rites of chiefly installation the chief and the ancestral deity were identified (Hocart 1952). The names of motifs used in *masi* pattern refer to the instruments of rituals of chiefly investiture as well as the ritual instruments (such as combs, ceremonial forks, kava bowls, carrying sticks) involved in the exchange between chiefs – transactions of clothing and feasts which once bound the confederation together under the leadership of Bau.

The conversion of the Bauan paramount chief, Ratu Cakobau in 1855 by members of the Wesleyan mission, which presaged the official conversion of Fiji as a whole, permanently ruptured Bau's exclusive connection to *masi*. In place of the Bauan chiefly style of wearing *masi yarabalavu*, which involved binding barkcloth patterned with stencils around the loins in such a way that a train dragged along the ground, channelling ancestral power into the world of the living,[4] Tongan native preachers required converted chiefs to adopt Tongan style – barkcloth (Waterhouse 1866). These were *sulu* (sarongs) made from *gatuvakatoga* (barkcloth patterned in the Tongan manner) which stretched down demurely from the waist to the ankle. As well as being used as items of clothing, huge sheets of Tongan-style barkcloth, often several hundred yards long, were commissioned from many different parts of Fiji as 'missionary offerings' and for the other aspects of chiefly ceremonial that accorded with the imported *lotu* (Tongan Wesleyan Church). The scale of these cloths was such that they effectively absorbed resources that might have been channelled into any other form ritual political activity. Although many European visitors expressed their concern at the strength of Tongan influence in the Methodist Church, and showed an interest in preserving Fijian native customs, their tendency to imagine Fijian traditions in the context of a primordial past, rather than present circumstances, served to reinforce the association between *masi* and heathenism. In a paradigmatic example, which resulted in some of the most iconic photographs of 'Fijian warriors' taken in the late nineteenth century, samples of Fijian *masi*, which had been collected by Baron von Hügel in exchange for Christian clothes, were used by the Dufty brothers as stage props to dress up members of the Fijian constabulary (who were allowed to wear their hair long) for highly stage-managed photographs (see Fig. 8.1) (Roth and Hooper 1990).

Given these associations with *qaravi tevero* (heathenism, literally 'facing the devils'), it is interesting to note that *masi* enjoyed two revivals during the period of colonial rule. In the light of the argument outlined above it should now be fairly clear why the largest revival of Fijian *masi* was precipitated by negotiations over British withdrawal from the islands, although it is very possible that the need to reassert independence from the Tongan *lotu* (Tongan Wesleyan Church) was another contributing factor (see Scott-Troxler 1971). However data from analysing museum collections of *masi* indicate that a smaller, but possibly more significant, revival occurred in the 1920s. The date of this revival, coming in the wake of a series of devastating pandemics of influenza, Spanish flu and measles, which killed almost a fifth of the entire population of the islands between 1914 and 1919, is highly significant since it indicates how *masi* was implicated in a controversy over the correct means of appealing for divine assistance. This controversy is

Responses to Revival of Chiefly Dress in Fiji

Figure 8.1 The photograph entitled 'A Fijian Mountaineer' shows how *masi yarabalavu* was used by photographers to project an image of Fijian identity to the outside world. Photograph Dufty Brothers (Pitt Rivers B3721a)

central to the story of *masi* in Fiji since it provides a vital insight into the way in which *masi* is used and presented in Fiji today.

It has been demonstrated that the non-conformist missionaries' assertions that 'disease was an agency of the Providence of God, a judgment on the sins of the people and the necessary consequence of their immoral state' was important to the progress of the Wesleyan mission and helped to secure the conversion of a number of chiefs in Fiji between 1835 and 1855 (Gunson 1978: 248). Similar sentiments were used to justify the intrusive colonial projects of social reorganization, house building and welfare reform for, in keeping with the European ideas on racial decay characteristic of the period, the idea of foreign origin of disease was not countenanced (Thomas 1994). Yet even before the pandemics, the rate of infant deaths and death from disease had become so alarming that many Fijians had started to lose faith in the efficacy of Christian prayer, and in the Wesleyan doctrine on justification through conduct or good works.

A theological essay on the subject, which was written by a Fijian Methodist minister/ trainee, and translated and published by A.M. Hocart in a religious journal in 1912, contains an explicit call for the revival of certain aspects of Fijian pre-Christian religious customs *alongside* Wesleyan piety and practice. The minister's thesis was that abandoning the native deities was the origin of infertility and disease. However the interesting theological rationale of his argument regarded the identity between the nature of the petition, the nature of the addressee, and the nature of the expected effect.

> I observe that there appear to be two kinds of prayers coming from heaven to us men who abide in the flesh. I think and believe that there really are two kinds of answers to prayers... Most rapid is the answer to prayer to matters pertaining to the spirit. But petitions addressed to the Spirit God concerning the flesh, that we may increase to be many, are delayed and not fulfilled. What is the reason? Because it is not possible for Jehovah to go past him who is already appointed leader of the flesh. And if the Vu were placed at our head and we then went up together to our goal, to wit the Spirit God Jehovah, there would be no still births and Fiji would then be indeed a people increasing rapidly, since our conforming to our native customs would combine with progress in cleanly living at the present time. Now in the past, when the ancients only worshipped the Vu Gods and there was no commandment about cleanly living yet they kept increasing. Then if the Vu Gods were worshipped in Fiji (the deputy pertaining to the life of the flesh), and this was also combined with the precept of cleanly living, I think the villages would be full of men. (Hocart 1912, 97; Küchler 1996)

The perceived need to present material alongside immaterial prayers remains a vital element of Fijian piety today, one that finds its expression not in church, but through the performance of chiefly ceremonial at fund-raisings, as well as at ceremonies that are ostensibly connected to life-cycle events. While belief in the identity of the petition, the addressee and the anticipated effects may account for the importance attributed to the enactment of *masi* that is discussed below.

Clothing, Pattern and Conduct

Masi was one of Natewa's traditional ceremonial valuables of the land (*iyau dina ni vanua*) yet the diverse motivations at play in its revival were evident from its growing dislocation from the old ritual hierarchy. In the past, rights to reproduce *masi* patterns had been highly restricted. Only a few women, called ladies of the leaf stencil *(marama ni draudra)*, had the right to make the leaf stencils for printing motifs. This situation had changed. Although ordinary women living in the area complained that the knowledge of stencil making had never been willingly shared, and described the stratagems and deceptions they had been forced to adopt to acquire the little they knew, stencils were becoming widely distributed. This change in the political economy had a material aspect: while stencils had been made from fragile banana leaves in the past, so that they could be torn up immediately after they had been used, they were now made from other materials, such as used X-ray film, on which the shadowy images of bones could be seen.

A comparison of the collections of *masi* housed in the British Museum with barkcloth collections from Samoa and Tonga indicates that *masi* patterns have been substantially less modified in the wake of conversion. Natewan women were proud to demonstrate the correct way of executing various *masi* motifs in bands and strips along the edge of the cloth. They indicated that while certain bands of imagery were invariant to all *masi* embellishment, others could be substituted, or added according to the intended use of the cloth, or in order to complement particular strips of pattern.

The stability of pattern imagery is central to understanding the ideology of image making in Fiji, that is the esteem and respect which *masi* is accorded, because it casts the tradition of image making within a frame of action that transcends the individual, and the immediacy of the here and now. During my time in Natewa, a few of the older women still maintained that *masi* patterns were of ancestral origin; their remarks suggested that reproduction of pattern was a means of channelling ancestral power into the world of the living. The notion that *masi* clothing was a vessel that could serve as a conduit for divine intervention was also suggested by the terms used to describe formal components of *masi* design which had an affinity with those used to describe spirit possession. Thus *masi* patterns are said to be comprised of a series of *waqa* (literally 'container' or 'vessel'; skin) and *lewena* (literally 'contents' or 'flesh') which are nested or embedded within one another; just as prior to Christian conversion seers and priests were said to become *vakawaqa* (possessed) through contact with a range of ritual media, including lengths of barkcloth (*vakacabe i soro*) that were attached to the rafters of the spirit houses. However in contemporary Natewa, the majority of women expressed the connection between traditional forms and external authority more obliquely, by saying that 'a woman from elsewhere' had brought the patterns to the village, or by describing the ideals of conduct associated with traditional practice.

In contemporary Fiji, ancestral intervention is still used to explain a range of phenomena such as dreams, or illnesses that have resisted Western medical treatment, or spirit possession (Becker 1986). However the evangelical tenor of the Methodist mission to Tonga and Fiji means that divine intervention *is also* an important facet of Christian piety and practice. Thus lay preachers' extempore prayers and sermons are often said to be the product of divine inspiration. Furthermore, just as traditional worship placed an emphasis upon adherence to ritual forms, so the relationship between Christian conduct and divine providence has become an established theme of Methodist doctrine (Gunson 1978). Attempts to consolidate these ideas explain why self-effacement through formalized expression and conventions of conduct is now idealized not only as a means of showing the respect and deference embodied by chiefly manners, but as the expression of Christian humility. Indeed, many people expressed their attachment to Fijian tradition on moral grounds by saying that they found deference moving and beautiful, and in contrast to the unseemly preoccupation with the self, which they felt was characteristic of Western individualism.

The moral idealization of Fijian tradition, discussed in terms of cultural alterity, remains one of the hallmarks of Fijian neo-traditionalist discourse and has assumed a prominent place in nationalist rhetoric. However, the diverse ways in which *masi* was presented suggested that the articulation between respect for ancestral forms and ideals of Christian conduct was often very difficult to achieve and prone to hazard or misinterpretation. It was not enough, apparently, that *masi* was now made in such a way that layers of *yarabalavu* were worn over a demure, ankle-length sarong made from *masi* (called *masi vakairua,* literally 'Two sides joined together'), which were in turn worn over modern Christian clothes.[5] *Masi* still seemed to unleash a sense of 'doubleness', or cultural mismatch, which provoked outbursts of hilarity. For example, when women spread their legs wide to beat and pattern their *masi,* adopting ritualized postures in keeping with its intended use in the promotion of fertility, their self-conscious laughter indicated their embarrassment at contravening conventions of posture and deportment which had been introduced by the Tongan Wesleyan Church (Fig. 8.2).

Due to this sense of slippage or cultural mismatch the potential for ceremonial participants' intentions to be misconstrued – to suggest either too little, or too much – seems to have required additional strategies of framing, suppression, displacement or management. Attempts to regulate the interpretation of *masi*'s materiality had become implicated in an ongoing *moral* argument between chiefly factions. For if conversion had involved transformations in the political economy and social organization of the land (*vanua*) or chiefly confederation (*matanitu*), post-colonial revisionism was exerting a counterbalancing force. Thus when members of the Bauan faction prepared *masi* for a marriage ceremony, they prepared the cloth *beneath* the house of their chief, in the proximity of the main village *yavu* (literally 'ancestral foundation' or 'burial mound', see Fig. 8.3) thereby demonstrating their superior claim to, and mastery of, traditional ritual resources. However when other factions presented *masi,* the seam between

Responses to Revival of Chiefly Dress in Fiji

Figure 8.2 A posture adopted for stencilling in Natewa 1998. Photograph author's own

appropriate Christian conduct and traditional ritual activity was reworked through the way in which the making and presentation of *masi* was enacted. For example, when the offspring of another chief (who claimed affiliation to a yet more archaic chiefly hierarchy that had been deposed by the new chiefs – *masi vou*, literally 'new cloths'- from Bau) were formally presented to their maternal kin dressed in *masi* the ritual was restructured in such a way that their presentation formed part of a series of offerings – including Tongan barkcloth, drums of kerosene and European cloth – whose sequence indicated the place of cloth substitution in the *vakararama* (conversion literally the coming of light) and the transformation of the ritual polity over time. By contrast, when the Senator's brother commissioned several lengths of *yarabalavu*, he pointedly did *not* allow the children to wear it, and presented it tied up, with its optically charged designs obscured from view.

Finding some excuse or another – a light shower perhaps, or maybe the pressure of time – to sidestep performance of *masi* in ceremonial contexts had become a convention at the Christmas fund-raising events for building new churches. I became accustomed to being led round the back of the ceremonial ground to see tightly bound bundles of *masi* (the product of several weeks' hard work) with bottles of scented oil arranged along their side. The suppression of *masi*'s material qualities indicated the growing anxiety that its enactment might be wrongly interpreted as *vaketevoro* (heathenish, literally 'in the way of the devils') by

Figure 8.3 Preparing the clothing for a Natewan wedding. Photograph author's own 1997

younger members of the community influenced by Christian fundamentalism. If they had the means to do so, *their* views were sometimes conveyed by wearing of a cotton sarong printed with the emblem of a Christian charismatic convention at a ceremony, or by refusing to drink kava in ceremonial contexts, or by sidestepping the call to participate in *masi* production.

Some of the older women responded to this moralizing by drawing attention to the dual nature of social reality in Fiji to comic effect. Thus when Varitema received a formal libation for supervising the highly ritualized production of a length of *masi bolabola* for the head of the Methodist Church, she wore a Deputy Dog T-shirt (Fig. 8.4) as a way of framing the association between this cloth and Narewa's ancestral deity, Mai Nabare, who assumed the form of a dog. When the primary school children were invested with *masi* in order to receive their school certificates, women's clowning was used both to evoke as well as to historicize ancestral presence. As the children performed a dance (*meke*) on the school lawn, their dance was interrupted by a group of women impersonating priests (*bete*) or prophets (*daurairai*) in the throes of spirit possession. This intrusion drew attention to the multidimensional character of Fijian social reality to comic effect – for while the performers' impersonations of the oracles and seers were irreverent, the fiction of spirit possession also gave them licence to subvert Christian neo-traditionalist codes of conduct and decorum (see also Hereniko 1995).

Figure 8.4 Two examples of the way that T-shirts are used to provide a commentary upon the contemporary manufacture of archaic barkcloth clothing in Fiji

Domestic Ritual: Clothing Displays and Patterns of Causation

The tightly wrapped bundles of intricately patterned *masi* have an affinity to the regulation of *masi* patterns that I have described above: both are techniques of knowledge management. They are ways in which competing chiefly factions have attempted to regulate or control the mediatory power of *masi* in ritual contexts. As such they reinforce belief in the consequence of the appearance of ritual forms. As we have seen, such beliefs were central to the *masi* revival, and may account for the redeployment of chiefly ritual among ordinary Fijians. Yet the prevailing characteristic of performing such rites in contemporary Fiji was delay. Thus, apart from funerary rites, which *had* to be performed promptly, other ceremonial obligations were ducked and delayed for years – if not decades – since the protagonists were unwilling to be a drain on their immediate kin's limited resources. Elopement had therefore become not only commonplace, but also expected (Colchester 1999). Yet elopement and other ceremonial delays were always clouded by the fear that things might go wrong. When people faced tragedy or personal misfortune they turned to the rituals they had overlooked. Thus 'marriage ceremonies' were often mounted decades after the event as offerings of 'reparation' or 'restitution' to address problems infertility, or the persistent malady of kin.

While other forms of cloth wealth, such as mats were typically used in these ceremonies, ordinary women sometimes used *masi* to mount personal petitions on the walls of their houses. If *masi* was displayed in a house it was hung high up, 'out of respect' because it is *ka vakaturaga,* a 'chiefly thing', and was suspended along the length of the transverse roof beam, which roughly divides the house into spaces for eating and sleeping. In Natewa, many households had a row of tall, spindly *masi* saplings growing outside the house, around the sleeping quarters, waiting to be coppiced and beaten into strips of barkcloth. Thus, *masi* in different states – growing saplings and printed barkcloth – could be seen to wrap or encircled the sleeping quarters. The selection of artefacts and religious imagery in these displays indicated many women's belief in the consequence of ritual action and Christian conduct. Packets of womb hair (cut when the child is four years old at a hair-cutting ceremony), a bundle of twigs, umbilical cords, together with strips of *masi* taken from garlands provided evidence of the number of feasts and ceremonies that had been performed on behalf of kin, while certificates of participation at Sunday school, or bookkeeping courses, diplomas, team photographs, degrees and awards, provided evidence of Christian conduct.

More generally, however, ordinary women mounted *masi* displays in order to prepare their houses for visits from family members living in town. I was told that these displays served to *maroroya na i tovo vuvale* ('maintain the manners of the household ancestors'). Refurbishing these displays often took place before Christmas. This was the time when offspring returned from studying or working in town to perform the necessary ceremonies and to register their children in the *Book of Living Genealogies* so that they would be entitled to use clan gardening land in the future. Many children brought new photographs with them as gifts and, during their stay, their mothers presented them with *masi* in return. On these occasions both family photographs and *masi* were described as *ka vakananuni* ('remembrances' or more literally, 'things for thinking with'). The photographs were typically mounted and framed and are hung high up on the wall, tipped at a slight angle towards the floor for greater visibility. They were 'dressed' or garlanded with plastic flowers and shell necklaces.

Ancestral figures that sprout subordinate figures are a characteristic feature of much Polynesian religious art. The anthropologist Roy Wagner has termed these kinds of images person-fractals, highlighting the way in which they portray self-similarity at different registers, and suggests that they represent genealogical models of personhood. The superimposition of photographs of kin on top of lengths of *masi* may be seen as an extension of this tradition that locates *masi* and photographs of kin within a world of natural causation by demonstrating the power of *masi* to bring new offspring into the world. Reproduction is also conveyed visually through reduplication. For example, a photograph of an old *masi* display, taken in 1912, indicates that the reproductive power of *masi* has long

Responses to Revival of Chiefly Dress in Fiji

been conveyed in terms of resemblance or self-similarity. Hocart's photograph of a paramount chief's house, taken in Vuna, on the island of Taveuni, shows a clock and three identical black and white family photographs, reprinted and framed as a continuous series – a pattern set against a backdrop of *masi* (Fig. 8.5). This photograph enables one to see that current displays of *masi* and photos are part of a much more extended *series* of displays, slowly unfolding, layer upon layer in space and time. It reveals the way in which the reproductive power of *masi* has been reinforced, or naturalized, through the repetition of a specific chain of association. Whether such conventions exert a conservative force on the formation of a 'Fijian Way' can be assessed through analysing the nature of the resemblance binding these displays together.

But there is more. It has already been shown that tapestry versions of Leonardo da Vinci's *Last Supper,* brought back by the Fijian UNAMSIL peacekeeping force that served in the Lebanon (1978: 81), have often featured on Fijian *masi* displays. The anthropologist Christina Toren has argued that the superimposition of tapestry images, which portray the prefiguration of Christ's sacrifice, along a length of *masi* establishes a series of resonant analogies, which suggest that the status quo was prefigured by the pre-Christian chiefly ritual polity (Toren 1999). The ideological power of organizing *masi* and the Last Supper into a commanding

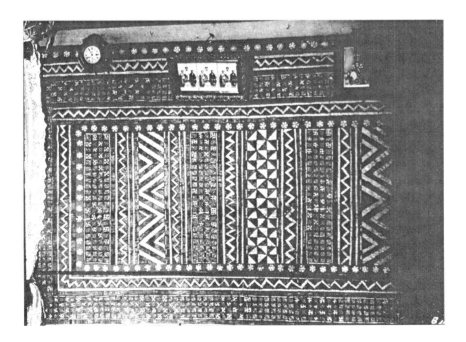

Figure 8.5 Making connections. The tui Vuna's House 1914. Photograph by A.M. Hocart. The Pitt Rivers Museum (Hocart, 996 Fiji neg 555771/2)

image, which confirms that the status quo conforms to a divine pattern need hardly be emphasized.

Anthropologists have not been accustomed to think of highly regulated areas of human activity, such as ritual or ritual imagery as being capable of suggesting a range of different possible outcomes, like a loose preparatory sketch. However *masi* displays I saw in the villages around the chiefly capital affirmed that *masi* had the capacity to suggest new realizations in different circumstances. In contemporary Natewa, the perception of objective relations between *masi,* photographs and other artefacts had started to be used in a humorous and ambiguous manner that undermined the power of convention to naturalize causal relations between *masi* and other images. For example, while square-faced clocks were displayed so that they 'matched' the section of barkcloth pattern behind them, their use as decoration (since few rural Natewans were prepared to waste batteries in them) worked like a pun: to frame the expression cultural *difference* to comic effect. The way that Fijians laughingly referred to 'black time' or 'Fijian time' indicating that cultural incompatibility had become a source of pride.

Masi displays were also a means of elaborating difference at the household level. Although certain objects and images were regularly displayed (such as family photographs, clocks, Christian maxims and imagery, calendars and pictures of political leaders) Christian images and texts and political images varied according to the denomination of the household. Their variety bore witness to sheer diversity of people's religious and political commitments. As well as images of the then prime minister, Colonel Sitiveni Rabuka, the Lauan president, Ratu Mara, or newer national icons such as Wesele Serevi, the leader of the Fijian rugby sevens team, or Lucky Dube, a reggae singer from South Africa, whose concert in Suva in 1996 was a much discussed event.

Religious and political images were supplemented with a range of apparently surprising objects which showed how the game of recognizing objective relations between *masi* and 'found objects' was being elaborated at a personal level. Thus displays featured audacious finds: an orange plastic beach bat in the shape of a grid; a turtle shell saved from a feast with a *Spider Man* sticker on it (kinship links are often said to be as intricate and fragile as cobwebs in Fiji); a photograph of a Fijian expatriate family, living in Sydney dressed identically in pinstriped suits.

Photographic displays also indicated how women and their children shared a common appreciation of the self-conscious elaboration of visual analogy. Most of the photographs of family members were taken in Fiji-Indian studios where, following the photographic conventions of the time, the subject was formally posed against a standardized painted or photographed backdrop. Many of these photos showed the family dressed in contemporary clothing posed against distinctively foreign backdrop of a park in spring. However I have before me a picture of a *masi* display which features a black and white photograph of a young Fijian

Responses to Revival of Chiefly Dress in Fiji

Figure 8.6 Using visual analogy subversively. A contemporary domestic display of archaic chiefly dress. Photograph author's own

man squatting, Indian-style, in front of a painted backdrop of the Taj Mahal (see Fig. 8.6). His mother has displayed the photograph so that the painted backdrop 'matches' the pattern of the *masi* behind it, while the boy's posture also evokes conventions of chiefly posture that prevailed in Fiji prior to the arrival of the Tongan *lotu*. It presents an image that says a great deal about the changing nature of associations featured in *masi* displays, which convey, in turn, the permutations of mediated expression in contemporary Fijian culture.

Conclusion

It is well known that the doctrine of prefiguration was both a guiding concept and a literary device which prompted the selection of events and sayings which make up the narratives of the Christian Gospels. By showing how the events and sayings of the New Testament were foreshadowed or anticipated in the Old Testament, the Gospel authors hoped to demonstrate that Christ's life had been planned from the beginning. The evocation of prefiguration through resonating images, or the re-enactment of biblical scenes was also a central facet of Renaissance piety and painting where it served in the attempt to reconcile the experience of radical cultural disjuncture between a revolution in the representation of social space-time and a pre-existing set of beliefs (Baxandall 1986). The arrangement of *masi* displays in Fiji shows how the elaboration of formal analogy or resemblance between the patterns on *masi* clothing and religious imagery has been used to assert that Fijian indigenous traditions are a fitting foundation for contemporary Christian practice and belief. Such attention to formal coherence shows the affinity between contemporary *masi* displays and its use by prophets and seers in the past, because it is a technique for projecting the past into the future. Yet even religiously powerful clothing and pattern is merely a function of the social relational matrix in which it is embedded, and has no intrinsic nature independent of a relational context. Beyond describing the social and political relations which contributed to the revival of masi and which inflect its contemporary use I have endeavoured to highlight the changing nature of the connections of analogy or resemblance which animate *masi* displays. Resemblance is always undertermined, which is why it opens even the most conventional artefacts up to new interpretations and new descriptions of the current state of things. Changes in the nature of resemblance found in *masi* displays indicate how the discovery of surprising formal correspondences to ancestral pattern imagery is now being used in a more self-conscious manner which undermines its claims to causality.

Acknowledgements

I am grateful to Susanne Küchler and Allen Abramson for their insightful supervision. I would also like to thank Daniel Miller, Christopher Pinney, Michael Rowlands and Chris Tilley for their constructive comments and encouragement. I am also grateful to Christina Toren, Nicholas Thomas, Marshall Sahlins Stephen Hooper and Fergus Clunie for their comments on earlier drafts of this paper. My fieldwork in Natewa was funded by the ESRC who have subsequently supported the *Clothing the Pacific* project. The Department of Ethnography at the British Museum helped by offering unlimited access to their collections.

Notes

1. Although I emphasize the significance of the revival of *yarabalavu* in this article it should be noted that many different styles of barkcloth were being manufactured in Natewa between 1995 and 1997. They included *Masi yarabalavu, masivakairua, na salativtiva*, masi kuvui, *masi vula, masi bolabola* and *kumi*. See Colchester 1999 for a fuller description.
2. The title, 'literally God of War', is of Bauan origin and indicates Natewa's historical attachment to a specific chiefly confederacy *matanitu*.

3. The popularity of this new term, *cakacakavakavuvale* ritual action in the manner of the household polity may be indicative of the political fragmentation of the *vanua*.
4. The power of these items of chiefly clothing also emerge from stories. According to one story of origin, the land of Natewa assumed its current shape as one of the ancestor's walked across it, dragging his train of *masi yarabalavu* behind him.
5. Images of doubleness abound in *masi* production. For example, the duality of chiefship is also conveyed by virtue of the fact that the bark from two saplings is beaten together to make a length of *yarabalavu*. The terms used to describe the beating of this bark indicate that the process is a form of sacrifice.

References

Baxandall, M. 1986 *Painting and Experience in Fifteenth Century Italy*. Oxford: Oxford University Press.
Becker, A. 1986 'Body Image in Fiji: the Self in the Body and in the Community'. PhD dissertation, University of Texas.
Bolton, L. 2003 *Unfolding the Moon: Enacting Women's Kastom in Vanuatu*. Honolulu: University of Hawaii Press.
Colchester, C. 1999 'Barkcloth, Reproduction and Endogamy in Natewa'. Unpublished PhD thesis, University of London.
France, P. 1969 *The Charter of the Land: Custom and Colonisation*. Melbourne
Gell, A. 1998 *Art and Agency*. Oxford: Clarendon Press.
Gunson, N. 1978 *Messengers of Grace: Evangelical Missionaries in the South Seas*. Melbourne: Oxford University Press.
Hereniko, Vilsoni 1995 *Woven Gods: Female Clowns and Power in Rotuma*. University of Hawaii Press.
Hocart, A.M. 1912 'A Native Fijian on the decline of his race'. *The Hibbert Journal*, pp. 80–99.
—— 1952. *The Northern States of Fiji*. Occasional Publication no. 11: Royal Anthropological Institute.
Keane, W. 1997. *Signs of Recognition: Hazards and Risks of Representation in an Indonesian Society*. University of California Press.
—— 1998 'Calvin in the Tropics'. In P. Spyer (ed.) *Border Fetishisms Material Objects in Unstable Places*. London: Routledge.
—— 2004 'The Hazards of New Clothes: What Signs Make Possible'. In G. Were and S. Küchler (eds) *The Art of Clothing: A Pacific Experience*. London: University College London Press.
Küchler, S. 1997 'Sacrificial economy and its objects: rethinking colonial collecting in Oceania'. *Journal of Material Culture*, 2(1): 39–60.

Nayacakalou, R. 1975 *Leadership in Fiji*. Melbourne: Oxford University Press.
Roth, Jane and Hooper. Steven (eds) 1990 *The Fiji Journals of Baron Anatole von Hügel*. Suva: Fifi Museum.
Sayes, S. 1982 'Cakaudrove Ideology and Reality in a Fijian Confederation'. PhD dissertation, Australian National University.
Scott-Troxler, G. 1971. *Fijian Masi*. Fiji: Suva Government Printer.
Thomas, N. 1994 *Colonialism's Culture: Anthropology, Travel and Government*. London: Polity Press.
Toren, C. 1988 'Making the Present, Revealing the Past: The Mutability of Continuity and Tradition as Process'. *Man* (new series), 23: 696–717.
—— 1999 *Mind, Materiality and History, Explorations in Fijian Historiography*. London: Routledge.
Waterhouse, J. 1866 *The King and the People of Fiji*. London: Wesleyan Conference Office.

–9–

Pattern, Efficacy and Enterprise: On the Fabrication of Connections in Melanesia

Graeme Were

Since the advent of European intervention in the Pacific, a huge and highly visible change in clothing and textiles has taken place there. The import of textiles, their rapid uptake and, in some cases, their radical alteration raises issues critical to our understanding of the role of key technologies in cultural change within a region. For pre-colonial Pacific societies were to a large extent based on fibre-based technologies, and an important series of studies has highlighted the continuing centrality of wrappings, clothing and textiles of all sorts to modes of thinking and being (Weiner 1989, Thomas 1995). Moreover, art theorists have invited us to consider clothing more seriously, to treat aspects such as cutting, stitching and sewing as artistic expressions of worldly concepts (Hollander 1988, Jones and Stallybrass 2000). Even so, only a limited amount of work has been carried out to investigate the relationship between imported textile forms and traditional fibre-based technologies in the Pacific.

One of the most overlooked aspects in Pacific colonial history is the story of calico[1] and clothing in Melanesia. We know from early encounters between Europeans and Pacific islanders that calico and clothing played as vital a role for mediating social relationships there as guns and scrap metal. However, whereas guns and metals transformed warfare and the production of local crafts respectively, calico and clothing carried potentially less harmful connotations. The sight of Melanesians dressed in a mismatch of striped calicoes or discarded Victorian clothing was often greeted as an innocent attempt to conform to missionary stipulations concerning the dressing of the body.

What makes the story of calico and clothing in Melanesia so especially interesting to study are the types of decorative designs they carried into the region. A wealth of historical records, museum collections and photographic evidence suggests that in fact some Melanesians selectively sought out printed garments of various types. If, as this observation implies, Melanesians were actually operating strategically in their take up of European dress,[2] we may challenge assumptions that

Melanesians passively adhered to the missionary stipulation of dressing the body. Crucially, by taking into account the relation of pattern systems to local modes of religiosity, it suggests that Melanesians may have invested these patterned fabrics with more important ideas than we are originally led to assume. The intention is not to trace the pattern of trade from calico manufacture to its consumption in the South Pacific, but rather to demonstrate the discrepancy between the intentions of Europeans and missionaries with regard to calico compared to its perception by Melanesians.

Europeans and the Distribution of Calico

Considerable quantities of calico and clothing were imported into the Pacific with the advent of regular trade voyages in the region, whaling expeditions and the establishment of the first Christian missions in the nineteenth century. As historical documents and literary texts show, explorers, traders and sailors travelling in the region during this era were acutely aware of the value calico and clothing represented to local populations eager to lay their hands on woven fabric. One of the best documented changes was the rapid uptake of imported ready-made calicoes by Polynesians which resulted in a major decline in traditional bark cloth techniques (see Koojiman 1972).

Calico is both highly durable and portable and would have been easily transported on board ships to the Pacific. European explorers, traders and whalers could thus exchange items of calico and clothing for local resources such as food and wood as well as other goods like traditional arts and crafts, turtle-shell and bêche-de-mer. For instance, records document in 1838 how the British whaler *Coronet* traded hoop iron, cotton and 'strips of red shirt' for arrows, spears and clubs in the Tabar–north New Ireland area (Gray 1999: 31). Though, while it is clear that for the main, calico was introduced to barter with the local people, several other motivations lay behind the European introduction of calico in the South Pacific.

In *Typee* (1993) [1846] – Herman Melville's classic account of a whaling expedition to the South Pacific – Melville documents the widespread use of calico as a tool in which to engage local people in social relations, and particularly for soliciting women. Melville draws on his own experiences of life on board a ship destined for the Marquesas Islands in the nineteenth century to portray the adventures of a young man whose life under a ruthless captain forces him to jump ship and roam the dark and perilous interior of these islands. His documented use of calico reveals European knowledge of the local responses to calico, bringing to light its role as mediator between Europeans and Pacific people. On jumping ship at the Marquesas Islands, Melville illustrates the motivating qualities of calico by

The Fabrication of Connections in Melanesia

describing how he fears the captain would offer a handsome reward of 'yard upon yard of gaily printed calico' for his arrest (1993: 32). Melville makes numerous references to the necessity to carry calico for barter with local people; one of the main characters carrying with him a package containing 'a razor with its case, a supply of needles and thread, a pound or two of tobacco and a few yards of bright-coloured calico' as security against attack (1993: 125).

Another American writer, Jack London, sailed in the merchant navy around the South Pacific at the turn of the century, and like Melville, he was inspired by the things he saw and the stories he heard. His acute observations led him to write about the darker sides of calico and its conscious use by Europeans in the South Pacific. In many of his short stories, he describes how unscrupulous plantation managers used calico to entice and often trick Melanesians to work on plantations in Queensland, Australia (see London 2001 [1911]). London's literary exposition on the shadowy use of calico is also reported by a Samoan missionary in the Tokelau Islands, who wrote a letter to Reverend Henry Gee of the London Missionary Society describing how a blackbirding ship took away many able-bodied men from the island of Atafu in the 1860s.

> Sir, all the people of this land are carried off. They have taken the chief Oli, who was in Samoa, and 34 other men.... Such, Sir, had been the cruelty of the ship to the people of this land. The good work which had begun on this island is now destroyed. Had we known the character of this vessel, no-one would have gone aboard. We are startled that such a thing should be done to these people. Two men who were returned to the shore by the captain, told us that when the people reached the ship with their things for sale, one of the crew collected these things together. Then the captain said to the men, 'Go and look at the cloth for your purchases'. But this was the contrivance of the captain: he placed some things in the hold of the vessel – the best of the cloth, red cloth, and shirts, and trousers, and white and blue calico; and some things he kept on deck. Then the captain said to the men, 'look for the cloth on deck and that in the hold, and see which to choose'. Some of the people were looking at the cloth in the hold, then went below. The captain told them to go below, and all went down. Then one of the crew gave them wrappers and shirts, and trousers and hats to put on. So the men rejoiced that they had got some clothing to attend worship in. But some of the crew were hidden in the hold armed with cutlasses. They were hidden so that the people did not know they were there. ... Then the hatchway was immediately closed down upon them.[3]

This excerpt highlights the kind of risks Pacific Islanders were prepared to take in order to seize calico. In fact, calico and blackbirding almost go hand in hand, as Pacific Islanders tricked into working on overseas plantations often brought back lengths or strips of calico on return home, though this was little compensation for the hardships they had endured. Many photographs depicting plantation life in the Pacific portray groups of men wearing a wrap-around cloth like a sarong, known in New Guinea as a *laplap,* handed out as standard attire by the plantation management.

Missionaries and Calico

Missionaries may not have been the first Europeans consciously to introduce calico to Pacific Islanders but they certainly benefited from European knowledge of its motivating value due to the networks of trade relations already existing in the region. In the Bismarck Archipelago, Gray (1999) documents how European whalers and traders first set up relations with islanders before mission stations were established. The missionaries profited from the influence the traders wielded in the area and exploited these contacts to promote their Christian teachings.

Yet the motivations that lay behind the missionaries' conscious decision to carry calico and clothing into the Pacific differed from those of other Europeans. Indeed, it needs to be remembered that in Melanesia in the nineteenth century, encounters were not always amicable and trading was often only chanced by anchoring close enough to the coast for locals to paddle out by canoe to exchange food and goods (Thomas 2000). Many Europeans dreaded setting foot on the beaches of Melanesia fearing attack. Prolonged residence at missionary outposts was precarious, and missionaries often suffered hostility, intimidation and violent attacks from local people. Since calico and clothing provoked so much reaction in the region, missionaries carried them as acceptable gifts along with knives and axes in a bid to gain rapport with local people and to pacify the region. They were no doubt aware of the violent and bloody encounters experienced by fellow missionaries attempting to set up base there.

Missionaries used calico as payment to trade for lives of captured headhunting victims or dissuade warfare between rival groups. In *Whale Tooth,* a short story written by Jack London (2001), he writes:

> The frizzle-headed man-eaters were loath to leave their fleshpots so long as the harvest of human carcases was plentiful. Sometimes, when the harvest was too plentiful, they imposed on the missionaries by letting the word slip out that on such a day there would be a killing and a barbecue. Promptly the missionaries would buy the lives of the victims with stick tobacco, fathoms of calico, and quarts of trade beads. (London 2001: 20)

Although excessively exoticized, this text underlines how Europeans adventuring to the South Pacific were generally aware of calico's attraction and thus carried it as a form of contingency. Moreover, it stresses how calico was utilized by both missionaries and Melanesians for their own strategic purposes.

The seizure of clothing and calico by Melanesians calmed the nerves of many missionaries, and presented them with proof that 'the grace of God can and does

The Fabrication of Connections in Melanesia

change the mould of a native's thought' (Mann, 15 August 1920). For missionaries, the clothing of the body was quintessential to the salvation of the soul and an ultimate sign of conversion to the Christian faith. The pretext existed that God was closer to those clean and clothed, so in assuming that the adoption of clothing was indicative of the act of conversion, missionaries received Pacific Islanders' willingness to adopt clothing as an outward sign of religious conversion. We can see therefore, why, on sighting clothed New Irelanders, the Methodist missionary George Brown recorded with real optimism: 'I was glad to see Le Bera (the chief) clothed in a shirt and waistcloth, and his wives and daughters each wearing a handkerchief or small piece of cloth' (1908: 135–6).

Christian missions became the new ritual spaces and church architecture was often covered in traditional pattern systems, reinforcing the link between pattern and religiosity (Fig. 9.1). Missionaries stipulated that local converts should appear for worship clothed, as naked people were deemed unfit for prayer and offended European sensibilities. There can be little doubt that missionaries thus saw folded calico as a material that could easily be wrapped, stitched or embroidered and transformed into an item of clothing to partially cover bodily extremities. Ready-made clothing imported into the Pacific, such items as calico skirts, shirts and so

Figure 9.1 'Church and people at Fagani, San Christobal', Beattie Collection (no 258), The British Museum (OC/A14/258). Courtesy of the Trustees of the British Museum

forth, needed simply to be worn as a covering to the body and provided a more rapid solution to Christian preoccupations with clothing the body.

Converts to the Christian faith would undoubtedly have been provided with calico or clothing quicker than non-believers so as to allow them to attend services held at the local mission and bolster numbers. Eager to impress officials back home, missionaries photographed local congregations sporting their 'Sunday best', displaying a modest range of skirts, shirts, trousers and *laplaps,* with some people even wearing hats, waistcoats or pieces of cloth draped around the shoulders. Much of the clothing they wore exhibited stripes, floral motifs and other decorative designs, yet to presume that these people were simply dressing so as to appear like Europeans would be a misleading assertion to put forward.

Not all Europeans received images of Melanesians dressed in Victorian clothing so fondly. For anthropologists and collectors, calico, clothing and their associated designs encapsulated the corrupting influences of European intervention in the Pacific so were systematically ignored. The Scandinavian anthropologist Hjalmar Stolpe – researching ornamentation on North America and Polynesian art – critiqued such hybrid works as 'inauthentic', choosing instead to focus on pattern systems that remained impervious to Western presence (Stolpe 1891). Patterns on traditional artefacts were believed to be analogues for mental ability, and a series of works (most notably Haddon 1894, 1895) sought to impose an evolutionary model on decorative art whereby abstract, non-figurative art was regarded as inferior to a Western tradition of figuration. In the light of such thinking, it is hardly surprising to find that ethnographic collectors were primarily concerned with acquiring artefacts produced with traditional materials, pigments and patterns and used in ritual contexts rather than hybrid entities that evinced signs of Western intervention.[4] But by treating introduced technologies such as strips of calico and discarded Victorian clothing as artificial and uninteresting, we run the risk of losing sight of their resemblance to local technologies that already existed in the Pacific.

The Transformation of Calico

The responses and reactions provoked by the introduction of calico and clothing suggest that Pacific Islanders had alternative perceptions that lay in the surface of the woven fabric. In Melanesia, it is important to remember that the patterned exterior of an object may not simply be construed as mere decoration but rather becomes a surface for enhancing the ritual effectiveness of an object. This efficacy associated with pattern is visible in the way patterned surfaces articulate notions of personhood, act as abstract devices through which to visualize genealogies, or allude to the power of ancestral presence bound up with the ritual display of the object. In the Solomon Islands, for example, patterns of shiny mother-of-pearl inlay embedded in carved artefacts are offset by the smoke-darkened wood, acting as attention-drawing devices which are linked to ideas of spiritual power (Waite 1987). Meanwhile, the intricately carved shell valuable, *kapkap,* manufactured across the Bismarck Archipelago, exhibits a dazzling circular arrangement of geometric patterns. In New Ireland, these *kapkap* patterns become material ways in which to conceive of genealogies that interlink clans from the region through a complex network of social relations while at the same time creating social distance (Were 2003). In the Trobriand Islands, the decoration of *kula* canoe-board prows with geometric patterns increases the potential success of *kula* expeditions through the efficacy attached to the mythical creatures to which the patterns relate (Campbell 2002); while across the Pacific, the patterns displayed on body tattoos make known social and political affiliations and histories (Thomas 1995).

Melville (1993) must have noticed the effects of calico and clothing (particularly those with bright colours and patterns) in Polynesia during his travels aboard a whaling ship in the mid-nineteenth century, as he pays particular detail to this in his work:

> Some of the natives present at the Feast of Calabashes had displayed a few articles of European dress; disposed however, about their persons after their own peculiar fashion. Among these I perceived two pieces of cotton-cloth which poor Toby and myself had bestowed upon our youthful guides the afternoon we entered the valley. They were evidently reserved for gala days; and during those of the festival they rendered the young islanders who wore them very distinguished characters. The small number who were similarly adorned, and the great value they appeared to place upon the most common and most trivial articles, furnished ample evidence of the very restricted intercourse they held with vessels touching at the island. A few cotton handkerchiefs, of a gay pattern, tied about the neck, and suffered to fall over the shoulder; strips of fanciful calico, swathed about the loins, were nearly all I saw. (Melville 1993: 189)

Similarly, in an account of the New Georgians of the Solomon Islands, Somerville (1897: 362) also notes a preference for bright colours and patterns. In referencing the use of trade calico in the design of the 'men's wrapper', he states that it should be of a single colour, preferably blue. He adds: 'Patterns or stripes of bright colours are invariably spoken of as "women's calico". Those who can afford it, bind additional strips of turkey red twill, with white and blue calico, over the hips in near ornamental bands, surmounted by a string of beads' (1897: 362). Although it is not clear whether missionaries or indigenous people imposed these classifications on clothing styles, we do know that patterns on shell ornaments and wooden carvings are inseparable from an understanding of local religious thinking as well as forms of identity. For instance, geometric shapes and patterns are named after creatures such as the frigate bird, bonito fish and sharks, and are deemed to carry with them regenerative forces as they emanate from the sea (Waite 1987). The question remains to be asked what exactly was the motivation behind the selective uptake of calico, and whether calico, as a new resource, presented New Georgians with a chance to bring about some kind of transformation to align themselves with the Europeans who brought with them ships, weapons as well as other material goods.

Other material qualities such as colour and texture were significant factors in the uptake of calico in many parts of Melanesia.[5] Those calicoes dyed in particular colours, such as red, mobilized local people to harness it for innovative uses in ceremonial contexts. Beasley (1936) describes how red calico was used as a composite part of red feather money in the Santa Cruz Islands, almost certainly because of symbolic associations attached to the colour as well as the ease with which it could be used. Meanwhile in the Polynesian outlier of Tikopia, Florence Coombe (1911) writes how local people hoped for calico, knives and hatchets when the opportunity arose to trade with Europeans. Three decades later, calico still maintained its importance in the islands: Firth (1947) documents how calico became easily integrated into local exchange systems in Tikopia, most likely because of its textural affinity to bark cloth. Calicoes were initially hard to acquire and, according to Firth, this inflated their prices, with dyed calicoes fetching the highest rates of exchange.

In fact, the manner in which Melanesians appropriated calico leads us to question the missionary understanding that the fervent seizure of calico was akin to dressing the body. We know this because, from the outset, calico was seized by Melanesians and acted upon in a range of innovative ways. Calico was not simply worn around the waist as a *laplap* or tied around the neck like an apron, but in many instances Melanesians radically transformed the calico sheets by tearing them into strips. Calico was even stored in houses, hidden away from sight, only to be revealed for ceremonial exchange as though its surface harnessed ancestral power.

In the Solomon Islands, for example, historical documents suggest that calico and clothing were adopted in places located within close proximity to mission outposts. Florence Coombe states that on the island of Malaita (where missionary influence was weak), women were rarely dressed in European clothes; while in South Malaita where the mission was strong, the men covered themselves in 'clean loin cloths' while the women wore 'gay petticoats' (Coombe 1911: 290). Even where missions did exist though, it did not guarantee that traditional dress was abandoned altogether. For example, in Bugotu on the island of Santa Ysabel, women dressed in a combination of both European and traditional clothing, 'with brilliant calico petticoats over thick grass girdles, which gave a very conical, almost Tudor-hoop effect!' (Coombe 1911: 344).

Ethnographic records also describe how local people appropriated calico and transformed its surface into a range of innovative forms. In New Ireland, for example, Duffield (1886: 116) observed how, 'The women took readily to clothing, but much preferred to make ribbons of calico petticoats to adorn their heads than to cover their bodies.' In some cases, its mere presence was enough to signal status and prestige within religious polities. Somerville, on commenting on local trade in New Georgia (Solomon Islands), mentions the fact that local islanders: 'seem to make no use of their wealth however; the mere fact of possession is sufficient, and *kalo* (whale's teeth), shell rings, calico, clothes – any article of European clothing is a great prize – are simply stored up, and scarcely worn or used at all'. Indeed, Somerville references the use of calico in bride-price payments in New Georgia, and shows that not only Europeans, but Pacific Islanders also saw the exchange value within local social networks (1897: 394).

The manner in which calico was appropriated, its transformation by shredding or it simply being hoarded demonstrates clearly how Melanesians revisualized its surface in a diversity of novel ways. These responses could only come about with the advent of Europeans and the new ideas and material resources they brought with them, suggesting therefore that Melanesians perceived something far more profound in the surface of the woven fabric.

Fabricated Connections

Explorers' journals clearly suggest that calico and clothing were greatly sought after and that patterned cloth was rated more highly than plain cotton cloth in many places in the Pacific. This observation becomes apparent when we take into consideration the notes of explorers in Melanesia during the end of the nineteenth century. One of these, the ethnobotanist H.B. Guppy (1887), took the time to remark on the appropriation of patterned calicoes by Solomon Islanders:

> Caution is required in studying modes of ornamentation of these islanders. The remark made by the Rev. Mr. Lawes, in reference to the women of the Motu tribe in New Guinea, that they are glad to get new tattooing patterns from the printed calicoes, is equally applicable to some of the Solomon Island natives. (1887: 139)

Melanesians' preference for patterned cloth was also acknowledged by Reverend Lawes (1879: 370), who notes that for the Motu, Koitapu and Koiari people of New Guinea: 'They were glad to get new patterns from some of our printed calicoes and other English designs. They attach great importance to the tattooing as a means of enhancing beauty'. This excerpt suggests that the English patterns carried on the surface of calico enhanced traditional pattern systems in New Guinea. In fact, tattooing designs among the south-eastern coastal people of New Guinea articulate social and ritual polities, suggesting therefore that the incorporation of various English designs could have offered a novel resource from which to express new modes of being and thinking with the advent of Europeans in the region.

Colonial and missionary photographs add weight to this argument and suggest that Melanesian people utilized calico and clothing for more strategic purposes rather than simply as a form of 'colonial mimicry' (Bhabha 1994). In the collection of historical photographs at the British Museum taken in Melanesia at the turn of the century, local people are captured wearing an array of calicoes and clothing in various fashions. What is significant is that many items are worn in local style as though they are replacing traditional bark cloth wraps or body ornaments. Stripes, checks and geometric shapes and patterns on calico and clothing feature predominantly giving no clue as to the origins of the cloth manufacture but they do give vital indications of local aesthetic preferences.

A number of photographs from the British Museum collection suggest that patterns carried on European cloth were seized upon and used for innovative purposes as they resembled existing traditional pattern systems. There are three particularly striking images that I want to describe here. In the first of these photographs (Fig. 9.2), the image portrays a Malaitan (Solomon Islands) labourer

Figure 9.2 'Malaitan native "a labour man" in Fiji'. The British Museum (OC/B36/15). Courtesy of the Trustees of the British Museum

The Fabrication of Connections in Melanesia

posted in Fiji adorned with traditional body ornaments. What is remarkable about this image is the beaded belt worn around the man's waist. One is left wondering whether the criss-cross pattern is an indigenous design or whether it is supposed to resemble the British Union flag. We can be virtually certain that the man would have seen a British flag either on a ship or government outpost, but it is entirely possible that the motivation behind its incorporation in the beaded belt was due to its close association to existing traditional designs.[6]

The second photograph is similar to the previous one for a number of reasons. In terms of subject matter, it depicts a group of Malaitan (Solomon Islands) labourers posted on a plantation in Fiji (Fig. 9.3). Three men pose together in front of a house wearing traditional Malaitan armlets as well as cloth *laplaps*. As in the previous photograph, the interesting thing about this image is the resemblance of the *laplap* patterns to the patterns on the indigenous body ornaments. We should recall that patterns on Solomon Islands body ornaments are a material means by which people communicate group identity: the patterns on armlets, leg ornaments and so forth articulate regional identities and thus project notions of

Figure 9.3 Solomon Islands men wearing patterned cloth, The British Museum (OC/B36/11). Courtesy of the Trustees of the British Museum

Figure 9.4 'British New Guinea bride and bride groom', S E Hill 1897, The British Museum (OC/B28/18). Courtesy of the Trustees of the British Museum

personhood. We could therefore hypothesize that in fact the lozenge shape designs on the *laplaps,* like the use of the British Union flag, have been appropriated as a material resource to articulate novel ways of being and thinking with the dawning of plantation life.

The final image (Fig. 9.4) is a portrait of a young man and woman from British New Guinea. Unfortunately, the exact provenance remains unknown, but other photographs in the series were taken in the Massim region of Papua New Guinea, so it would be reasonable to assume that this photograph also depicts the people of the region. The young woman only wears a grass skirt – typically in red and white for the Massim (though we can only infer this from the black and white photograph) – while the man stands with face paint and a headdress. Armlets with leaves suspended from them adorn his upper arms, and he wears a European belt with metal buckle, suggesting he may be a village police constable (appointed by the colonial administration). Interestingly, tucked inside his belt and appearing to hang on his waist suspends a piece of check cloth which appears to be white with several contrasting darker shades. In his right hand he holds a carved wooden object, possibly a decorated club or weapon of some kind, with curvilinear designs incised into the upper section of the 'blade'. As Haddon (1894) documents in his catalogue of decorative art from British New Guinea, Massim artefacts such as wooden clubs, lime spatulas and canoe board prows are incised with curvilinear patterns, many featuring white lines while others are coloured with red, black and white pigmentation. If indeed this photograph proves to be of a Massim couple, it would be reasonable to hypothesize that the check patterns are reminiscent of the traditional patterns found in Massim material culture.

The common thread linking these three images is the way by which patterned surfaces act as devices for making connections. This process of connecting things contrasts markedly with the way we in the West categorize things, a process that usually involves drawing differences between things (see Stafford 1999 for a lengthy discussion). These insights should urge us to reconsider the role of decorative art in the Pacific by thinking instead about what pattern makes possible. Interestingly, a similar history exists at the interface of European and native North American social relations in the eighteenth and nineteenth centuries; there, ready-patterned calico and clothing also became powerful media through which to convey the influence of Christianity and the shaping of the mind. As Ruth Phillips notes in the case of floral imagery in the native American Northwest: 'Floral images were incised on trade silver and painted on ceramics, but the most common carriers of these images were undoubtedly textiles. The pleasure that Aboriginal people took in European textiles and their preference for calicoes (many of which bore small floral designs) are well documented in European diaries, letters, and travel literature' (1998: 171). The native North American appropriation of European pattern systems reads in a similar fashion to the Pacific experience.

Conclusion

The manner in which patterned calico was selectively utilized in Melanesia leads me to suggest that the strategies of appropriating cloth and clothing were used as a kind of technology towards a new way of being in the world. What the wearing of garments meant to Melanesians in the late nineteenth century is not easy to gauge, but we can be certain that these meanings differed somewhat from those inferred by Europeans. As Nicholas Thomas points out in his discussion of the Polynesian poncho, Christian superiority (with access to tangible resources such as ships and guns) impressed on Pacific Islanders such that the fully dressed body was perceived as an empowered body (Thomas 1999). In the context of Melanesia, we may infer that the power of that body was facilitated by patterns. Therefore, if Pacific Islanders were transforming themselves in response to European intervention, they were also instigating a shift that was internal to Melanesian culture and material culture. Thus we can hypothesize that the patterns on European cloth and clothing offered a new resource through which novel ways of being could be displayed. This would therefore explain why many of these patterned garments were worn as 'Sunday best', reserved for special use when attending services at the mission, which acted as the new space for the ritual display of patterned artefacts.

To bring this paper to a close, I believe that the study of the calico thus offers us new insights into Pacific histories with the innovations and inspirations it brought as an agent of translation. We can see how the abductive qualities that Alfred Gell (1998) attaches to patterned surfaces offered Melanesians the opportunity to make connections to existing pattern systems and the ideas carried with them, presenting Melanesians with novel ways of being and thinking in the light of change. In doing so, it thereby allows us to reconsider the materiality of the woven fabric and the thoughts associated with it as a *process* involved in promoting new modes of religiosity rather than simply the *product* or *outcome* of religious conversion.

Acknowledgements

This research was funded by the Pasold Research Fund as well as the ESRC *Clothing the Pacific* project. My thanks go to Ben Burt, Elizabeth Cory-Pearce, Sean Kingston and Lucy Norris for commenting on earlier drafts of this paper and to Christian Kaufmann and the staff of the Museum der Kulturen in Basel, the Pitt Rivers Museum in Oxford, the Cambridge Museum of Archaeology and Anthropology and Jill Hasell in the British Museum for their kind assistance.

Notes

1. In this paper, calico is used as a general term to describe cotton cloth. Calico is a type of cotton cloth that was originally produced in Calicut, a port on the west coast of India, where textiles were collected for shipment by the East India Company.
2. See Thomas (1991) for this argument discussed more generally.
3. This excerpt from the missionary diary is sourced from the internet site: http://www.janeresture.com/

4. Christian Kaufmann informed me that the Museum Der Kulturen in Basel, Switzerland still has an active policy not to collect ethnographic artefacts evincing signs of Western influence. See also O'Hanlon (1993) for a lengthy discussion on authenticity in the practice of museum collection and display with reference to the Papua New Guinea Highlands.
5. Bolton (in press) adds that in Vanuatu, the Bislama term for colour (*kala*) is often used to refer to pattern; when women describe island dresses, colour actually equates to the pattern of the dress.
6. Two of these beaded belts exist in the collections of the British Museum (+5541, 1931.7–22.81). One belt is coloured in red, white and blue as the British Union flag although there are too many red portions. The other employs black, white and red beads with an interesting innovation: a black 'George' cross with black diagonals, all outlined in white. The remaining spaces are filled in with red beads.

References

Beasley, H.G. 1936 'Notes on Red Feather Money from Santa Cruz Group New Hebrides'. *Journal of the Anthropological Institute of Great Britain and Ireland*, 66: 379–91.

Bhahba, H.K. 1994 *The Location of Culture*. New York: Routledge.

Bolton, L. (in press) 'Dressing for Transition: Weddings, Clothing and Change in Vanuatu'. In Susanne Küchler and Graeme Were (eds) *The Art of Clothing: A Pacific Experience*. London: UCL Press.

Brown, George 1908 *George Brown, D.D.: Pioneer-Missionary and Explorer. An Autobiography*. London: Hodder & Stoughton.

Campbell, Shirley 2002 *The Art of Kula*. Oxford: Berg.

Coombe, Florence 1911 *Islands of Enchantment*. London: Macmillan.

Duffield, A.J. 1886 'On the Natives of New Ireland'. *Journal of the Anthropological Institute of Great Britain and Ireland*, 15: 114–21.

Firth, Raymond 1947 'Bark cloth in Tikopia, Solomon Islands'. *Man*, 47: 69–71.

Gell, Alfred 1998 *Art and Agency: an Anthropological Theory*. Oxford: Clarendon Press.

Gray, Alastair C. 1999 'Trading Contacts in the Bismarck Archipelago during the Whaling Era, 1799 – 1884. *The Journal of Pacific History*, 34(1): 23–44.

Guppy, H.B. 1887. *The Solomon Islands and their Natives*. London: Sonnenschein, Lowrey and Co.

Haddon, A.C. 1894 *The Decorative Art of British New Guinea: a Study in Papuan Ethnography*. Dublin: Academy House.

—— 1895 *Evolution in Art: As Illustrated by the Life-Histories of Designs*. London: Walter Scott Ltd.

Hollander, A. 1988 *Seeing through Clothes*. New York: Penguin Books.
Jones, A.R. and Stallybrass, P. 2000 *Renaissance Clothing and the Materials of Memory*. Cambridge: Cambridge University Press.
Koojiman, S. 1972 *Tapa in Polynesia*. Honolulu, Hawaii: Bishop Museum Press.
Lawes, W.G. 1879 'Ethnological notes on the Motu, Koitapu and Koiari tribes of New Guinea'. *Journal of the Anthropological Institute of Great Britain and Ireland*, 8: 369–77.
London, Jack 2001 [1911] *South Sea Tales*. London: Dover Publications.
Mann, Rev. I.J. 1919–41 *Diaries and Papers*. Canberra: Pacific Manuscripts Bureau PMB 630.
Melville, Herman 1993 [1846] *Typee*. London & Vermont: Everyman (reprinted 1998).
O'Hanlon, Michael. 1993 *Paradise*. London: British Museum Press.
Phillips, Ruth B. 1998 *Trading Identities: the Souvenir in Native North American Art from the Northeast, 1700 – 1900*. Seattle & London: University of Washington Press.
Somerville, Boyle T. 1897 'Ethnographic Notes in New Georgia, Solomon Islands'. *Journal of the Anthropological Institute of Great Britain and Ireland*, 26: 357–412.
Stafford, B.M. 1999 *Visual Analogy: Consciousness As the Art of Collecting*. Cambridge, MA: The MIT Press.
Stolpe, Hjalmar 1891 [1927] 'On Evolution in the Ornamental Art of Savage Peoples'. In H. Stolpe (ed.) *Collected Essays on Ornamental Art* (foreword by Henry Balfour). Stockholm: Aftonbladets Tryckeri.
Thomas, Nicholas 1991 *Entangled Objects: Exchange, Material Culture and Colonialism in the Pacific*. Cambridge, MA: Harvard University Press.
—— 1995 *Oceanic Art*. London: Thames & Hudson.
—— 1999 'The Case of the Misplaced Ponchos: Speculations Concerning the History of Cloth in Polynesia'. *Journal of Material Culture*, 4(1): 5–21.
—— 2000 'Epilogue'. In Michael O'Hanlon and Robert L. Welsch (eds) *Hunting the Gatherers: Ethnographic Collectors, Agents and Agency in Melanesia, 1870s – 1930s*. New York and Oxford: Berghahn Books.
Waite, D. 1987 *Artefacts from the Solomon Islands in the Julius L. Brenchley Collection*. London: British Museum Press.
Weiner, A.B. 1989 'Why Cloth: Wealth, Gender, and Power in Oceania'. In A.B. Weiner and J. Schneider (eds) *Cloth and Human Experience*. Washington DC: Smithsonian Institute Press.
Were, Graeme 2003 'Pattern, thought and the construction of knowledge: the question of the *kapkap* from New Ireland, Papua New Guinea'. Unpublished PhD dissertation, University of London.

–10–

Why are there Quilts in Polynesia?
Susanne Küchler

We generally assume that, like language, goods too tend, over time, to become 'merely symbolic' or else merely functional. The theory of the 'sliding scale' of value was famously coined by George Simmel in his *Philosophy of Money,* where he pointed out that 'a high degree of sensitivity distinguishes very precisely between the amount of satisfaction that a certain possession provides, through which it becomes comparable and exchangeable with other possessions and those *specific qualities* [my emphasis] beyond its ordinary effects which may make it just as valuable to us and in that respect completely irreplaceable' (Simmel 1978 [1907]: 123). The idea that goods are *bundles* of iconicity and indexicality, and are thus relatively *symbolically dense,* was developed by Annette Weiner (1992; 1994: 394–6) to help explain how certain objects are capable of resisting exchange while, simultaneously, their value is enhanced by the exchange of other things. Symbolic density, she argued, literally weighs objects down, restricting their potential or actual movement from one social or economic encounter to another, while other, often similar, objects lack such density and thus enter rapid circulation as they are sold or lost.

I am less interested here in debating the merits of Weiner's notion of inalienable possessions for a theory of value, than I am in the idea that objects can have relative 'density' or indexicality. For Weiner such density was only partially materially construed, as one and the same type of object could exude its lack or its abundance in equal measure. Density, rather, was seen to result from an *attribution* of what she called 'gender-based-power' (Weiner 1994: 297). In what one might describe as a typically 'Trobriand fashion', Weiner linked rapidly moving valuables, such as the famous Kula shells, to male-dominated wealth; and the Trobriand banana leaf bundles and skirts, which stay attached to a place, to women's wealth. As she extended this logic across the Pacific, symbolic density came to be equated with cloth wealth, as evidenced by an abundance of examples: Trobriand bundles, Samoan fine mats, Maori and Hawaiian cloaks, as well as eastern Polynesian quilts.

Arguably, important though it was in breaking down the gender stereotypes that have riddled the theories of exchange and value in anthropology, Weiner's blanket association of cloth with gender-based power skewed a simple question – why cloth? From Weiner's perspective, the authentication of political succession through cloth in the Pacific does not derive from any intrinsic qualities of the cloth itself, but results from its production and control as emblem of female power. Therefore, the materiality of cloth wealth matters very little in Weiner's writing, as the ascription of density to it appears to be a matter of interpretation and knowledge alone, quite independent from the actual feel of a thing – its weight, texture and the resemblances enticed by its visual surface.

A little observation allows us, I believe, to move forward in our understanding of the relation between cloth and indexicality in the Pacific. This observation is directed to the material translation that has occurred, in some parts of the Pacific, from cloth wealth made from plant fibre to stitched quilts produced from imported cotton fibre and second-hand clothing. For while in Samoa and many other parts of western Polynesia fine mats woven from pandanus have continued to be produced together with barkcloth made from the mulberry tree; across the eastern Polynesian islands of Hawaii, Tahiti and the Cook Islands quilting has largely replaced the production of fine mats; and in Tonga mats have come to be richly embellished with embroidery sewn with cotton. In eastern Polynesia, where sewing has replaced lattice-work, precise quantities of coloured cloth are cut and shredded into pieces before being stitched into intricate and vibrant patterns. The material resonance of such shredded and restitched cloth with death and ideas of renewal shows most clearly that the iconic and the indexical is not just *ascribed* to generic cloth things, but is an intrinsic part of the fibrous, fragile and transformative property of cloth made from introduced cotton which shrinks, tears and yet can be reassembled in ever differing ways. It is with such qualities in mind, which draw attention to what fibres are perceived to do, that we can approach the differential appropriation of new fibres in Polynesia. While this may be seen to be a matter of regional ethnography, this case study points to the complex resonance evoked by fibre, as ephemeral cover or as material capable of transformation, which reduce the form it is given to a mere functional thing or elevate it to a symbolically dense icon of sociality.

Sacred Cloth and Modes of Domesticity in Polynesia

It is a curious fact that, although fashion has become one of the features of Pacific modernity, in Polynesia it tends to be less preoccupied with dressing the body than with the visual effect achieved by choosing materials that call up other resemblances. Garlands may be worn that are made of plastic bags; bags, in turn, may be woven out of packaging tape; cotton dresses are printed in barkcloth designs. The use of recycled and 're-seen' materials may indicate the feeling of 'in-between-ness' many Pacific Islanders experience – moving frequently between island and urban

Why are there Quilts in Polynesia?

diaspora communities, living in either for long stretches of time (Raymond 2003: 201). Quilting, which reuses cut up cloth and clothing, has thus emerged, perhaps not surprisingly, as a major occupation of some communities that consider it to be the most apt form of a highly contemporary cloth wealth. Doing things with and to cloth and clothing is seen as a demonstration of respect for its *kaupapa,* its cultural foundation or value, and expresses a 'feeling' for clothing that demands a brief excursion into the ideas that are bound up with cloth-like things.

Literature provides ample descriptions of the sacred nature of cloth in Polynesia, where it functioned as an important vehicle for exchange between an exterior, wild and nocturnal world, which was the source of light and life, and an interior, domestic and diurnal world that depended upon the harnessing of light and life from the invisible and immaterial (Sahlins 1985; Valeri 1985; Bababdzan 1993; Tcherkézoff 2003: 57). Cloth-like fibre had always played a profound role in life-giving and life-affirming ceremonies associated with marriage and investiture (as well as death) – yet only after a brownish bark or darkened leaf of a pandanus palm had been arduously lightened and stained with a luminous yellow and reddish colouring (through such laborious techniques as washing, burying and painting). Shiny things, such as shells and feathers, had served to heighten luminosity. By exploiting the qualities of reflected light, cloth-like things were seen as effective mediators with the immaterial world.

White, patterned or coloured – and sometimes even odorous – cloth made from introduced cotton fibre offered new technical possibilities for harnessing, containing and controlling luminosity. By sheer coincidence the fabric which Europeans had brought to barter, together with glass beads and mirrors, was often of a vivid red or blue – they intended to attract people by the colour and dazzle of their wares. Then again, in one sense, this was not a coincidence, as both Europeans and Polynesians were interested in similar material qualities, if for different ends. From the Polynesian perspective, as the material embodiment of light, cloth made from new fibre required domestication, yet how that was done differed substantially across the Pacific. The literature distinguishes between two responses to the introduction of cloth, each involving different assumptions about the potential of luminosity: to reside in the containment of light, or in the refraction of light through cutting up and restitching cloth into a map that traces the passage from the immaterial to the material (Colchester 2003). Both responses imply distinct attitudes to social space and domesticity: the former stressing the formality of an interior social space contained within ephemeral, yet firm covers suitably provided for by the plant-based fibres of plaited pandanus mats; the latter, by contrast, amplifying permeable spatial boundaries suitably amplified by fragile and fractal fibre of introduced cotton.

In western Polynesia the manufacture and use of indigenous cloth made from plant-based fibre was not interrupted by missionary activity or by the arrival of new types of cloth. 'Cloth' was and is 'barkcloth' made from beaten strips of mulberry bark, or it consists of woven material made from dried strips of pandanus leaves or fibres, both materials that were grown close to the house. The bark was treated so as to appear white, and had patterns imposed through stencilling or rubbing; while the leaves of the pandanus palm were softened and whitened and subsumed into the weave of a mat, showing how lineages became interwoven. Such cloth of bark or leaves ('tapa' and fine mats) served to wrap people of rank and to complete a presentation of wealth by being placed over the top of a pile of other ceremonial gifts. Other forms of dress, such as leaf skirts, were never presented as gifts, and in Samoa people still make a clear-cut distinction between fine mats and imported fabrics or clothes (Tcherkézoff 2003: 53). The emphasis on the containment of light can also be seen in the fact that formal dress is still worn inside the house (which is largely regarded as a formal public place, not a place of intimacy): 'Once this formal dress worn inside was 'tapa'; today it is a length of spotless, vibrantly coloured printed cotton or, for very formal occasions (Church or political meetings), a dark fabric without any printed patterns' (Tcherkézoff 2003: 53). Like blood, which cannot be seen and yet connects as the principle of vitality, so the white or luminous cloth (in Samoa: *mea sina*) required wrapping for the imposition of a second layer of colour or pattern that gives evidence of the enclosure of the luminous inside.

Likewise, in Tonga the preference expressed by missionaries that people should don white clothing as a lesson in industriousness – because of the work required to keep the clothing clean – brought about an unsuspected response. As respectability had generally been associated with the wearing of mats or various forms of woven covering around the hips, the association of plain white clothing with the white barkcloth worn by commoners demanded that a woven fibre waist ornament, either in the form of a mat or a crocheted apron, be worn over white dress material (Addo 2003: 142). Regardless of religious or political convictions, a Tongan of the twenty-first century wears a short waist mat (*ta'ovala*) wrapped around the midriff and fastened with a braided cord at the waist; it is these wraps that have become synonymous with a notion of clothing that, in Tonga, alludes to wrapping and layering. Ping-Ann Addo (2003) describes the metaphoric potential of such 'covering', which covers or overlays one's other clothing, as extending to the practice of covering freshly slaughtered pig or taro in order to bake it in an earth oven: 'Certain *ta'ovala*', she reports, 'are indeed "baked"; for example, *ta'ovala lokeha* are customarily soaked in seawater and then buried in the ashes of burnt lime coral to give a yellowish tint to the light brown fibres, which are soft to the touch and acquire a smoky smell' (Addo 2003: 145). Other metaphorical allusions of the mat are to motion at a distance, as *vala* can be interpreted as a composite of *va*, translatable as 'distance apart', and *la*, translatable as 'a sail from a boat' – the older forms of which were closely woven pandanus mats.

Why are there Quilts in Polynesia?

In eastern Polynesia, on the other hand, the destruction of clothed wooden sculptures by members of the London Missionary Society halted the ritual use of bark cloth and fine mats forever. Here, in a move that was as swift as it was unremarkable, techniques of cutting and of sewing transformed the work that went into the patterning of layered funerary cloaks made of barkcloth, and into the covering of genealogical figures with fine mats and protruding feather holders that were intricately knotted into the shape of flowers. An efflorescence of pattern innovation using the ready-made mediums of dress-material and cut-up, used clothing has shaped the development of so called *tivaivai* across the Cook Islands, the Hawaiian Islands and the Society islands. Described mistakenly as 'quilts', *tivaivai* are 'sewings' (Fig. 10.1): for it was the imprinting of designs – through embroidery and appliqué techniques using pre-coloured and pre-patterned material – that led, through the folding and cutting of cloth, to quilt-like garments that were invested with new uses and ideas (Jones 1973; Arkana 1986; Hammond 1986; Pogglioli 1988; Rongokea 1992; Shaw 1996).

Collections from the Pacific made during the nineteenth century show a preoccupation with coloration in eastern Polynesian barkcloth that is distinctively absent from barkcloth collected from Fiji and Tonga during the same period. Cook Island barkcloth, in particular, came in large and rectangular sheets, some of which were bright yellow on both sides and measured 2920 × 1720 cm – the size of a

Figure 10.1 Tivaivai *taorei* (patchwork), Cook Islands, ca. 1965, Owner and maker Moparau Taruia, Avarua, Raroonga.

latter-day *tivaivai* (Buck 1944: 72). Other pieces were dark, matt brown on one surface, and had a shiny almost black appearance on the other surface. According to Buck (1944: 73) this form of decoration was achieved by soaking the cloth in the mud of the sago swamp, washing and drying it, and then rubbing the other side with a mixture of grated turmeric and grated coconut. Buck also refers to the use of flowers, as well as coconut cream, to perfume the cloth – a fact that will become significant when considering the later use of floral imagery in *tivaivai*. It appears that stitching not only enabled the realization of technical concerns with layering, but also with the capturing of olfaction.

Colour in eastern Polynesia was not so much thought of as a symbolic referent to the luminous caught beneath, but as a substance whose coloured state indicated the performative, fractal properties of light. Contained within a material thing, coloured light reflected its past passage as well as its potential escape; and thus became inseparably anchored to odour as something that is also known only as it escapes its container. One can perhaps explain, as David Howes (1988) has argued convincingly, the predilection for regarding colour as substance akin to a smell with the fact that in eastern Polynesia the dead were istanced from the living in elaborate ceremonies at the height of which sculptures wrapped in cloth were undressed (also Babadzan 1993).

Unlike the woven mats of western Polynesia, which trace the interweaving of lineages, the forever changing appearance of the cut up and the restitched *tivaivai* reveal no definite surface and thus no definite inside, displaying only a ceaseless passage of odour and light. It is in this passage that the mystery of animation is seen to lie. In eastern Polynesia genealogical knowledge reveals a strikingly similar passion for the tracing of an unceasing, almost vertical, passage from a male ancestor to a present person in either the male or female line, quite in contrast to the emphasis on the branching and interweaving of genealogical lines that predominates in western Polynesia.

The idea that light refracts as it is contained within things connects the fractal god figures of the Cook Islands with the fractal images of *tivaivai* today. At the top of such god figures was a head, carved as if folded in upon itself, that was replicated many times in miniature down the front of the shaft. Reflecting a notion of the 'fractal person' (see Wagner 1991), the figure instantiated an ancestor not 'as one body, but as many bodies into which his one body has transformed itself' (Gell 1998: 140). This classical Polynesian image, which consists of an amalgamation of replications of itself, thus recalls the idea of an individual person as a multiple, rather than singular and unique, entity – in the sense of being the precipitate of a multitude of genealogical relationships. Figures of this kind express a 'genealogical theory of mind' that accounts for agency in terms of an 'enchainment' of internal and external relations in ways that have been explored by Marilyn Strathern (1988), Alfred Gell (1998) and Roy Wagner (1991).

Why are there Quilts in Polynesia?

The images protruding from the skin of the carving seem even more significantly enmeshed with a relational notion of personhood when we become aware of the fact that, for consecration and ritual animation, it was covered in red feathers and wrapped in layers of sennit, cotton and string. While the barkcloth was covered in hand-drawn lines and stained with rich yellow and red natural dyes that also perfumed it, it was preferably striped cloth that was used for the wrapping of the god-staff in the early 1900s (Buck 1944: 45). This outermost cloth layer of the wrapping constituted the visible 'social skin' of the carving and, significantly, recalled in its hand-drawn lines the act of writing. For this outer layer was made as a likeness to the temple complex, known in the Cook Islands and eastern Polynesia as the *marae*. The *marae,* square stone structures filled with sacred words and odours, have to this day remained a microcosm of society, as all land-court records and title disputes have to refer to the genealogical relations laid down in the treatises of the *marae*.

However, the written testimonies of the *marae* were not conceived as the impermeable and permanent barriers their stone structures may suggest, but as passages to a more essential interior that reduplicates in image form what is written outside. We can make sense of the nature of this outer layer by turning to Alain Babadzan's (1993) description of the ritual of the *pa'iatua,* the ritual gathering and undressing of the gods, which the Cook Islands shared with the neighbouring Tahiti. This ritual consisted of three stages, mirroring the three cycles that composed the agricultural calendar, each stage being defined in relation to the manipulation of the mummy-like object:

1. the unwrapping of the object, effecting the death or departure of the gods;
2. the exchange of feathers and of cloth as the 'sharing' of the remains of the gods;
3. the reassemblage or 'renewal' of the object invoking the return of the gods and the period of abundance.

The *pa'iatua* ritual established a contractual relation with the multitude of the dead, whose bodies had become unified in the image of the god in a sacrificial exchange that used olfaction as powerful medium for the translation of an object into a concept (cf. Gell 1977).

With the banning of the *pa'iatua* ritual by the mission and the burning of the idols in the early nineteenth century, it was clothing that emulated new ways of marking passages along which ideas and things could flow as an outward manifestation of a successful economy of vitality. The new importance that was assigned to coloured cloth, which was to be severed, ripped apart and refigured is evidenced by the fact that cotton production and printing was well established in Rarotonga, the largest off the Cook Islands, in the 1860s (Gilson 1980: 35).

Ostensibly, the new use to which the genealogical markers were put across eastern Polynesia extended to the realm of domesticity, with its newly invested moral connotations and attendant practices and social relations. Revealingly, however, the new space afforded to this domesticity – the house – also became the site for the anchoring of genealogical powers distanced at death. So it is that, in the Cook Islands, graves are still erected in house-like structures at the entrance to the residence, and are filled with quilt-like garments that wrap the body at death. Surrounded by a floral garden, the grave should be visible from the doorway and veranda of the residence, the passage from inside to outside that is the true formal and public place in eastern Polynesia. It is here that guests are welcomed and fed, while the inside of the house is considered to be a place whose often chaotic state – with piles of worn clothing, sheets and dress material – reveals the intimate nature of this sphere. As domesticity is thus marked as a passage to be performed, rather than a means of containment, it continues to be allied to a sacrificial economy that today, in eastern Polynesia, revolves around 'sewing bees' (which organize regular massive displays and distributions of sewing).

There are three distinct types of quilt-like garments that are made to be presented at life-cycle events, such as significant birthdays, a boys' first haircut, weddings and funerals. The most valuable is a type of patchwork called *taorei* (handkerchief), in which several thousand tiny diamond or rectangular pieces are sewn together. Patchworks of this kind recall the painted *moenga* or sleeping mats that are still used today to work out the design. The pattern, always consisting of multiply replicated motifs (*pu*) connected by trails (*tarere*), is broken down into coloured pieces that are threaded in exact number and sequence onto a string. The string of coloured pieces is then sewn into one of eight triangular pieces of cloth before the entire sewing is assembled, and the overall pattern becomes apparent. Each triangular piece is to be sewn by a different woman, usually by sisters or, today, work colleagues. Individual triangles can be kept and used as a template for re-creating similar pieces when the sewing has been taken off its backing and begun to disintegrate. Women recall their friendships or familial ties by referring to these pieceworks. *Taorei* are personal possessions that, if they are not wrapped around the owner at death, are gifted as a token of succession – usually to a favourite grandchild.

The most popular sewing is called *ta taura* (piecework). It is an appliqué work, usually of floral motifs with leaves, with detailed embroidery that gives the design, composed of four separable layers, the impression of three dimensions. Pieces of appliqué are frequently resewn onto new backings and may even be altered in their composition over time. It is such *ta taura* that are the preferred gift at weddings and sons' hair-cutting ceremonies when they inspire recollections of the personal attributes of the maker. Some women are expert in embroidery, while others are renowned as cutters or as seamstresses.

Why are there Quilts in Polynesia?

The design of quilts called *manu* (bird) closely resembles a snowflake. In construction, the material is folded four times before cutting the design into it, taking care to create an even balance of positive and negative space. Tracings of cut-out designs are commonly drawn on tissue paper and carefully stored for future reference. Such *manu* are the quickest to make and, as they generally do not involve more than two colours, are in comparison to the other sewing less expensive to produce and less arduous to plan for. They are the preferred gift to those outside the lineage.

A complex, analogous relation thus exists between the visual and material composition of the quilt-like garments and the quality of women's relational and emotional attachments, which – from the moment they set up their own house upon marriage – oscillate sharply between intense experiences of loss and severance, and heightened awareness of connectedness (which are ironically usually associated with experiences of movement such as travel or work-induced relocation). It is not that each type of sewing would be made by women as a reflection upon these states, rather that the partibility (into two, four or eight parts) and the layered composition of the sewing, as a sequential whole, reflect on the composite and partible nature of social relations that coalesce around those that pass in and out of the house.

As the living house – full of people, noise and chatter – faces the house of the dead, density in being and thinking is fragile indeed. The easily shredded cloth material used for the quilting, the ripping sounds of which etch deeply into the silence of houses abandoned by all but the lonely quilter, recalls the careful stitched lines that trace the connections that may yet be hoped to mature. It is from the material evocation of luminous threads of connection patched into cloth that we may glimpse an answer to the question of the value that quilting assumed as it took over the production of mats in this decidedly poignant manner.

Fragile Connections

Cook Island *tivaivai* are perhaps the most complex of Polynesian quilts. There are several distinct, named types of quilts, each being composed of up to four layers made of pieces of cloth and cotton thread. Yet, it is not just the visual and conceptual complexity of the quilt that suggests the Cook Islands as a suitable starting point for a discussion of the Polynesian quilt. It is also the Cook Islands' geographical and political position on the edge of the old and the new worlds that allows one to observe sewing in action, paving new connections along which people and ideas move back and forth. In fact, we can observe Cook Island quilts as genealogical markers that have come to undercut the divisive properties of institutionalized hierarchy and nation building. It may not come as a surprise to learn that the Cook Island quilts are the most vividly coloured and luminous sewings of eastern Polynesia, and that they expand visually beyond their own so very permeable boundary.

Located within a small triangle of the Pacific defined by Fiji, Samoa and French Polynesia, Cook Islanders have as close ties to Tahiti as they do to New Zealand, Sydney or Los Angeles, where three quarters of its population live today. Like the foreign flowers that decorate Cook Island quilts, prosperity is found elsewhere, yet reaches the Cooks along the paths stitched into the quilts. Young men and women living far away will cherish the *tiavivai* given to them by their mothers, and recall the place to which they will make many future returns. Through the eyes of quilters, the Cooks are not an abandoned or a small place, but one that is teeming with memories of lives lived and paths to be taken (Herda 2002).

Geographically, the Cook Islands fall into two clusters: a northern group of seven coral atolls and a much larger southern group of eight islands, most of them upraised coral formations. Today, quilting is mostly found in these southern islands. Culturally, Cook Islanders belong to Polynesia; yet with the exception of Manihiki and Rakahanga, no two islands had the same cultural origin. Pukapukans in the far north originated from western Polynesia, centuries ago, while most of the peoples of the other islands came from various parts of eastern Polynesia. Tradition holds that the Maori-speaking population of the southern Cook Islands came from Tahiti and Samoa some time in the thirteenth century, but that the islands were already populated by immigrants from the Marquesas. Rarotonga, today the main administrative centre of the Cook Islands, is also the location of the mythical departure of canoes to New Zealand.

Trails of often distant connections appear to have been traced in the hand-drawn lines that are so clearly visible and distinctive on the surfaces of Cook Island barkcloth of the late nineteenth century. Such trails can be found again in the twentieth-century *tivaivai*, but now on the underside. When judging the quality of a piece of sewing, women flip over a corner to look at the stitching visible beneath, which should traverse the cloth in regular and neat lines. These lines bind the layers of cloth. Often multicoloured, because of the use of shaded thread, the stitches appear on the surface as rich embroidery that covers layers of cloth pieces cut and arranged to resemble floral arrangements in almost microscopic clarity (Fig. 10.2). The layering of cloth, once an important yet invisible aspect of all composite and mediatory objects in eastern Polynesia, emerges as the distinctive visual trait of the sewing in which colour and luminosity, once so powerfully linked to olfaction and verbal recollection, appears synonymous with the dazzlingly intricate geometric pattern.

Significantly, the outermost coloured and patterned layer of the stitched *tivaivai* is comprised of flowers. Flowers have been described by Ruth Phillips (1999) as the principal iconography of 'trading identities', and thus as icons of the most potent and yet also fragile connections that link those who have departed to those

Why are there Quilts in Polynesia?

Figure 10.2 Detail of tivaivai *tataura,* cut out with rich embroidery, 2003, owner and maker Moparau Taruia, Avarua, Rarotonga, made as a gift for her daughter at her wedding.

who stayed behind. Ruth Phillips refers to the salient trade that linked Victorian England and the Northern Iroquois tribes in the late 1900s, yet this perspective is also relevant to Pacific material. In eastern Polynesia, the flower was not just the common aesthetic icon of Chinese traders and the chiefly class of predominantly female *ariki*. Beneath the common symbol of humanity and compassion lies an infinitely more complex way of forging connections, however fragile.

When we look more closely at the floral representations of *tivaivai* stitchings, we notice three features that upon reflection make us wonder. Firstly, the flowers that are represented are not commonly found in the flora of eastern Polynesia: they are roses, margaritas or even water-lilies, not frangipani or hibiscus. The images of those foreign flowers reach the Cooks via pattern or cross-stitch books sent home by departed relatives or brought by incoming missionaries, or they occasionally arrive as cuttings, brought back as images from the many journeys abroad that people entertain as frequently as possible. Secondly, the flowers that are depicted on the *tivaivai* are magnified, highly naturalistic representations that tend to visualize that which is usually invisible to all but those involved in flowers to the extent of controlling fertilization. On the surface of the *tivaivai* are the capillaries and stamens of flowers from an unusual 'inside' perspective, which more frequently than not makes the identification of the flower quite difficult. The third feature is perhaps the least obvious, but also the most pertinent to the symbolic potency of flowers: the flowers represented are not standing in full bloom, but are instead cut, and are as carefully arranged as the flower cuttings that decorate the headbands without which no women will be seen in public places.

The importance of the headbands or the single flower tucked behind the ear lies not in their look, but in their odour, an odour that is known to increase with the wilting of the flower. The flowers that we see in the sewing are thus, above all, markers of the passage of time that are themselves inherently temporal, simultaneously marking endings and foreshadowing new beginnings. That flowers are thus both situational and relational is appreciated and exercised on a daily basis when deciding which flower to wear in the hair, as this anticipates encounters and potential new attachments even more than commenting on the existing biographical status of the wearer.

Given the precision with which neatly replicated flowers are arranged symmetrically across the planar surface of the sewing (Fig. 10.3), one cannot help being reminded of the carved staff god of the Cook Islands or the Rurutan fractal god that consisted of amalgamated replications of itself in a succession of budding protuberances (cf. Gell 1998: 138–9). In fact, it is an open secret that in the Cook Islands, at the very least, women's sewing took over where men's carving stopped. Like the staff-god, a sewing can be said to be a genealogical object par excellence: when women arrange the flowers on the surface prior to stitching them into the frame they may do so in not a too dissimilar manner to the men touching the protruding knobbly extensions of the carved *rakau whakapapa* of New Zealand Maori that aids the memory in the recitation of genealogy (Mead 1984: 218). Yet, just as the touching of the staff-god was restricted to the momentary ritual 'undressing' of the gods so brilliantly described by Babadzan (1993) for ancient Tahiti, so the sewings are taken out of their storage box merely once a year, to be shaken out, cleaned, inspected and, if need be, mended by being given a new backing that covers the sewing when it is folded up again and returned to the box for another year (like the dressing of the staff-god with a new layer of cloth). Poignantly, the time for the unfolding of the *tivaivai* falls around Christmas and is marked by an 'inspection' of the house that used to be organized by the local health official, but which today is usually carried out by women of the same sewing group.

Most, though by no means all, women have their own 'collections' of *tivaivai* that are kept hidden in a box. They consist, in part, of their own sewing, most if not all of which has already given away, but which is kept in care for their sons and daughters while they lead busy working lives abroad. Other items in the collections

Figure 10.3 Tivaivai *manu*, 2003, Rarotonga, Cook Islands, owner unknown, exhibited at a tivaivai exhibition at Titekaveka village.

are received at major gifting occasions, usually at sons' first haircuts, children's twenty first birthdays, weddings and funerals. Among the women who are known to be members of a sewing group, only one or two are generally responsible for the designing and cutting of the pattern, irrespective of what type of *tivaivai* is to be made. In return, they will either be recompensed by the group for their work or receive help with their own stitching.

Women who are known as the originators of patterns are considered *taunga*. This term is usually conferred on ritual specialists, and designates the special status afforded to these women, who also stand out as superior organizers of public functions (such as in acting as president of non-governmental organizations or as leader of a youth group). However, what these women tend to have in common are not their public personas, but something we would consider intensely personal. For, rather surprisingly, the designers of *tivaivai* tend to have been adopted across tribal boundaries. To take on a 'feeding child', as they are known, is a common practice in the Cook Islands, and is most commonly undertaken by a couple whose own children have already left the house. The 'feeding child' is taken into the house, severed from their roots in family and place, and designated to grow into the carrier of all knowledge bound up with its new house. Children who are raised in this manner can be observed sitting next to the elderly, plaiting pandanus headbands, or learning the skill of sewing when all the others are playing after school.

'Feeding children' are generally girls, though this appears to be a preference stretching back to the increased status of female chiefly leaders (*ariki*) encouraged by the church in the latter part of the nineteenth century. As the child is 'like a cutting', the knowledge that is conferred upon the feeding child about relations over land, labour and loyalty, in the form of floral patterns, is not individuated, but retains the plurality of the tribe as an aggregate of persons. The feeding child thus acts as the impersonation of an assemblage of relations, conflating the plurality of the persons comprised by the lineage. Like the staff-god, the notion of personhood conferred upon such a child consists of amalgamated replications of itself, and it is this internalized self-similarity that is carried forward into their creative ability to replicate relations externally into the cuttings and sewing of patterns.

Conclusion

'Proper' sewing of *tivaivai,* and of tablecloth and pillow-covers, is usually only started upon marriage, or sometimes even only when a woman's children are ready to leave the house. More often than not, the first sewing will be prompted by a death or a marriage in the spouse's family (for which a wife is expected to provide a *tivaivai* to be placed into the grave or to be given away as a gift to the new in-laws). Every *tivaivai* made to be given away is eliciting the expectation of a similar return when a woman's own children get married, or when there is a death in the woman's own close family.

The giving and receiving of *tivaivai* connects those who may be living apart for most of their lives, but they also demarcate moments of rupture, when relations are transformed forever. In more ways than one, each new *tivaivai* anticipates a future yet to be lived. We may think of these sewings as skin-like, self-replicating and layered cloth-things, whose successive opening and folding traces the passage of persons through the household. Marking points of departure and new beginnings, the sewing is a shroud that conjoins, as its wraps, those that are divided by fate and circumstance.

As over the years new backings are sewn onto old stitching, and damaged patchworks (*taorei*) are replaced by new replicas, a woman settles to sewing with thoughts in mind of those who may depart without ever returning. As she faces the house of the dead, just outside her doorway and often marked by the grave of her husband, the passage through the household that she has anticipated and called forth through her work takes on another meaning. No longer does it appear to lead from an inside to a world outside, but instead from a place of plurality and public responsibility synonymous with the inside of the house to a place of 'oneness' where the *many* social relations that are recalled by the *tivaivai* are transformed into *one* as the sewings are wrapped around the corpse inside the grave.

Yet what about clothing? How is the dressing of the body affected by such overwhelming expectations of cloth as a luminous thing that requires shredding and reworking? When walking around the few clothes stores that exist in the main town on the main island of Rarotonga, one notices a striking absence of Cook Island shoppers. It is not that dressing the body is not important; quite to the contrary, to wear a new dress is a must for every event, whether this a sports competition or one of the many competitive and public meetings that mark the yearly events calendar in the Cook Islands. Not to be able to sew would be a terrible handicap for any woman here, as new dresses are required all the time – while the old are shredded and turned into cloth. The predilection for cut cloth has made fashioning the body a domestic affair, not because of necessity, but out of principle.

It is time to return to the beginning of this essay, where I called on the notion of the density of cloth-things that so profoundly affects their value and the quality of their movement in exchange. Cook Island *tivaivai* show that in turning to the material resonance evoked by what cloth is perceived to do, the nature of this density and of the notion of value that resides within – left vague and almost mystical in Annette Weiner's account of treasured possessions – can be seen in a new light. Genealogy and its attendant train of objectification may never be the same again, as things lay bare the threads of connection.

Across eastern Polynesia, it was undeniably the materiality of cloth, its capacity to be cut and restitched, to absorb and to decay, which allowed it to materially translate ideas of performance and resemblance into new media and new social relations. In this sense, the case study of the uptake of quilting in parts of the Pacific draws out a recurrent theme across all the papers collected in this volume; this is, that clothing is uniquely capable of elucidating ideas about who we are and how we should behave not because it is worn on or of the body, but because it brings ideas of consumption up against the realities of production. Threads, after all, are a frame for ideas whose enduring effects belie fibre's frequently ephemeral nature.

Acknowledgement

Research for this paper was funded by the Economic and Social Research Council of Great Britain and was conducted as part of the funded project 'Clothing the Pacific: The Study of the Nature of Innovation' (R000 23 91 98).

References

Addo, P.A. 2003 'God's kingdom in Aukland: Tongan Christian Dress and the Expression of Duty'. In C. Colchester (ed.) *Clothing the Pacific*. Oxford: Berg, pp. 141–67.

Arkana, E. 1986 *Hawaiian Quilting: a Fine Art*. Honolulu, Hawaii: The Hawaiian Mission Children Society.

Babadzan, A. 1993 *Les Dépouilles des Dieux: Essai sur le Religion Tahitienne à L'époque de la Découverte*. Paris: Editions de la Maison des Sciences de l'Homme.

Buck, P. 1944 *Arts and Crafts of the Cook Islands*. Honolulu, Hawaii: Bernice Bishop Museum Bulletin 179.

Colchester, C. 2003 'Introduction'. In C. Colchester (ed.) *Clothing the Pacific*. Oxford: Berg, pp. 1–25.

Gell, A. 1977 'Magic, Perfume, Dream...'. In I. Lewis (ed.) *Symbols and Sentiments*. London: Academic Press, pp. 25–39.

—— 1998 *Art and Agency: A New Anthropological Theory*. Oxford: Oxford University Press.

Gilson, R. 1980 *The Cook islands 1820–1950*. (Ed. Ron Crocombe.) Wellington and Suva: Victoria University Press in association with the Institute of Pacific Studies of the University of the South Pacific.

Hammond, J. 1986 *Tifaifai and Quilts of Polynesia*. Honolulu: University of Hawaii Press.

Herda, P. 2002 'Cook Island's tivaevae: Migration and the display of culture in Aotearoa/New Zealand'. In A. Herle, N. Stanley, K. Stevenson and R. Welsch (eds) *Pacific Art: Persistence, Change and Meaning*. Adelaide: Crawford House Publishing, pp. 139–46.

Howes, D. 1988 'On the Odour of the Soul: Spatial Representation and Olfactory Classification in Eastern Indonesia and Western Melanesia'. *Bijdragen Tot de Taal-land- en Volkenkunde,* 144: 84–113.

Jones, S. 1973 *Hawaiian Quilts*. Honolulu: Hawaii University Press.

Mead, S.M. (ed.) 1984 *The Maori: Maori art from New Zealand Collections*. Auckland: Heinemann.

Phillips, R. 1999 *Trading Identities: The Souvenir in Native North American Art from the North-East 1700–1900*. Seattle: University of Washington Press.

Pogglioli, V. 1988 *Patterns from Paradise: The Art of Tahitian Quilting*. Pittstown, NJ: Main Street Press.

Raymond, R. 2003 'Getting Specific: Pacific Fashion Activism in Aukland during the 1990s'. In C. Colchester (ed.) *Clothing the Pacific*. Oxford: Berg, pp. 193–209.

Rongokea, L. 1992 *Tivaevae: Portraits of Cook Islands Quilting*. Wellington, NZ: Daphne Brasell Associates Press.

Sahlins, M. 1985 *Islands of History*. Chicago: Chicago University Press.

Shaw, R. 1996 *Hawaiian Quilt Masterpieces*. New York: Hugh Lauter Levin Associates.

Simmel, G. 1978 [1907] *The Philosophy of Money*. Trans. Tom Bottomore and David Frisby. London: Routledge & Kegan Paul.

Strathern, M. 1988 *The Gender of the Gift*. Berkeley: University of California Press.

Tcherkézoff, S. 2003 'On Cloth, Gifts and Nudity'. In C. Colchester (ed.) *Clothing the Pacific*. Oxford: Berg, pp. 51–79.

Valeri, V. 1985 *Kingship and Sacrifice: Ritual and Society in Ancient Hawaii*. Chicago: Chicago University Press.

Wagner, R. 1991 'The Fractal Person'. In M. Strathern and M. Godelier (eds) *Big Men and Great Men: Personifications of Power in Melanesia*. Cambridge: Cambridge University Press, pp. 159–73.

Weiner, A. 1992 *Inalienable Possessions: The Paradox of Keeping-While-Giving*. Berkeley: University of California Press.

—— 1994 'Cultural Difference and the Density of Objects'. *American Ethnologist*, 21 (2): 391–403.

Index

Addo, P.A. 178
Ahmed, L. 77, 78
Appadurai, A. 83, 125
Arkana, E. 179
Ash, J. 117
Atatürk (Kemal, G.M.) 7, 62
Attfield, J. 4

Babadzan, A. 177, 180, 181, 186
Balasescu, A. 61, 72, 78, 79
Bannerji, M. 15–16, 41, 103
Barthes, R. 21, 42
Baudrillard, J. 43
Baxandall, M. 156
Bayly, C.A. 33, 83
Bean, S. 54
Beasley, H.G. 166
Becker, A. 148
Benstock, S. 42
Best, E. 128–30, 132–3, 135
Bhabha, H.K. 167
Binark, M. 62
Bloemen, S. 107
Bolton, L. 135, 140
Bourdieu, P. 116
Braddock, S.E. 54
Braham, P. 42
Breward, C. 42
Bruzzi, S. 41
Buchli, V. 1, 44
Buck, P. (Te Rangihiroa) 126, 131, 180, 181
Buckley, R. 21
Butts, D. 134

Cakobau, R. 144
Campbell, C. 42
Campbell, S. 165
Cavallero, D. 42
Cerny, C. 99
Clarke, A. 13, 52

Colchester, C. 10, 12–13, 151, 177
Cole, S. 21
Coombe, F. 166
Coote, J. 99
Craik, J. 23, 42
Crewe, L. 101

da Vinci, L. 153
Dalby, L. 41
Davis, F. 3
du Gay, P. 44
Dube, L. 154
Duffield, A.J. 167
Dupont Company 48–52, 54

Eicher, J. 4
El Guindi, F. 78
Engelke, M. 13
Entwistle, J. 3, 4, 23, 41, 116, 117
Epstein, A.L. 109
Esposito, J.L. 79

Featherstone, M. 33
Ferriss, S. 42
Fine, B. 83
Finkelstein, J. 108
Firth, R. 166
Foucault, M. 79
France, P. 140
Freeman, C. 4

Gee, H. 161
Geertz, C. 126
Gell, A. 5, 6, 13, 22, 24, 35–7, 125, 139, 172, 180, 181, 186
Ger, G. 7–8, 15, 62
Gibson, P.C. 42
Gilson, R. 182
Goffman, E. 23
Gray, A.C. 160, 162

Index

Greenfield, V. 84
Gregson, N.
Gundle, S. 21
Gunson, N. 146, 148
Guppy, H.B. 167

Haddon, A.C. 164, 171
Hakiwai, A. 125
Hammond, J. 179
Handler, R. 126
Handley, S. 47
Hansen, K.T. 4, 8–9, 41, 47, 88, 97, 107, 112, 114, 118
Hanson, A. 125–6
Harrison, H. 126
Harrison, S. 122
Haug, Frigga 75, 77, 79
Haynes, M. 5
Heath, D. 4
Hebdige, D. 42
Hendrickson, H. 41
Herda, P. 184
Hereniko, V. 151
Hetet, E.P. 133
Hetet, R. 131, 133
Hocart, A.M. 143–4, 146
Hodkinson, P. 43
Hollander, A. 42, 159
Hooper, S. 144
Howes, D. 180

Ingold, T. 44

Jackson, P. 44
Jolly, M. 122
Jones, A.R. 159
Jones, S. 179

Keane, W. 2, 13, 139–40
Keesing, R. 122
Kılıçbay, B. 62
Kondo, D. 4
Koojiman, S. 160
Kroeber, A.L. 4, 18, 41
Küchler, S. 2, 9, 14, 46, 54, 127, 146
Kunzle, D. 43

Lander, M. 126
Latour, B. 83

Leach, J. 122–3, 124, 133
Leitch, V.B. 42
Lemire, B. 84
Leopold, E. 83
Liechty, M. 4
Lipovetsky, G. 108
London, J. 161, 162
Lowe, M. 44

MacKenzie, M. 11
Makhlouf, C. 64
Mandel, R. 62
Mann, Rev. I.J. 163
Mara, R. 154
Marchand, R. 47
Marcus, G. 126
Marcus, G.E. 42
Mauss, M. 11, 23, 108, 132, 133
Maxwell, E. 126
McCracken, G. 30, 75
McRobbie, A. 42
McVeigh, B. 4–5
Mead, H.M. 130, 131–2, 196
Melville, H. 160–1, 165
Mernissi, F. 78
Miller, D. 2, 3, 6, 13, 15–16, 21, 41–2, 44, 47, 107
Mintz, S. 45
Mitchell, J.C. 109
Moore, S.F. 46
Mort, F. 44
Morton, C. 99
Munn, N.D. 84
Myers, F. 11

Napier, D. 21
Nava, M. 78
Navaro-Yashin, Y. 62
Nayacakalou, R. 141
Neich, R. 124
Ngata, A. 131
Nicholson, J. 99
Nixon, S. 42
Noble, D.F. 47
Norris, L. 9–10, 85

O'Barr, W.M. 47
O'Biso, C. 125, 134
O'Connor, K. 6–7, 16, 42, 44, 49

Index

O'Halliday, C.O. 48
O'Hanlon, M. 6
O'Mahoney, M. 54
Ortner, S.B. 43

Paki-Titi, R. 131
Palmer, A. 42
Pamuk, O. 8
Pastoreau, M. 46
Peiss, K. 22
Pels, P. 125
Phillips, R. 171, 185
Pierce, C.S. 84
Pogglioli, V. 179
Powdermaker, H. 109
Pryke, M. 44

Rabuka, S. 154
Ranapiri, T. 132
Raymond, R. 177
Renne, E.P. 41
Richardson, J. 41
Rongokea, L. 179
Roth, J. 144
Rubinstein, R.P. 42
Rutledge, C.H. 50

Sahlins, M.D. 44, 53, 54, 177
Salmond, A. 127, 133
Sandıkcı, Ö. 7–8, 15, 62
Sayes, S. 141
Schlachter, T. 54
Schneider, J. 3, 41, 45, 61, 83
Scott-Troxler, G. 144
Sennett, R. 3, 22
Serevi, W. 154
Seriff, S. 99
Shaw, R. 179
Showalter, E. 47
Simmel, G. 3, 78, 175
Sissons, J. 124
Smosarski, G. 92
Somerville, B.T. 165, 167
Sontag, S. 79
Stafford, B.M. 171

Stallybrass, P. 84, 159
Steele, V. 42, 43
Stewart, S. 84
Stolpe, H. 164
Strasser, S. 47
Strathern, A. 11
Strathern, M. 3, 5, 6, 11, 26, 32, 181
Styles, J. 83
Summers, L. 4, 43

Tambiah, S. 126
Tapsell, P. 122, 133–4
Tarlo, E. 84
Taylor, L. 4, 83
Tcherkézoff, S. 177, 178
Te Rangihiroa (Peter Buck) 126, 131
Te Whatahoro 128
Thomas, N. 11, 13, 122, 124, 146, 159, 162, 165, 171–2
Thompson, M. 85
Tonkinson, R. 122
Toren, C. 142, 154

Vakalalabure, R.T. 140
Valeri, V. 177
von Hügel, Baron 144

Wagner, R. 122, 152, 180, 181
Waite, D. 165, 166
Warwick, A. 42
Weiner, A.B. 3, 45, 61, 83, 84, 127, 133, 159, 175–6
Were, G. 13, 54, 165
White, J. 80
Wigley, M. 3, 21
Wilford, J.N. 126
Wilson, E. 23, 41, 42, 78
Wilson, G. 109
Winnicott, D. 15
Wolf, R. 54
Woodward, S. 5–6, 7, 9, 10

Yeğenoğlu, M. 78
Young, D. 22

CPSIA information can be obtained at www.ICGtesting.com
Printed in the USA
LVOW091241020213

318280LV00017B/186/P